THE GUARDIAN
MON£Y GUIDE

THE GUARDIAN
MON£Y GUIDE

Margaret Dibben

WILLOW BOOKS
Collins
8, Grafton Street
1984

WILLOW BOOKS
Collins
8 Grafton Street, London
1984

Willow Books
William Collins & Sons plc
London · Glasgow · Sydney
Auckland · Toronto · Johannesburg

First published in Great Britain 1984
© Margaret Dibben 1984

Dibben, Margaret
The Guardian Money Guide
1. Finance, personal
I. Title
332.024   HG179
ISBN 0 00 218133 9

Filmset in Plantin by W & G Baird Ltd,
Greystone Press, Antrim, Northern Ireland.
Printed and bound in Great Britain by William
Collins & Sons plc, Glasgow

Contents

ACKNOWLEDGMENTS

The detailed checking of a book like this is a monumental task. I hope I have expressed adequately my deepest gratitude to the very many people who provided and checked the facts and figures.

But, in particular, I would like to name the following who generously gave an enormous amount of time and care to reading individual chapters of the manuscript. Without them, the book would have been only halfway useful:

The Automobile Association; British Gas; British Insurance Association; British Insurance Brokers Association; British Telecom; the Building Societies Association; Stephanie Cooper; Department of Health and Social Security; Electricity Council; Hinton & Wild, the Law Society; Legal & General Assurance Society; Life Offices Association; Lloyds Bank; National Girobank; National Savings; Office of Fair Trading; the Post Office; the Royal Institution of Chartered Surveyors; Royal Insurance; Trustee Savings Bank; Unit Trust Association.

Tim Good patiently demystified the subject of tax. And David Simpson bravely and scrupulously read the whole manuscript. My thanks to everyone.

Introduction

When I first started writing about personal finance for *The Guardian*, I was surprised to discover how little most people knew about managing money. The hardest question, which I am asked many times, is still 'where can I go for independent financial advice?'

In this book I have tried to show that personal finance is not a complicated subject or beyond the understanding of anyone without a degree in applied calculus. With a knowledge of basic principles, you can answer many money questions for yourself, and certainly learn enough to know that, when your affairs become more involved, just what the expert should be doing for you.

I have also tried to point out that the professionals should not be allowed to perpetrate the illusion that they have inside knowledge not available to anyone else and that they are doing you a favour by letting you in on the secret.

You are the customer; you pay the bill (or provide their livelihood if they earn commission); you are the important element. They need your custom to be in business at all, whether it is a one-man insurance broker or a multi-national bank.

If you understand the level of information, advice and service you should be getting from these people, you can gauge how well they are doing their job. You will almost certainly end up with a better deal if you know what to ask for than if you approach them cold and say 'tell me what I need'. The experts do not necessarily know what is best for you.

From the readers' letters I receive, I can see that there is no limit to the variety of money problems people have. But also, there is no end to the number of times that different readers will ask for the same advice.

I hope this book is comprehensive enough to answer the basic questions that crop up regularly in everyone's life and also to give you the information to solve more unusual problems.

I also hope it will give you the knowledge to pester the professional. If you are not satisfied, or do not understand, make them explain to you. They are there to look after your interests and to provide a service in the same way as your local corner shop.

The chapters are grouped together to cover the broad periods of your life that create financial problems: the need for basic budgeting; borrowing and saving; your home; your work; your family; and your future.

MARGARET DIBBEN   JULY, 1984

1/Budgeting

How to pay the bills • *rates / gas and electricity / meters / Scotland / water / telephone / television licence / road fund licence / season ticket* • Bank budget accounts • *shopping* • Letter

Humans come in two forms: one can manage its money and enjoys budgeting; the other can't, and doesn't. Most people belong to the second category and it is for them that *The Guardian Money Guide* has been written.

If you are totally incapable of keeping tabs on your finances but nevertheless muddle through life quite happily, then the distress of trying to balance 'cash in' with 'cash out' is not worth while. However, if you really do want to feel in control of your finances but do not know how to go about it, then read on.

The first step in learning how to sort out your money problems is discovering exactly how much you have coming in each week or each month. Surprisingly, many people cannot say with any precision.

You then need to work out a fairly accurate idea of how much you will be paying out regularly. If you do not know the exact figure, make a guess, but remember to make an allowance for inflation. Bills have a habit of growing larger, rarely smaller. This is how to start:

Write down and then add together:

● net pay after all deductions	£..........
● dividends and interest from savings	£..........
● occasional bonuses	£..........
● social security payments	£..........
	£..........

Next, total your regular expenses:

- mortgage or rent   £..........
- rates   £..........
- ground rent   £..........
- water rates   £..........
- telephone   £..........
- gas   £..........
- electricity   £..........
- oil or coal   £..........
- season ticket or commuting costs   £..........
- insurance premiums – house building   £..........
  - – house contents   £..........
  - – life insurance   £..........
  - – mortgage protection   £..........
  - – car   £..........
- road fund licence   £..........
- TV licence   £..........
- TV rental   £..........
- hire purchase and credit repayments   £..........
- credit card bill   £..........
- subscriptions to – publications   £..........
  - – associations   £..........
- school fees   £..........
- children's pocket money   £..........
- other   £..........

£..........

The next main item to allow for is:

- food   £..........

followed by the other necessities of life; estimate how much for:

- cleaning materials   £..........
- dry cleaning and laundry   £..........
- kitchen and bathroom accessories   £..........
- dentist's and optician's bills   £..........
- vet's fees   £..........
- travelling   £..........
- petrol   £..........
- car repairs   £..........
- household repairs   £..........
- haircuts   £..........
- medicine   £..........
- other   £..........

£..........

Next come the less essential expenses; items that you can manage without, or delay buying, if you really have to:

- meals out   £..........
- drinks and cigarettes   £..........
- sweets and toys   £..........
- books, magazines and newspapers   £..........
- records, tapes, video cassettes   £..........
- theatre, cinema, music, gambling   £..........
- postage   £..........
- evening classes   £..........
- birthday and Christmas presents   £..........
- holidays   £..........
- clothes   £..........
- hobbies and sport   £..........
- decorating   £..........
- cosmetics   £..........
- garden tools   £..........
- miscellaneous items   £..........

   £..........

Add together all the outgoing totals and subtract this from your income.

If you have already run out of money before you reach the end of the list, then hopefully you will, on the way, have seen areas where you can cut back. Each of us has our own priorities.

If you are fortunate enough to have money left over after allowing for these predictable outgoings, the next step is to start an emergency fund. Build up a pool of money, say up to £500, perhaps in a bank or building society where it will earn interest but where you can get hold of it quickly.

This is money to tide you over when the unexpected happens: the car breaks down or you receive a large bill from the vet.

With that taken care of, you can please yourself. You can save a bit more, you can gamble, or you can spend it.

This is how an average family divides its money:

housing	15·7%	durable household goods	7·5%
fuel, light, power	5·9	other goods	7·5
food	21·7	transport and vehicles	15·0
alcohol	4·8	services	11·0
tobacco	3·0	miscellaneous	0·5
clothing and footwear	7·4		

   100·00%

At least 80 per cent of the population reckons it saves regularly and, on average, people save 13 to 14 per cent of their disposable incomes.

HOW TO PAY THE BILLS

Now you know where you stand, the next step is to discover how to manage your money. There are various ways.

You could, for example, line up half-a-dozen empty jars and every week put a few pounds in each. But apart from the safety risk, you are losing money. If the money were put in a deposit account instead, it would be earning interest. There are many kinds of convenient savings schemes which you will find in Chapter 3: Savings.

Here are some better ways of spreading the costs of living.

Rates

Most local authorities will let you pay your rates on a monthly basis instead of all in one go at the beginning of the year. When you receive the bill in March, you can ask to pay either in two halves or, better still, in ten monthly instalments.

Look at it this way. If you regard rates as a monthly instead of annual expense, you can fool yourself that you have two 'free' months in February and March or March and April depending on where you live. This is not true, of course, but the trick can help you feel richer.

You can pay the bill by standing order from your bank account, by sending a cheque each month through the post, or by calling in person at the town hall.

A few local authorities have introduced savings stamps and some have made arrangements for payment through post offices or gas and electricity showrooms. Ask at your town hall if your authority has any such scheme.

The advantages of spreading the cost of the rates bill are that it helps you budget and delays payment; you are holding on to your money for as long as possible and paying only at the last moment. The situation is different if you spread the cost of gas and electricity bills because you are paying in advance for these.

Gas and electricity

Gas and electricity bills are far higher in winter than in summer and, to even out the expense, you can buy savings stamps at gas and electricity board showrooms whenever you can afford it. This is called a pay-as-you-go scheme. The disadvantage is that you are paying for the fuel before you use it. The gas and electricity boards get their hands on your cash sooner than if they had to wait for settlement of a quarterly bill.

Another way of smoothing out big bills is to open a budget account and pay in an amount each month. The board estimates your annual bill and divides by 12. You pay the same amount each month so that in summer you pay for more energy than you use but in winter you pay less.

If you start the account at the beginning of winter at least you are immediately getting the benefit of paying less for the heavy winter bills.

The monthly payment can be made either by standing order, direct debit, or in cash at the showrooms.

The two utility authorities have different philosophies when it comes to settling up at the end of the year. Part of the reason for this is that they are organised differently: the British Gas Corporation is centralised – you make a cheque out to 'British Gas'. But the 12 regional electricity boards are financially autonomous, so you may find different rules apply in different parts of the country.

As far as the gas board is concerned, at the end of the year, you settle up: either you pay them what you owe, or if you have paid too much, they refund your money.

The electricity board will probably take any money overpaid or underpaid forward to next year. Here cheques are made out to the regional board, for example, 'London Electricity'. If you are paying too little each month to pay off the whole bill at the end of the year, the local manager will probably get in touch and ask for more.

If you have paid too much, this will be offset against next year's account. If you do not like the arrangement, however, it is worth talking to your local branch to see what they can do.

Both gas and electricity board showrooms sell stamps at £1 each. They are interchangeable between the two and a few sub-post offices also sell them. The savings stamps scheme is a poor way of managing your money unless you really have difficulty meeting the quarterly bills. In effect you are giving the gas or electricity boards an interest-free loan: except in the coldest months they collect your money sooner than they otherwise would but they do not pay you any interest.

The same criticism applies to a budget account. You would be better off opening a building society account, depositing the same monthly payments there and earning interest on the money.

Some electricity boards allow payment by credit card – Access or Visa card. If you pay off your credit card bill in full each month, you will not pay any interest and gain another six weeks of free credit.

The gas board does not permit this and argues that because you pay for the gas after you have used it anyway, it sees no reason to give you yet more time to pay up.

Meters
If you find paying your fuel bills very difficult, you can have a slot meter installed. There is no charge for the meter but the running costs are higher. Unless you use fewer than 30 therms a quarter (about the amount a gas cooker takes a quarter) it will work out more expensive.

Scotland
The Royal Bank of Scotland runs its own savings stamps scheme. These

stamps can be used towards paying gas and electricity bills or cashed in.

The stamps are sold in denominations of 50p, £1 and £2. They can be bought at bank branches or in the showrooms. At the bank, they can be exchanged for cash or used to pay any bill you would otherwise settle through the Giro system (see p. 114 for explanation of the Giro System).

Water

The regional water authorities will let you spread the bill over eight months of the year. One or two of them issue savings stamps and some allow payment by credit card. Water is a utility that qualifies for social security assistance.

Telephone

You can buy savings stamps at the post office to go towards paying the telephone bill. British Telecom issues the stamps in £1 and £5 denominations. Like gas and electricity board stamps, these are a bad buy.

Television licence

You can buy 50p savings stamps at the post office to help pay for a television licence.

Road fund licence

Car tax can be paid half yearly but it costs more this way. A six-month licence is half the cost of a 12-month plus 10 per cent. One year costs £90, six months £49.50. There is also the chance that the fee will go up during the year. If you have already paid for the full year, you will avoid the increase until your licence is due for renewal. If you pay half yearly, you might get caught for the second six months. However, if you cannot meet the whole cost all at once, paying in two halves is a help.

The licence for a motorbike has to be paid in one go unless the bike is larger than 250cc. That costs £36 a year.

Season ticket

You may be able to persuade your employer to give you an interest-free loan to buy an annual season ticket: if you can this is a very good deal.

Otherwise, a British Rail annual ticket saves 10 per cent more than four quarterlies; a quarterly is 4 per cent cheaper than three monthlies; and a monthly 4 per cent cheaper than buying four weeklies.

BANK BUDGET ACCOUNTS

Some banks, but not all, will organise a budget for you. You add together everything you expect to spend on regular bills for the coming year, add the service charge, and divide by 12. You pay this amount each month into a special account at the bank.

You can write out cheques from this account using a special cheque book, without worrying if there is enough money to meet the cheque.

Under the Midland Bank's system, there is a £10 annual service charge. When the account is overdrawn, you pay interest charges calculated at 15 per cent or 15·8 per cent APR. However, you receive nothing at times when the account is in credit.

The National Westminster Bank's scheme works differently. You are not charged interest, neither do you receive any. But there is a service charge of £30 a year to cover the first £500 you will be spending. Above that, there is a £1 charge for every £50 you spend.

Some banks offer a 'save and borrow' account. You pay a predetermined amount each month and then can automatically borrow 30 times that figure. This is called 'roll-over' credit; as your monthly cheque is paid in, your borrowing limit is topped up. Again you will pay interest charges when the account is in the red.

For paying bills, it is economically sounder to deposit the money in a building society or bank deposit account to benefit from the interest.

Shopping

There are various other ways of stretching your money further when you go shopping. These include paying by credit card, mail order or joining a store's own credit scheme. You can learn more about buying on credit in Chapter 4: Borrowing.

LETTER

Q. I always wait until I receive a final reminder before paying my bills. A friend who does the same has just moved house and he was asked by the electricity board to put down a deposit before they would connect him. Why did they do this?

A. *The gas and electricity boards and British Telecom can ask you for a deposit if they know you to be a bad payer, or if they know nothing about you. The amount is likely to be between £50 and £100 but on the plus side they do pay you interest on the money.*

2/Banking

How to choose a bank ● *how the banks line up* ● Current accounts
● *writing out a cheque / cheque guarantee card / stopping a cheque /
getting cash / how to get cash when the banks are closed / standing orders/
direct debiting / paying-in* ● Deposit accounts ● Budget accounts
● *night safes / bouncing cheques / joint accounts / statements* ● What
your bank manager can do ● *investment advice / tax advice / executor /
storage / insurance* ● Sending money abroad ● *taking money abroad*
● Plastic cards ● *credit cards / charge cards* ● If you are blind
● Tomorrow ● *authorisation terminals / fraud / safety* ● Letters

Many people are nervous about approaching a bank manager; the
pin-striped image which bank managers have cultivated can frighten
away potential customers before they have even taken the first step
through the door. But despite feeling more like robbers than customers,
many people still need a bank account, especially for moving money
around. So, how can you make the best of it?

HOW TO CHOOSE A BANK
It is difficult to advise anyone how to choose a bank since you must
weigh up the relative merits of each one and decide how important these
are to you. Most often people pick the bank that their parents used, or
the one with the most convenient branch to their place of work.

If you want to compare bank charges, 'free' banking is offered by all
the banks, but it is only genuinely free among the smaller banks.
However, these have fewer branches so may be less convenient for you.

Usually 'free' banking does not mean what it says. At most banks
you have to keep a minimum of £100 in your current account to avoid
paying charges. But remember, that same £100 could be earning you
interest if you were to put it on deposit somewhere. So, even 'free'
banking is in effect costing you money.

The charges that a bank adds to your statement are, to some degree,
at the manager's discretion: a formula is programmed into the computer
but the manager does not have to keep to those charges if he does not
want to. He will usually let the computer work out the figure. But, if he

does take a personal interest, he will weigh up the amount of money you have in credit in your current account (this money is, in effect, a free loan to the bank) against how good a customer you are. Does he have to bounce your cheques regularly? Do you call into the branch frequently to pester him? You are not a 'good' customer if you do.

If you think you have been charged too much on your statement, telephone the manager and tell him so. He may reconsider if you point out an inequity in the calculations.

The bank already has the upper hand because the bank manager deducts the charges directly from your account before telling you, and without asking your permission. You then have to persuade him to reimburse your account if he agrees to waive the charges. No other system of payment works this way.

Always, a bank manger will respond more positively to a reasoned request rather than an irate outburst pointing out the injustice of such a large profit-making institution having the audacity to milk its impecunious customers.

How the banks line up

The best-known banks, the Big Four, are: Barclays, Lloyds, Midland and the National Westminster. They became enormous due to many mergers before the turn of the century.

Next in size and familiarity come the Trustee Savings Bank and Williams & Glyn's, followed by the Co-op Bank, Yorkshire Bank and National Girobank which operates through post office branches, see also p. 114. The Williams & Glyn's name will disappear shortly when the bank is absorbed into its parent, the Royal Bank of Scotland.

Scotland has the Bank of Scotland, Clydesdale Bank and Royal Bank of Scotland. The Scottish banks produce their own bank notes. Scottish notes are acceptable in England and Wales but if you cannot persuade a shop to take them, go to any clearing bank branch and they will exchange them.

If you are unhappy with the service you receive from your bank, you can always change. You can move banks, but it may be that **by simply switching to a different branch you find a more sympathetic manager.**

CURRENT ACCOUNTS

A bank's cheque book is more useful than anyone else's because it includes a cheque guarantee card. The card enables you to shop almost anywhere and pay by cheque, up to the maximum mostly of £50 a cheque. Without a cheque guarantee card, you are mainly limited to paying household bills.

Then, with a bank current account you can run up an overdraft. A bank manager will usually allow you to do this if you ask him politely first, or if you have obviously had an unusually stressful month which will be offset by a regular salary cheque. For more information about overdrafts see p. 54 and for high interest cheque accounts see p. 46.

Writing out a cheque

You must write clearly in ink and you must ensure that no one can add a few noughts to your figures. If you make a mistake when writing the cheque, you can tear it up and write out another. Or you can correct and initial the mistake.

Cheques are either 'crossed' (two vertical parallel lines drawn through) or 'open'. 'Open' cheques are used less often now and they can be cashed only at the branch where they are drawn. Crossed cheques can be paid into a bank account or they can be cashed at a local shop by endorsing, that is signing your name on the back.

If a cheque has been made out in your name but you want to pay it into someone else's account, you can shorten the procedure of paying it into your bank and writing out a separate cheque if you endorse the back of the cheque.

Always remember to fill in the cheque stub or record sheet so you can check your bank statement when it arrives.

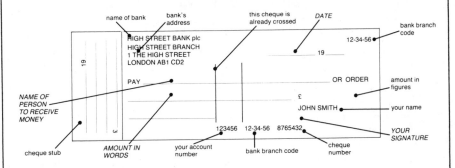

Cheque guarantee card

Provided the number of the cheque guarantee card is written on the back of the cheque, anyone who accepts it knows that, whatever happens, he will receive his money up to the usual £50 limit. When you use a cheque guarantee card, you cannot, under any circumstances, stop payment of the cheque.

Remember this if you are buying goods that you might change your mind about. Even if the card is stolen and misused, or you do not have sufficient funds in your account, the bank will have to pay up. But you should not write the number on the back of the cheque yourself. This must be done by the person accepting the cheque or the guarantee is invalidated. **Do not keep your cheque guarantee card with your cheque book: if both are stolen together, fraud is easier.**

If you lose your cheque guarantee card, inform the bank immediately. Once the bank knows that your card has been misplaced, you will not be liable if anyone uses it fraudulently.

Stopping a cheque

If you have not used a cheque guarantee card to support a cheque, you can telephone and instruct the bank not to pay up when the cheque is presented. You need to act quickly and it will cost you around £2 or £3. If you have simply changed your mind about buying an item, although the bank will obey your instructions not to pay, you still legally owe for the goods.

Getting cash

This is the most frequent transaction you will conduct with your bank. You can withdraw cash from a bank even if you have no account with them by using a cheque book supported by a cheque guarantee card but there will probably be a charge of 50p for doing this. Barclays charge other banks' customers £1 on Saturdays.

At your local branch you can withdraw as much cash as you like (as long as you have enough money in the account), but at other branches of your own bank or other banks, you are limited to the £50 a day rule under the cheque guarantee scheme. You can make special arrangements if you regularly withdraw large amounts from one particular branch of your own bank away from your home branch.

A useful innovation in recent years has been the cash dispenser: a machine which gives you cash at any time of the day or night (except at Lloyds Bank which closes the machines from 11·30 p.m. to 6·30 a.m.).

Customers have shown that they would rather queue outside in the rain to use the cash machine (known in the business as automated teller machines or ATMs) than face a cashier inside. If you are paying bank charges it is cheaper to use a machine than write out a cheque, and you can withdraw up to £100 a day.

Cash machines are mostly sited on the outside wall of a bank branch, but they are increasingly being installed in factories and shopping centres. By using a plastic card, you can withdraw cash, order a statement or cheque book and check how much you have in your account.

In future these machines will become even more sophisticated. They will be able to hand you a printed statement; take in cash; and obey instructions to pay bills.

How to get cash when the banks are closed

1. use a cash dispenser: your Visa and Access credit cards will also work in the machines.
2. cash a cheque at your corner shop or garage.
3. use a tourist *bureau de change*: these are mostly in London and are extremely expensive.
4. raid the children's piggy bank.
5. exchange a recent purchase from Marks & Spencer.
6. look under the stairs for returnable bottles.

7. have a meal with friends, pay the bill by cheque or credit card and collect their contributions in cash.
8. use the Co-op bank for longer opening hours.
9. some hypermarkets have facilities for cashing cheques.
10. open a Girobank account at the post office (this is open longer hours).
11. write a cheque in exchange for the contents of the church offertory plate!

To operate the machines you must remember a four-figure number. This is your Personal Identification Number or PIN which you key into the cash machine. The computer then matches your PIN against the code in the magnetic stripe on the back of your plastic card to make sure you are who you say. You have three chances to key in the right number, then the machine swallows your card.

Do not, whatever you do, keep your PIN with your cash card because if you were to lose them together, anyone finding them could easily get the cash. In fact, you should not keep you PIN number written down anywhere. If you do not trust your memory, try disguising the number, preferably more cleverly than by simply reversing the order.

Standing orders
Your bank will automatically make regular payments on your behalf by standing order. You simply fill out a form which can be cancelled at any time, and then you can forget about paying mortgage instalments, insurance premiums, annual charity subscriptions, or whatever.

Direct debiting
This is a similar system to standing orders but is more popular with the banks because it is cheaper for them to operate. The amount of any regular payment is bound to change (usually upwards) from time to time.

For payments such as annual subscriptions you might have a variable direct debit which authorises the bank to pay a different amount when the recipient asks for it.

For regular payments which do not change very often, such as monthly insurance premiums, you could have a fixed direct debit under which the bank will need your permission to pay a higher amount.

Paying-in
Most people choose to have their monthly salary paid directly into their bank account, indeed you often do not have any option about how you are paid. (See p. 140 about being paid in cash.) Both banks and employers prefer paying you this way because it is cheaper and avoids the enormous security hazard of handling large amounts of cash.

If the bank manager knows that you have a regular pay cheque arriving each month, he is more likely to agree to your request for overdrafts and loans.

For other amounts of money, you will be given a paying-in book with your cheque book, or you can pick up an individual paying-in slip at the branch. If you are paying into a bank which is not your own, you may have to pay an extra charge of 30p. To avoid this you could, for the cost of a second-class postage stamp, send it through the post.

If someone has sent you a cheque which is crossed, then you can convert this to money by paying it into your bank account. If it is not crossed, you can exchange it for cash at the bank, but only at the issuing branch. And so too could anyone who found the cheque if you lost it.

DEPOSIT ACCOUNTS
All the banks have various savings schemes. See p. 35 for details.

BUDGET ACCOUNTS
Your bank may offer a budget account to help spread the cost of household bills. You estimate how much you expect to pay out over the next year, divide by 12 and pay this amount in regular monthly instalments to the bank.

At some periods you will be in credit and at others in debit, but the bank will honour all cheques paid out of a special account. You pay a charge for the service. Two banks mainly offer this service: Midland and National Westminster. See p. 13.

Night safes
If you regularly have a lot of cash which you would like to bank after the branch has closed, you can ask for access to a night safe. Small shopkeepers, for example, do not like keeping the day's takings in their premises overnight. Night safes are in the outside wall of a bank and can be opened only with a special key. You then simply drop the money in a bag down the shute.

The next working morning the cashier will check the cash and send you a receipt. If the cashier's reckoning differs from yours, the bank will sort this out the next time you call. In any case, if you regularly use a night safe, the branch staff will know you well and you should be able to clear up the discrepancy.

There are two systems. As well as having your money or cheques counted by the cashier the next morning, you can have the bag of money kept intact for you to collect. The cost is around £2.50 a quarter for each wallet you have, plus 50p every time the wallet is used.

Bouncing cheques
If you write out a cheque but have no money in the account, unless the

manager allows you to be overdrawn, he can bounce your cheque.

When the payee, that is the person to whom the cheque is made out, pays the cheque into his account he will not get the money as he expected. Instead, the cheque is returned to him with the invitation: 'refer to drawer, please represent'. This gives you, the bad payer, a few more days to come up with the money, and the next time he presents the cheque, the manager may authorise payment.

But sometimes the cheque has the blunt message, 'refer to drawer'. This tells the payee that he is not going to get his money, so he better speak to you urgently.

Joint accounts

You can ease the cost of a bank account by running it with another person, needing only one £100 minimum to avoid bank charges. Many married couples open joint accounts. There are various permutations. You can both sign cheques separately, or you can arrange that one can sign alone, but the other can sign only jointly. Or, very restrictively, you can insist that neither can sign a cheque without the other's signature as well.

Statements

All banks will send you a statement of your account, monthly if you ask for it, or every few months if it suits them better. The service is free unless you ask for a statement too frequently, in which case you can be charged.

You should always check your statement against the cheque stubs or record sheet because mistakes can, and do, happen. If you discover you have wrongly been credited with someone else's £1000, do not rush out to spend it. When Customer B discovers the shortfall he will demand it back and the bank will trace it to your account.

Unless you can prove that you genuinely believed the money was yours and you have already spent it, you will have to give it back.

WHAT YOUR BANK MANAGER CAN DO

Investment advice

You can ask your bank manager to help sort out your savings problems. But, the worth of this advice will depend on how clued up the individual manager is and how much time he is prepared to spend on you.

You can reasonably expect his attention for half-an-hour and there will be no charge. If he then arranges a loan for you, or helps you to set up a company, the arrangement fee and his investigation time will be charged. There is no charge for savings advice.

However, if you treat a bank manager as a problem counsellor and use up a great deal of his time, he will mentally list you as a time waster and might very well raise your bank charges in revenge.

The banks have a specialist financial advice division, called the

Trust Division, which will, for a fee, look after large sums of money, say from £20,000.

Each bank has its own savings schemes and unit-trust investments so, of course, the bank manager may well recommend one of his bank's own investments rather than that of a rival. Whether you could have done any better, you will probably never know, but it does mean that your choice is limited.

Bank managers are less likely to know all about every savings opportunity than they were a few years ago. They will give you guidance on buying stocks and shares and gilt-edged securities and will carry out the deal on your behalf. In this case the bank acts as broker, operating through a stockbroker. Ask him what the charge will be because you will have to pay commission just as you would to a stockbroker.

Tax advice

The manager will give advice on simple tax problems. There may be no set scale of charges for this, but if you have complicated affairs, the branch manager will refer you to the bank's taxation specialist who will give you a quote for the likely cost.

Executor

A bank can act as executor of your will. You may prefer the idea of leaving this chore to the bank rather than putting the onus on a friend or relative. **But a bank's fees for this can become very expensive.**

There is a set scale relating to the value of the estate and banks will charge accordingly, regardless of how much or how little work is involved. But you can be confident of continuity. If you appoint your own executors, they may die before you, but there is always another bank manager to succeed the present one. As a guide, you might pay 5 per cent plus VAT on the first £50,000 and 2 per cent plus VAT above that with a minimum fee of £500.

If the estate remains unsettled after one year, the bank will take over as trustee and probably charge 1 per cent of the total amount a year.

Storage – safe custody

Any valuables you own, jewellery, silver, documents or whatever, that you feel would be more secure in the bank's vault than in your own home can be deposited for safe custody.

The charge will be about £7 a year plus VAT for small deed boxes and parcels, or £27 for large ones. The more space you take up, the more you will pay.

If the bank is burgled and you lose your valuables, the bank is not responsible for compensating you. You should, therefore, make sure you have insurance cover. Only if you can prove that the bank was negligent will you stand any chance of claiming against them.

Insurance

Your bank manager can provide the same insurance services as an insurance broker. And he works on the same principle – his own branch is accredited with commission on every deal. You can arrange all your insurance needs through your bank: life insurance; house; car; holiday.

The banks even have their own insurance packages, but they are quite happy to recommend other insurance companies if they think these are more suitable because they will earn the commission anyway.

SENDING MONEY ABROAD

This can be extremely expensive, particularly for small amounts. There are various ploys to keep down the cost but, with the cheapest ways, there is a greater element of risk.

If you ask your bank to transmit the money, it is guaranteed to arrive safely but the charges run as follows: cable transfer is the fastest system; it costs 25p per £100 but there is a minimum charge of £5 and a maximum of £30 plus the cost of sending a cable, which is probably a couple of pounds.

Money going to Europe is sent by a special electronic interbank system called SWIFT. This costs 25p to send £100 with a minimum charge of £4 and a maximum of £30. The money will take about three working days to arrive.

An international payment order can be sent in any currency but travels airmail, so it is slower. The charge is 25p per £100 with a minimum of £2.50 and a maximum of £30. Both telegraphic transfer and international payment orders are sent to foreign banks and not to individuals and named for the recipient.

Another way to send small sums overseas is through Girobank at the post office. This is called Transcash and costs £2.50. See p. 115 for more details.

The cheapest scheme is run by Barclays Bank which charges only £2 to issue a money order in either sterling or American dollars.

For very small amounts you could risk sending cash and registering the letter, but this is not advisable. In any case the person at the other end will then have to pay a fee to convert the sterling to his own currency.

Taking money abroad

Again, this costs money – you are paying for security and convenience. See pp. 225 to 228 for details.

PLASTIC CARDS

There was a time when owning a plastic card was a status symbol. Now there are so many you need a separate wallet to keep them all in. And what have the credit card companies done to maintain the cachet, or rather wealth distinction? They have invented 'gold' cards. These are charge cards rather than credit cards but, to qualify for one you must have an income of at least £20,000 a year. So flashing a gold card around tells the world that you are rich.

The run of the mill, everyday credit card or charge card is quite good enough for people who want to pay by plastic.

Credit cards

There are two main international credit card systems: Visa and Mastercard. Both are widely accepted in most parts of the world, but in some countries one is more popular than the other.

Among the UK banks, Barclays, Yorkshire Bank, Co-op Bank, Bank of Scotland, Allied Irish Bank and TSB belong to the Visa organisation while Midland, Lloyds, National Westminster, Williams & Glyn's, Royal Bank of Scotland, Clydesdale, Bank of Ireland, Northern and Ulster Banks have joined Mastercard.

The credit card company will give you a limit of how much credit you are allowed to run up in a month. If you do not think this is enough, you can try asking for more or you could have both cards. **You do not need to have an account with the bank that gives you the card.**

Once a month, you will receive a statement detailing what you have spent with your card, how much is outstanding and what is the minimum amount that you must pay off each month. You will have to pay a minimum each month: either £5 or 5 per cent, whichever is the greater. You are given a date, usually two weeks hence, by which you must have paid at least the minimum on the bill. If you pay the whole bill, you will incur no charge for interest. So in total, you can have about six weeks' free credit from the time you buy the goods until the date you have to pay for them.

If you pay off part of the bill only, you will pay interest on the outstanding amount from the day the money is due.

The danger with these cards is for those who are completely irresponsible when it comes to spending. If you are the sort of person who will use the card because it is there, then it is probably best not to put yourself in the way of temptation. You can easily fall deeply into debt very quickly.

But there are advantages. You can save bank charges by using a credit card: you need write out only one cheque a month instead of separate cheques for each purchase. You carry less cash around with you. You can use the card in a cash dispenser, although you will pay interest on the money immediately.

Charge cards

Another variety of plastic is the charge card. There is no limit to the amount you can spend using one of these, but you must settle the whole bill every month.

There are no interest charges because you do not have any period of credit. But there is an annual charge and also a joining fee. American Express charges £15 to join and £22.50 a year. Diners Club costs £17.50 to join and £22.50 a year.

Charge cards started out as a convenient way of paying for goods without using cash. Now they also provide cash facilities, free life insurance, and various other services.

IF YOU ARE BLIND

All the banks will send Braille statements to blind customers and there is no charge for this. Lloyds Bank can also issue large print statements and has a cassette tape describing its services with five Braille and large print booklets; Midland has Braille booklets while National Westminster and Lloyds have a Braille office which transcribes blind customers' correspondence.

The banks will supply free cheque templates which guide you to the correct position for filling out cheques and Lloyds Bank has a note gauge to help you identify your bank notes.

TOMORROW

New technology is changing the face of banking. Already technology exists to make money transactions so advanced that only some of it will ever work through to the high streets.

A recent innovation which will eventually be available to everyone is home banking. This means you will be able to sit in front of your television screen, punch numbers into a console and then see your bank account appear on the screen.

The next step will be to instruct the televised bank account to move money out of your account into another, pay out, show you your up-to-the-minute statement, or display a list of your standing orders.

Something else which will soon become a reality is EFTPOS, or Electronic Funds Transfer at Point of Sale. This means that your bank account is debited at the same instant as you pay for the goods.

Authorisation terminals

These are beginning to appear in shops, though mainly in large department stores near town centres at first. They can almost completely eliminate fraud once the loss of a card has been notified.

When you pay for an item at the check out, your cheque guarantee card or credit card is run through an instrument that looks like a telephone with a slit along the top. While the assistant is wrapping your goods, a message is passed electronically to a central computer which reads the information on your card and then authorises, or refuses, acceptance. This takes a few seconds.

Fraud

The banks' overwhelming worry in the 1980s is the growing problem of fraud. One reason for their reluctance to raise the limit on cheque guarantee cards beyond £50 is because this would increase the amount of fraud.

They are urgently looking for ways of cutting down the opportunities for fraud and will be introducing these ideas whenever they can.

Safety

Any money deposited with a British bank is largely secure from loss. The Bank of England has set up a Protection Scheme, run by the Deposit Protection Board, to which the banks contribute. If any bank or licensed deposit taker (someone registered with the Department of Trade and Industry) collapses, customers are guaranteed 75 per cent of the first £10,000 they have in a UK sterling deposit account.

LETTERS

Q. When I queried my bank charges, my bank manager said I was getting 'notional' interest on the credit balance. Is this the same thing as an interest bearing current account?

A. *No. You do not actually receive 'notional' interest; the bank manager (or more accurately, the computer) works out the notional interest your account has earned and offsets this against the bank charges you have to pay. If you do not pay charges you are not credited with the interest. And anyway notional interest is a very low figure indeed.*

Q. I object to paying 50p to cash a cheque in someone else's bank. How can I avoid it?

A. *Apart from obviously using your own bank, if you have an American Express or Diners Club card you can cash up to £50 a day at Lloyds or National Westminster banks for free.*

Q. I think the £50 limit a day is too low. I sometimes need more than that but I am never in the same area to make a regular arrangement. Why don't the banks make the limit £100?

A. *They probably will raise the limit but the reason for keeping it down is fraud. One trick you can use is to keep back a few cheques from an old cheque book so you can cash two £50 cheques in one day. You will need to use different branches but at least when the cashier marks the back of your cheque book he will not stop you having the money.*

3/Savings

Your tax position / charges / safety ● Children's savings ● Saving for retirement ● *The effect of inflation on your money* ● National Savings ● *National Savings certificates / 2nd issue index-linked certificates / monthly income bond / investment account / deposit bond / save as you earn / yearly plan / premium bonds* ● National Savings bank ● *ordinary account* ● National Girobank ● *deposit account* ● High street banks ● *deposit account / investment account / monthly savings account / monthly income account / save and borrow accounts* ● Trustee Savings Bank ● *savings account* ● Building society accounts ● *share account / monthly savings account / monthly income account / high interest account / save as you earn* ● Stock market ● *gilt-edged stock* ● Unit trusts ● Investment trusts ● Local authority loans ● Finance companies ● Alternative investment ● Life insurance ● *endowment policies with-profits / unit-linked policies / purchased annuities / growth or income bonds / home income plans* ● Letters

As an investor, you are a highly-valued customer and many different companies will try to tempt you to save your money with them rather than with a rival.

So, the more you know about investment decisions, the better able you will be to judge any advice you are given. There are just a few basic points to get straight in your mind first.

● can you afford to lose some or all of the money in the hope of gaining a higher than average return?
● can the money be put away and forgotten about, or might you need to get it back quickly?
● do you pay tax and, if so, at what rate?
● do you need a regular income from the investment?
● are you saving regularly or occasionally?

Now ask yourself the following questions:
● do I want to take a risk with my money? or   yes/no
● do I want to know that the capital is safe?   yes/no
● do I want to be able to withdraw the money quickly? or   yes/no
● do I want to tie it up for a longer period?   yes/no
● do I pay tax?   yes/no
● do I pay tax at a higher rate?   yes/no
● do I want to receive interest monthly?   yes/no
                 half yearly?   yes/no
                 annually?   yes/no

- do I want the capital to grow and receive less in dividends? or   yes/no
- do I want to receive more income?   yes/no
- do I have a lump sum to invest? or   yes/no
- do I want to save a set amount regularly?   yes/no

As you learn more about each of the savings schemes explained below, you will see how an understanding of these basic principles of saving helps you come to a decision.

Your tax position
It is important to get this point straight first, because the amount of tax you pay can turn a good investment for a taxpayer into a bad one for the non taxpayer.

If you pay no tax at all, you should first look for savings that pay the interest to you gross (that is, without deducting tax). Next, you should consider savings where, even if the interest is paid net (after the tax has been deducted), you can reclaim it from the Inland Revenue.

For example, if you pay no tax, you should not put your money into a building society because here the tax is paid on your behalf and you cannot reclaim it, even if you do not earn enough to pay tax. From April 1985 the banks will pay interest this way too.

If you pay a high rate of tax (that is, more than the basic 30 per cent rate), then you should look first at tax-free or tax-exempt savings such as national savings certificates or SAYE contracts. These are worth even more to you than to a basic rate taxpayer.

Charges
Another question to remember when you are looking for a savings slot is: will there be a fee or charge for putting my money here? For example, if you buy shares in the stock market, you will have to pay commission, stamp duty and contract stamp charges. But there is no cost if you open a building society account.

Safety
The security of your money is an important question. Some groups have organised a fund to bale out any of their members that get into trouble.

Building society savings are protected by a scheme run by The Building Societies Association. If any building society collapses, anyone with money deposited there will, at worst, receive 75 per cent of it back. If the society is a member of the protection scheme then you will get at least 90 per cent back.

In practice, a larger society would almost certainly step in and take over the troubled society so you would probably lose nothing. It is worth while the societies doing that to preserve confidence in them.

The banks also have a Deposit Protection Bond which will pay out 75 per cent of the first £10,000 in a UK account if any bank or licensed deposit taker (that is someone licensed with the Bank of England) collapses.

Insurance policies are covered by the Policyholders' Protection Act which states that, if an insurance company fails, policyholders will receive at least 90 per cent of the money due to them. See p. 132 for more details.

CHILDREN'S SAVINGS

If children want to save, then the criteria they use to pick one investment rather than another are no different from the ones adults use. There are various special schemes aimed at attracting children's pocket money which include colourful magazines, drawing books, piggy banks and other bits and pieces that appeal to the marketing men from time to time.

But the important factor to look at when choosing an investment for a child is the rate of interest paid: if the interest is less than with a conventional account, you could be paying dearly for, say, a set of colouring pencils.

Building societies, for example, are a poor place for children's money, unless the children are wealthy enough to pay tax. However, several of them, working on the principle of 'catch them young and keep them and their mortgage for life', actively encourage children's savings.

If a grandparent, or family friend, wants to give regular sums of money over a number of years to a child, then this should, without question, be done by deed of covenant. You will not be signing away money for life, but you will receive a tax rebate, at basic rate, from the Inland Revenue. To find out exactly how to go about creating a covenant, see p. 164.

SAVING FOR RETIREMENT

The sooner you start saving for retirement, of course, the more money you will have. You should begin planning your retirement finances as soon as you can bear to think about it.

What pensioners mostly need is extra regular income: an investment which pays interest every month is more valuable than one paying out every six months. Indeed, anyone seeking an income from their savings rather than capital growth should pick a scheme that pays interest more frequently. If you take the interest out to spend, you have the money earlier. And if you leave it on deposit, the interest itself starts earning interest sooner.

THE EFFECT OF INFLATION ON YOUR MONEY

The value of the pound has changed enormously over the years.

This table shows how the pound has shrunk in value

1920	£100
1945	£111.40
1970	£45.60
1983	£9.90

This table shows how much more you have had to pay over the years to buy the same goods

1920	£100
1945	£89.80
1970	£219.20
1983	£1014.10

The interest rates on all these savings schemes show the position at July 1984. They will in time change.

NATIONAL SAVINGS

These are all schemes run by the Government which each year raises money from the public to fund the difference between its spending and its income from other sources such as taxes.

National savings certificates

They are sold in units of £25 and are meant to be kept for five years. You can' cash them in sooner but will get less interest if you do.

The national savings certificates on sale at the time of publication are the 28th Issue. The interest on these will never change; when the Government wants to alter the rate, it will issue a new certificate.

interest rate	after 1 year 6·52%, in 2 years 7·08%, in 3 years 7·69%, in 4 years 8·33%, in 5 years 9·00% Average rate over five years: 9·00% A £100 certificate is worth £153.88 after five years
interest paid	when certificates are cashed in
tax	free of all income and capital gains tax
minimum investment	£25 (each unit costs £25)
maximum investment	£5000
charges	nil
safety	secure
how to invest	at a post office or bank
money tied up	five years to receive full benefit
cashing in	ask at post office for application form and pre-paid envelope addressed to: Director, Savings Certificate and SAYE Office, Durham DH99 1NS. It will take about eight working days You do not have to cash in the certificates after five years. They will continue to earn interest at the common extension rate applying at the time. In July 1984 it was 8·52%.

2nd Issue index-linked certificates
The value of these, after one complete year, rises in line with the increase in the retail prices index. When inflation is high, the certificates increase in value sharply, but when inflation is low, the return is smaller. The aim is to maintain the spending power of your money.

The first index-linked certificates were nicknamed 'granny bonds' when they came out because they were available to elderly people only. The 2nd Issue can now be held by anyone of any age, even babies.

interest rate	no interest as such is paid. The certificates grow at the same speed as inflation; in addition there is a 4% bonus after five years; an additional second bonus worth 4% will be paid on the tenth anniversary. There is also a supplement, accumulated monthly, worth 3% a year if the certificates are held for a full 12 months until 1 November 1985. At least three further annual supplements will be paid. The value of index-linked certificates, updated monthly, is shown on a chart displayed in post offices
interest paid	when certificates are cashed in
tax	tax free
minimum investment	£10 (each unit costs £10)
maximum investment	£10,000. This amount can be held in addition to any other national savings certificates
charges	nil
safety	secure
how to invest	at post offices or banks
money tied up	one year to receive any index-linking
cashing in	same as ordinary certificates. For up-to-date rates (24-hour service), South: London (01-) 603 8646/603 8672, North: Lytham St Annes 0253 723714, Scotland: Glasgow (041) 632 2766

Monthly income bond
This is for tying up large sums of money for long periods to receive an income each month.

interest rate	12·75% but can change
interest paid	either straight into a bank account or sent to you through the post on the 5th of every month
tax	paid gross but taxable
minimum investment	£2000
maximum investment	£50,000

Monthly income bond continued

charges	nil
safety	secure
how to invest	at post offices or from: Director of Savings, Bonds & Stock Office, Blackpool, Lancs FY3 9YP
money tied up	at least one year
cashing in	after six months, and with three months' notice without loss of interest; otherwise there are penalties. In the first year you receive half the rate of interest, after one year and with three months' notice, there is no loss of interest. You can withdraw only in multiples of £1000.

Investment account

This is sometimes abbreviated to 'Invac'.

interest rate	12%
interest paid	same as ordinary account
tax	interest paid gross but taxable
minimum investment	£1
maximum investment	£50,000
charges	nil
safety	secure
how to invest	at post offices
money tied up	one month's notice
cashing in	application form at post offices which is sent to: National Savings Bank, Glasgow G58 1SB.

Deposit bond

This offers a competitive rate of interest if you tie up a large sum of money for a long time.

interest rate	12·75% but can change
interest paid	once a year on anniversary of purchase; it is added on to the capital investment
tax	paid gross but is liable to income tax
minimum investment	£250; can be bought in £50 units only
maximum investment	£50,000
charges	nil
safety	secure
how to invest	at post offices or through newspaper advertisements
money tied up	at least one year, otherwise there is a penalty
cashing in	you can withdraw only in multiples of £50; after one year at three months' notice; in first year still three months' notice but you

will receive only half the published interest rate, unless repayment is due to the death of bondholder. Apply to your local post office or Deposit Bond Office, National Savings, Glasgow G58 1SB.

Save as you Earn (SAYE)

These are no longer available but contributions under existing contracts will continue until 1989. A 3% supplement for the year to 1 December 1985 will be paid.

Yearly Plan

This is a new scheme for national savings, introduced in July 1984, to replace the index-linked Save as you Earn. It gives a rate of interest guaranteed for five years on regular savings.

interest rate	in saving year 6%; certificate cashed in 1 month to 2 years 7%; 2 years to 4 years 8%; if held full four years 9·5%; average overall rate over 5 years is 9·06% compound
tax	tax free
minimum investment	£20 a month
maximum investment	£100 a month
charges	nil
safety	secure
how to invest	at any post office but you can pay by bank standing order only
money tied up	one year but you can leave it at the same rate of interest for five years
cashing in	application forms at post offices or from: Savings Certificates Office, Durham DH99 1NS.

SAYE share option issue series B

This contract is available only for anyone entitled to buy shares under a share option scheme. A share option scheme is organised by your employer but must be approved by the Inland Revenue. If you leave your job, you can continue the SAYE contract.

interest rate	none as such but bonuses equal to 14 and 28 monthly instalments are paid after five and seven years
interest paid	when contract is cashed
tax	tax free
minimum investment	£10 a month, deducted from pay
maximum investment	£100
charges	nil
safety	secure

how to invest	ask your employer
money tied up	at least five years. If you fail to keep up the payments, interest is paid on a cancelled contract at 6%
cashing in	ask your employer. For more details see p. 149.

Premium Bonds

These are a gamble, not an investment. A prize draw is held every month, with a smaller weekly draw each Saturday. The winning numbers are selected by ERNIE, the Electronic Random Number Indicator Equipment. The amount of money paid out in prizes is equivalent to 7·75% of all the money invested in premium bonds. Winners are notified by post.

interest rate	nil
tax	prizes are tax free
minimum purchase	£5
maximum purchase	£10,000
charges	nil
safety	the capital is guaranteed to be returned
how to buy	at post offices and banks
money tied up	about eight working days to get it back
cashing in	repayment forms from post offices or banks should be sent to: Bonds & Stock Office, Lytham St Annes, Lancs FY0 1YN.

NATIONAL GIROBANK

Deposit account

This works the same way as a deposit account with any high street bank but you must have a current account with Girobank before you can open a deposit account. You will find Girobank at post office branches.

interest rate	9%
interest paid	every six months
tax	interest paid gross but taxable until April 1985, then net
minimum investment	25p
maximum investment	none
charges	nil
safety	secure
how to invest	from Girobank current account using transfer slips in cheque book
money tied up	no notice period, but loss of seven days' interest
cashing in	at post offices, via current account.

NATIONAL SAVINGS BANK

Ordinary account

interest rate	6% on £500 or more held for one calendar year. 3% on smaller sums and until the start of the calendar year. For example, if you invested £600 on 9 January 1984, you will receive the lower rate until 1 January 1985
interest paid	once a year on 31 December
tax	first £70 of interest is tax free. Interest is paid gross and taxable after £70
minimum investment	£1
maximum investment	£10,000
charges	nil
safety	secure
how to invest	at post offices
money tied up	up to £100 on demand; up to £50 at any post office without sending pass book away. With a regular customer account, you can cash up to £250 a day at one nominated office
cashing in	at post offices or from National Savings Bank, Glasgow G58 1SB. Will take a few days.

HIGH STREET BANKS

The precise terms and conditions will vary from bank to bank but the broad outlines remain the same. From April 1985, the way banks are taxed will change. They will then be on a 'composite' rate of tax like building societies and will deduct tax before paying interest to savers. Non-taxpaying investors will not be able to reclaim the tax paid on their behalf.

Deposit account

interest rate	variable: 9%
interest paid	every six months, sometimes quarterly
tax	interest paid gross but taxable. From April 1985 will be paid net and tax not reclaimable
minimum investment	£1
maximum investment	none
charges	nil
safety	depositors' protection scheme
how to invest	at any branch of a high street bank
money tied up	seven days
cashing in	seven days' notice at branch.

Investment account or money at notice
This will pay a higher rate of interest than a deposit account but your money is tied up for a longer period of time: the longer the period, the higher the interest.

interest rate	½% to 2% above deposit rate
interest paid	half yearly or monthly
tax	interest paid gross but taxable until April 1985, then net
minimum investment	from £50 to £5000
maximum investment	usually none
charges	nil
safety	depositors' protection scheme
how to invest	ask at any bank branch
money tied up	one, three or six months as agreed
cashing in	at agreed notice period or with loss of interest.

Monthly savings account
An agreement to save a set amount each month.

interest rate	about 2% to 3% above deposit rate
interest paid	half yearly, either into a current account or added to savings account
tax	interest paid gross but taxable until April 1985, then net
minimum investment	£10 a month; some banks allow alterations
maximum investment	none
charges	nil
safety	depositors' protection scheme
how to invest	at any bank branch
money tied up	six months, sometimes more
cashing in	at six months' notice.

Monthly income account

interest rate	1% to 3½% above deposit rate
interest paid	monthly
tax	interest paid gross but taxable until April 1985, then net
minimum investment	up to £2500
maximum investment	can be £50,000
charges	nil
safety	depositors' protection scheme
how to invest	at bank branches
money tied up	could be one or two years
cashing in	ask at branch.

Save and borrow accounts
These are half and half accounts where you invest a fixed amount each
month and can borrow up to 30 times that figure. For more details, see
revolving credit on p. 55.

TRUSTEE SAVINGS BANK (TSB)
This is similar to the high street banks. The TSBs at present are divided
into autonomous groups around the country, but in 1985 they will be
merged into one.

Savings account

interest rate	variable: 4%
interest paid	annually on 20 November
tax	interest paid gross but taxable until April 1985, then net
minimum investment	5p
maximum investment	none
charges	nil
safety	secure
how to invest	at any TSB branch
money tied up	money back on demand, or a few days for large amounts
cashing in	at the branch.

Investment account

interest rate	higher for longer periods of notice
interest paid	annually, as savings account
tax	interest paid gross but taxable until April 1985, then net
minimum investment	£1
maximum investment	none
charges	nil
safety	secure
how to invest	at any TSB branch
money tied up	one or three months as agreed
cashing in	at the branch.

Term deposit account
For lump sums over a long period.

interest rate	higher than for more flexible accounts
interest paid	quarterly, half yearly or annually
tax	interest paid gross but taxable until April 1985, then net
minimum investment	£100 to £1000
maximum investment	none

Term deposit account continued

charges	nil
safety	secure
how to invest	at any TSB branch
money tied up	for several years
cashing in	at the branch.

Maxiyield

This is for very large sums of money and the terms can be varied to suit each customer.

interest rate	2% to 3% higher than other TSB rates
interest paid	annually on 20 November
tax	interest paid gross but taxable until April 1985, then net
minimum investment	£10,000
maximum investment	none
charges	nil
safety	secure
how to invest	at any TSB branch
money tied up	for an agreed period of months or years
cashing in	at the branch.

Money markets

All the banks will allow you to put very large sums of money on deposit with them for a few weeks at the going money market rates, which are higher than the ordinary rates. See also p. 46 for money funds.

BUILDING SOCIETY ACCOUNTS

If you do not pay tax, you should think twice before putting money into a building society account. The building societies have a special arrangement with the Inland Revenue whereby they pay a 'composite' rate of tax on behalf of investors. At around 25 per cent, this rate is lower than basic rate income tax.

This tax cannot be reclaimed from the taxman, even if you are not a taxpayer. If you pay tax at basic rate, there is no more to pay but, if you are a higher rate taxpayer, you will have to pay the extra above basic rate. From April 1985, banks will operate on the same system.

The maximum amount of money you can invest in any one building society is £30,000 or £60,000 in a joint account. But you can invest this maximum amount in as many different building societies as you like. If you have several separate accounts with one society you are still limited to £30,000 or £60,000.

As well as the basic types of account, individual variations appear from time to time at different societies. Ask several building societies with branches near you what they have to offer.

Share account

interest rate	basic rate which most societies pay is 7¾% net at August 1984
interest paid	half yearly
tax	paid for you at basic rate
minimum investment	£1
maximum investment	£30,000 (or £60,000 for a joint account)
charges	nil
safety	investors' protection scheme
how to invest	at any building society branch, or by post or bank transfer
money tied up	instant withdrawals usually allowed of several hundred pounds; a few days for larger sums
cashing in	at any branch or by post.

Monthly savings account

This is for regular savings.

interest rate	a little higher than basic
interest paid	usually annually
tax	paid for you at basic rate
minimum investment	about £1 a month
maximum investment	£30,000 (£60,000)
charges	nil
safety	investors' protection scheme
how to invest	anv building society branch, or by post
money tied up	normally immediately available
cashing in	at any branch or by post.

Monthly income account

A few societies offer this account.

interest rate	varies between societies
interest paid	monthly
tax	paid for you at basic rate
minimum investment	around £1000
maximum investment	£30,000 (£60,000)
charges	nil
safety	investors' protection scheme
how to invest	at any branch or by post
money tied up	varies
cashing in	at any branch or by post.

High interest account
These offer higher interest rates in exchange for longer periods of notice.

interest	about 1% above basic
interest paid	half yearly
tax	paid for you at basic rate
minimum investment	varies
maximum investment	£30,000 (£60,000)
charges	nil
safety	investors' protection scheme
how to invest	at any branch or by post
money tied up	typically 28–90 days' notice to withdraw or immediate access with loss of interest on the amount withdrawn
cashing in	at any branch or by post.

Save as you Earn (SAYE)
The terms are the same at all building societies but you can join only one scheme. You make monthly payments for five years and can leave the money for a further two years for an additional bonus.

interest rate	after five years a bonus worth 14 months' savings (equal to 8·3%) after seven years, a bonus worth another 14 months' savings (equal to 8·6%)
tax	tax free
minimum investment	£1 a month
maximum investment	£20 a month
charges	nil
safety	investors' protection scheme
how to invest	at any branch or by post
money tied up	you can stop payments at any time. In the first year, you will receive no interest at all, but after that, 6% on the amount you have paid in. If you were to die, you would get 8%
cashing in	at any branch or by post.

STOCK MARKET

Much of the business of buying stocks and shares is done by large institutional investors. But there is still room for the small man.

It is an investment for anyone whose main aim is capital growth and not income.

This is a high-risk investment (the stock exchange is sometimes compared with a casino) and you should use only spare money you do not need and can risk losing to buy shares.

Ordinary shares

dividend	depends on the success of the company
dividend paid	half yearly
tax	basic rate tax is deducted before you receive the dividend but can be reclaimed if you are not a taxpayer. If you pay higher rate tax, you will have to pay more. Capital gains tax is payable on the profit
minimum investment	probably £800 to £1000 in each company to be worth while but it is better to spread several thousand pounds over a few different companies
maximum investment	none
charges	buying: 1·65% commission (minimum £8 upwards) + 1% stamp duty + 60p contract stamp; selling: the same commission and contract stamp. Ask before you buy
safety	high risk
how to invest	through a stockbroker or bank manager
money tied up	you can get your money back within a couple of weeks if you are forced to sell but, of course, at the price ruling at the time
cashing in	will take a couple of weeks.

(See also share option schemes p. 149.)

Gilt-edged stock

These are commonly known as 'gilts' and are Government stock issued by the Government to raise money. They are traded on the stock market with names like Treasury $9\frac{1}{2}$ per cent 1988 or Exchequer $10\frac{1}{2}$ per cent 1997.

Each one has a par value of £100 and you are guaranteed to get that back on the date mentioned in the title. But the actual cost will vary from day to day because the value is affected by the rate of interest, which is called the 'coupon'. This can be as low as 3 per cent or as high as 15 per cent.

There are two elements to the return from an investment in gilts: the interest rate and the difference in price between what you pay for the stock and the redemption value, that is the price you get at the end.

As well as the problem of choosing which gilt to buy, it is also important to get the timing right for the best chance of increasing your money. Professionals exercise their brainpower all day long worrying about this, but broadly the aim is to **buy gilts just before interest rates go down and to sell them just before interest rates rise.**

dividend	variable
dividend paid	half yearly
tax	income tax to pay but, if you hold gilts for more than one year, there is no capital gains tax.
	If you buy through the post office or TSB, the dividend is paid gross; if you buy through a stockbroker it is paid net
minimum investment	£250 to be worth while
maximum investment	none
charges	commission charges to pay for the small investor but they are lower if you buy through a post office. Then the charge is £1 for investments up to £125 and another 50p for every extra £125. Selling costs are £1 for every £100 to £250 realised; below £100 the cost is 10p for every £10; over £250 it is £1 plus 50p for every additional £125. There is no stamp duty to pay
safety	the nominal value is guaranteed at the date of maturity but the value of the investment can go up or down before the redemption date
how to invest	through a stockbroker or bank; a limited but broad selection is available on the national savings stock register at the post office
money tied up	a few days to get back
cashing in	will take about a week from the same source as you bought.

Index-linked gilts

These have a lower coupon than ordinary gilts, usually 2 or 2½ per cent, but at the redemption date you receive the nominal value plus an amount linked to the retail prices index which makes up for what inflation has taken away. It is the capital itself which is index-linked.

UNIT TRUSTS

Unit trusts spread the risk of investing in the stock market. Your money is added to everyone else's in the same fund and is managed by a professional fund manager.

There is still a risk because the value of units can, and on occasions will, go down as well as up, just as the price of shares on the stock market fluctuates. The fund manager's job is to get as good growth as he can. **Unit trusts mainly provide capital growth rather than income**.

Sometimes there are dramatic rises in a specialist fund but, because highly specific funds are more volatile, they can also collapse.

There is a plethora of unit trusts to choose from – around 650 – ranging from all-purpose general funds to the highly specialised. For a beginner, the best advice is to go for a general fund, on the basis that the wider the fund manager can spread his investments, the smaller the risk.

One way of picking a fund is to look at the performance tables published in specialist magazines for previous years. But remember that, while a fund may come out top of the league one year, it may not do as well the next.

Also, the funds that come top are as likely to be the ones that come bottom another year because spectacular growth will have been caused by exceptional circumstances.

You can use the performance tables to see how different funds in the same sector (for example gold) compare.

It seems unnecessary to have so many different trusts to choose from and more are launched almost every week. One reason why there is such a large number is that fund managers find it easier to sell a 'new' fund, like 'new improved' packets of washing powder. Also, financial advisers, the middle men, appear to be doing their job if they advise you to switch out of, say, 'Japan' and into 'small UK recovery' funds.

Unit trusts are essentially a long-term investment. There are charges involved in buying and selling, just as there are with stocks and shares, so you would need a very good gain to cover the costs of selling units you have held for a short time only.

Ever since unit trusts began to increase in number and popularity in the 1950s, no investor has lost his money through fraudulent mismanagement. This is because of the way trusts are set up. There are three elements: the unit holder; the manager; and the trustee. A trust deed is drawn up and the companies are strictly controlled by the Department of Trade and Industry.

The unit holder, or investor, hands his money to the manager, who passes it on to the trustee. The trustee is an independent company, often a large bank or insurance business.

The manager decides where to invest the money, but the trustee buys the shares and holds them. Because of the tight control, the manager would find it difficult to fiddle the books or run off with the money.

Money in any fund is divided into small units of equal value. The prices are quoted daily in the *Financial Times* but two different figures are given: one is the 'offer' price and the other the 'bid'. The offer price is what you will have to pay to buy the units; the bid price is lower and is what the company will pay to buy them back. The difference between the two is the amount which covers administration costs.

As well as investing a lump sum in a unit trust, you can sometimes take up a monthly savings plan and buy so many pounds worth of units; the minimum is £10 a month. Some months you will get more units for your money and in others less because of the changes in price.

dividend	the dividend you will receive depends on how high a dividend the unit trust receives from the companies it has invested in. But more important is how much your capital grows.
capital profit	the gain from an investment in unit trusts depends on how the price of the units has risen or fallen since you bought them
dividend paid	usually half yearly; the money can be paid to you or used to buy more units
tax	to pay; the main burden will be capital gains tax
minimum investment	around £250 to be worth while
maximum investment	none
charges	initial charge 5% to 5½%; annual charge ¾% to 1%
safety	trust fund arrangement protects your money against fraud but the value can go up or down
how to invest	contact a particular unit trust direct (they are listed in the *Financial Times* and advertise in all newspapers) or ask your bank manager, stockbroker, an insurance broker, or financial adviser
money tied up	immediate withdrawal possible but you want to choose your timing to take best advantage of the price
cashing in	same as investing.

INVESTMENT TRUSTS

These are not unlike unit trusts but there are certain important differences. You invest in the shares of an investment company whose business is buying and selling shares.

The value of your investment is not directly linked to the value of the investments that the company owns, as it would be with unit trusts, and generally the market price of the shares is worth less than this portfolio. This is why investment trust shares are often said to be traded at a 'discount'.

Unlike unit trusts, investment trusts are not limited to investing their money in the stock market.

dividend	varies
dividend paid	half yearly
tax	basic rate is deducted before you receive the dividend but it is reclaimable; higher rate taxpayers will have to pay more

minimum investment	at least £600 to be worth while
maximum investment	none
charges	same as buying on the stock market
safety	high risk
how to invest	through a stock broker or bank manager. For more information contact the Association of Investment Trust Companies, address on p. 248
money tied up	couple of weeks
cashing in	couple of weeks.

LOCAL AUTHORITY LOANS

Like the Government, local authorities need to raise money and one way is to take loans from the public (the other way is through the rates). Once fixed, the terms will not change during the period of the loan.

Fixed term loans

interest rate	varies daily, but comparable with high street banks; higher rates paid on very large sums (£15,000+)
interest paid	half yearly
tax	basic rate tax deducted but reclaimable
minimum investment	around £500 to £1000
maximum investment	none
charges	none
safety	secure
how to invest	contact individual local authorities or Local Authority Loans Bureau (address on p. 249). There is a fee of £2.50 if you send stamped addressed envelope for list but the information is free if you telephone in the afternoon 01-920 0501
money tied up	for period of loan
cashing in	at end of period only.

Negotiable yearling bonds

These can be sold before the end of the period of the loan and operate very much in the same way as gilts.

interest rate	agreed each Wednesday for new issues; variable for bonds in issue
interest paid	half yearly
tax	income tax or capital gains tax to pay; benefit to high rate taxpayer in selling before redemption
minimum investment	£1000
maximum investment	none

charges	stockbrokers' commission if you buy or sell in the market but none if you buy when the bonds are first issued and hold to redemption
safety	as with gilts
how to invest	through a bank or stockbroker
money tied up	no
cashing in	takes a couple of weeks.

FINANCE COMPANIES

These are usually subsidiaries of large UK or foreign banks and are commonly known as money shops. Make sure you know the parentage of any finance company before placing money with it.

Deposit account

interest rates	varies but probably about the same as banks
interest paid	quarterly or half yearly; sometimes only at the end of period
tax	to pay; interest can be paid gross or net until April 1985
minimum investment	up to £50
maximum investment	none
charges	none
safety	first 75% of up to £10,000 guaranteed
how to invest	look for newspaper advertisements or write to Finance Houses Association
money tied up	three or six months
cashing in	at end of period only.

Money funds or high interest cheque accounts

These are run by some finance companies and banks. Your money is aggregated with other people's to take advantage of the higher rates of interest offered for very large sums of money on the London money markets. Some money funds give you a cheque book but there will probably be a minimum size cheque you can write, say £200.

interest rate	varies but a little better than the banks
interest paid	half yearly or quarterly
tax	to pay
minimum investment	£1000 to £2500
maximum investment	none
charges	yes, varying between companies
safety	first 75% of up to £10,000 guaranteed
how to invest	write to the individual companies whose names you will find in the *Financial Times*
money tied up	seven days
cashing in	apply to the company.

ALTERNATIVE INVESTMENT

There is a myriad of artifacts under this heading: investing in gold coins, diamonds, wine, busted bonds, antiques, stamps, paintings, clocks, limited editions, silver, Persian rugs, or anything else you can think of that might increase in value after you have bought it.

These are investments best left to the experts. If you specially want to own, say, finely-printed second-hand books and enjoy seeing them on the shelf, then by all means buy. But if you are acquiring for the sole purpose of investing, then there are far surer ways of increasing the value of your money.

However, you may be tempted by two well-advertised forms of alternative investment: commodities and foreign currencies.

COMMODITIES

Commodity prices can show spectacular gyrations; so many of the factors affecting the price are beyond anyone's control: bad weather; a bumper crop; a political uprising; fluctuating exchange rates.

Commodities break down into two categories: the metals (such as copper, tin, lead, silver, zinc); and the soft (including coffee, rubber, wool, barley). The commodity markets trade in either physicals or futures: that is you either take delivery of the actual commodity or you buy for delivery at a future date, though in practice you never take delivery.

You can join a syndicate and buy through a commodity broker but the best way for a small investor to start buying commodities is through commodity funds or specialist trusts: a unit trust, an investment trust; or an offshore commodity trust.

CURRENCIES

The simplest way of investing in foreign currencies is to open a foreign currency deposit account at a bank. You will be earning interest and you will make a gain if the foreign exchange rates move in your favour. You can do this only when, as at present, there are no exchange controls.

If you want to leave the timing to professionals, you can put your money into a currency fund which will almost certainly be based offshore. You will see advertisements for them. None ties your money up for more than a few days.

A managed currency fund operates on the unit trust principle: your money buys units in a fund. The money is aggregated and used to buy and sell currencies. The minimum investment will be at least £1000 and you will have to pay charges at about the same rate as unit trusts charge: 5 per cent initially and about 1 per cent a year.

LIFE INSURANCE

You can take out a life insurance policy which will pay money to your dependants when you die, called term insurance, But you can also take out a different type of policy which is a long-term investment with life insurance included. This is an endowment policy.

There are other life insurance policies which are used for savings: unit-linked insurance, annuities, which are a kind of pension, and growth or income bonds. There is no longer tax relief on new insurance policies.

Endowment policies with-profits

interest rate	comes in the form of bonuses: regular (reversionary) bonuses which are added to the sum assured (they are not guaranteed); and terminal bonuses determined when the policy matures. The size of bonus varies from company to company but it is not guaranteed by any of them
tax	income tax or capital gains tax is not generally payable on life insurance policies
minimum investment	£5 to £10 a month
maximum investment	none
charges	premiums include fees
safety	Policyholders' Protection Act
how to invest	contact an insurance company direct or as an insurance broker to obtain quotations
money tied up	at least ten years
cashing in	you can but will get poor value especially in the early years of the policy. See p. 130 for an example of early surrender values.

Unit-linked policies

Most of the premium you pay buys units in a fund of investments run by the insurance company.

interest rate	variable
interest paid	when you cash in the policy or die
tax	same as endowment policies
minimum investment	£5 to £50 a month
maximum investment	none
charges	premiums include fixed fee, about $5\frac{1}{2}\%$ and annual charge of around $\frac{3}{4}\%$
safety	Policyholders' Protection Act
how to invest	same as endowment
money tied up	ten years
cashing in	you can but will get poor value if units are low at the time.

Purchased annuities

This is a way of receiving extra money in retirement. An annuity is an investment of capital to receive a regular pay out. You can take out an 'immediate' annuity which starts paying straightaway or a 'deferred' annuity which begins at a later date.

How much you receive depends on how old you are when you take out the policy and what type of annuity you buy. There is no going back once you have bought an annuity; if interest rates improve, you are stuck with the rate at which you bought, but if rates fall you stay better off.

interest rate	variable but fixed when you sign the policy
interest paid	in form of pension when you retire and until you die
tax	as above but interest content of pension is taxed as earned income; capital content is tax free
minimum investment	up to £1000 lump sum or £10 a month
maximum investment	none
charges	yes
safety	Policyholders' Protection Act
how to invest	as above
capital tied up	until you die
cashing in	not possible.

Growth or income bonds

A lump sum or single premium investment offering a guaranteed rate of interest. You invest your money for a fixed period of years and for a fixed rate of return. These bonds are often available for limited periods only.

While the interest on income bonds may be high, the capital does not increase, so will be eaten away by inflation.

interest rate	fixed at the outset
interest paid	annually for income bonds; on maturity for growth bonds
tax	tax paid at basic rate, higher rate taxpayers will have to pay more
minimum investment	£500 to £2500
maximum investment	none
charges	none built-in
safety	Policyholders' Protection Act
how to invest	as above
money tied up	one to ten years
cashing in	not possible.

Home income plans

This is a way of raising money from your house when you are elderly. See p. 107 for details.

Friendly societies

These have almost disappeared since they were cut back in the March 1984 Budget. See p. 131.

Offshore insurance companies

If you are thinking of putting your money into an insurance company which is based outside the United Kingdom in order to save tax, be very careful. Not all of these companies are as closely controlled as UK companies and some have collapsed leaving policyholders without any money.

The Department of Trade and Industry now insists that, when an overseas insurance company advertises in the United Kingdom for business, it must declare in the advertisement that it is an offshore company and that your investment is not covered by the same protection as UK companies offer.

HOW YOUR SAVINGS GROW

If you save £20 a month:

	6%	7%	8%	9%	10%	11%	12%
after 12 months	248	249	250	252	253	254	256
after 2 years	510	516	521	526	531	537	542
after 3 years	789	801	813	825	837	850	862
after 4 years	1084	1106	1128	1151	1174	1198	1222

If you invest a lump sum of £1000

	6%	7%	8%	9%	10%	11%	12%
after 12 months	1061	1071	1082	1092	1103	1113	1124
after 2 years	1125	1147	1170	1192	1215	1239	1262
after 3 years	1194	1229	1265	1302	1340	1379	1418
after 4 years	1267	1317	1368	1422	1477	1534	1594
after 5 years	1344	1410	1480	1553	1629	1708	1791

LETTERS

Q. I know that inflation eats into my savings but just how much does it take away?

A. *The easy formula to remember is that, if inflation is running at 10 per cent, your money is halved every seven years. But inflation is not always so high. In 1983 it fell to less than 4 per cent, and you were getting a 'real' return on your savings.*

That means that the rate of interest is higher than the rate of inflation. In previous years, interest rates were lower than inflation which is why index-linked investments became popular, to restore some of the gap.

Q. I have seen several advertisements offering 'guaranteed' interest rates. Are these a good buy?

A. *They are if interest rates fall after you invest; they are a bad deal if rates rise. At times when interest rates are moving down, you are unlikely to see many 'guaranteed' rates. The disadvantage is that you are tying your money up for some years, during which time interest rates could move in any direction.*

National savings certificates and local authority loans always offer a guaranteed return.

You may have seen an advertisement for guaranteed income bonds. These are life insurance policies designed as an investment; they have a limited life and a fixed rate of interest.

Q. How can index-linked national savings certificates actually be worth less one month than in the month before when inflation is still rising?

A. *To work out the cash-in value of your certificates, you multiply the purchase price by the retail prices index figure shown during the month you want to cash in. Then divide by the index figure ruling in the month you bought the certificates.*

When the rate of increase of inflation was falling, although prices were still going up, the formula resulted in lower values some months.

4/Borrowing

Where to borrow • Bank loans • *overdraft / personal loan / revolving credit / budget account / impressing the bank manager / security* • Money shops •Money lenders • Money brokers • Life insurance policy • Credit schemes • *credit cards / bank credit cards / stores' credit cards / shop's revolving credit* / Other ways to borrow • *hire purchase / mail order / trading checks / credit unions* • Your rights • *credit scoring / credit reference agency / Consumer Credit Act / problems repaying*

Debt is no longer the dirty word it used to be and, certainly, using someone else's money instead of your own is an acceptable practice today. Indeed, if you are considered a good risk, you are positively encouraged to borrow.

But if you want, or in fact, need to borrow, obviously you want to do so on the best possible terms. Do not be fooled by deliberately misleading advertisements that say: 'only £5 a week to buy this three-piece suite' or '£10,000 no questions asked at 10 per cent per annum'. There is more to it than this and anyway, this sort of wording is illegal. You need to know far more details before signing any agreement.

You should know:
● exactly how much you are going to pay each month
● for how long
● whether you can pay off the loan sooner than planned
● what the APR is
● whether you are allowed to miss one or more payments without penalty

The initials APR stand for annual percentage rate and this figure enables you to compare more precisely the rate you are paying. This is because it must include any hidden charges which the lender adds on. The sort of unseen extras that might be sneaked in are an arrangement fee for setting up the loan; the frequent calculation of interest; or the cost of insurance to cover you if you become unable to repay the loan.

Whenever you are applying for credit, you have the right to ask for a quotation. This will give you all the details of the terms of the agreement.

A 'flat' rate loan at 10 per cent can work out far more expensive than a 'true' rate of 10½ per cent. 'Flat' rate is the basic rate; 'true' rate means the same as APR.

So, remember always to look at the true rate of interest, or APR, rather than the flat rate. All lenders, must by law show the APR whenever they mention interest rate figures. Building societies must start doing so from September 1986.

By law, until you are 18 years old, you are not legally liable for your debts. So, in practice, you are unlikely to be given credit until you reach that age.

WHERE TO BORROW

There are various places you can go to ask for a loan and you should approach the cheapest and most appropriate one for you.

The questions to decide first are:
● how much you want to borrow
● how quickly do you want to pay it back
● how much you can afford to repay

If you want to borrow a large sum, the best buy is an insurance policy loan or a bank loan.

For smaller amounts linked to buying a specific item, you can sometimes buy using a shop's own credit scheme or compare prices in a mail order catalogue. If you want the loan for a short time only, use a credit card or ask for an overdraft.

The best deal is an interest-free loan which some large stores offer from time to time. But check the price of the item first: you might still be able to buy it cheaper for cash elsewhere.

The places you will see offering loans are:
● a bank
● a money shop
● money broker
● money lender

or you can borrow money against an insurance policy.

You can buy on credit with a credit card, on mail order, hire purchase, provident checks and using stores' own credit schemes.

Just how much you can, or want, to borrow depends on the circumstances. If you desperately want a motor bike and do not mind spending less money in the pub, then you will borrow as much as you need. But there is a point at which the lender will say NO you simply cannot afford this.

This is not a show of concern for your welfare, only with the likelihood of getting his money back.

With some loans you can claim tax relief: these occasions are mainly when you borrow money to buy or improve a home. There is a limit to the amount on which you can claim tax relief and this is £30,000 including all the loans you have for the purpose.

For more details about home loans see Chapter 5: Buying your Home.

BANK LOANS

The bank is the obvious place to start if you need a little extra money. The bank manager has several schemes to offer but it is his duty to make the best deal for the bank that he can.

However, what is a good deal for him is not necessarily the best for you.

Overdraft

The cheapest way of borrowing from a bank is by arranging an overdraft. It is also very flexible. There is no set interest rate at any bank – the manager makes up his mind about exactly how much to charge depending on how highly he values your custom. You can negotiate this but the rate will be somewhere between 3 and 5 per cent over bank base rate. Base rate itself is a flat annual rate, not an APR.

Note that National Girobank and the Trustee Savings Bank do not allow customers to become overdrawn, unless they come into an unusually difficult patch for a brief period of time, when the manager might agree to allow a short overdraft.

The beauty of an overdraft is that **you pay interest charges only when your ordinary bank account is in the red**. So, each time you pay in a cheque or receive your monthly salary, you swing back into credit for a time and do not pay interest.

Bank managers do not take kindly, however, if you help yourself to this facility. It is not 'your' money that you are taking but the 'bank's'. It is a courtesy, and a more likely way of succeeding in future, if you ask the manager first.

The request could be either for a specific amount over a limited period, or a regular agreement for you to spend more money than you have in the account. It is entirely up to the manager what he allows you to do.

But, if you want to borrow money for a longer term, he will point you to a personal loan.

Personal loan

Particularly if you want to buy consumer goods, the bank manager will prefer you to take out a personal loan rather than an overdraft.

His argument for this is that with a personal loan you will know exactly where you stand each month and just how much money you have to repay.

The loan will probably be spread over two years and it will cost you more than an overdraft.

Revolving credit

Many banks run schemes which offer continuous credit. You pay an agreed sum of money each month into a special account and in return you can borrow up to 30 times the monthly figure. No questions are asked about how you want to spend the money.

The money is paid into a separate bank account with a separate cheque book but your usual cheque guarantee card. Interest is charged at around 5 per cent over base rate when the account is in the red but you receive interest at a lower rate if you have built up a credit balance. You will pay a charge each time you write out a cheque.

Budget account

Only a few banks offer a budget account and they operate in different ways. Basically, you calculate how much you will spend in the coming year on all your foreseeable bills, add on the charge for running the account, divide by 12 and pay this amount each month into a special bank account with a separate cheque book.

In theory, you will be all square by the end of the year but, if not, you settle the difference. See p. 13.

Impressing the bank manager

Really, all he cares about is that you will repay the loan when you say you will. Any other consideration is secondary.

Quite likely the bank will use credit scoring (see p. 61) to assess your request; this gives less opportunity for impressing the manager.

It does not matter what you want the money for, as long as the purpose is legal. So, when deciding whether or not to let you have the loan the bank manager will be looking for a good track record.

Perhaps you have borrowed before and repaid a loan. Or you may have been saving regularly with the bank for some time. These are both very good points in your favour.

If you do not have any such proof of your reliability, having a monthly salary cheque paid into your current account is a good sign.

But, even without this, you can still convince a bank manager of your creditworthiness. Does your appearance matter? This will depend entirely on the bank manager. Some will expect you to look clean and tidy when you sit down on the imitation-leather visitor's chair.

Others, and probably the majority, **would rather see you in your normal work clothes, even if you have just come off a building site**. They are not misled by someone who has rushed home to change, hoping to impress with an uncharacteristically smart appearance.

Security

If the bank manager does not know you already when you approach him, he may ask for security for a loan. You may have thought it essential anyway, before asking for a loan, that you have something such as an insurance policy to offer the bank manager as a guarantee against the loan. But this is not so.

Banks do not like having to resort to selling a customer's personal belongings if you default on a debt. They would much rather make sure that the customer is creditworthy in the first place.

So, security becomes a very small consideration, unless you wanted an unusually large loan, when the bank might insist on your taking out a second mortgage on your home.

Never hesitate to ask your bank manager for a loan: he will always listen to a proposition. But, the better you have prepared your case for meeting repayments and organising your finances, the more likely he is to accede.

MONEY SHOPS

Not everyone wants to use a bank to raise a loan. Recognising this fact, some finance companies have set up shops in the high street to lend money and provide financial services for the individual in less forbidding surroundings.

These have become known as 'money shops'. Their aim is to be readily accessible to anyone wanting to borrow money, and in particular to those who might be nervous about walking into one of the high street banks.

The names you will see in the street are subsidiaries of large organisations, sometimes foreign ones. The well-established money shops can be divided into two groups: those owned by a finance company and those owned by a bank. The names you are most likely to come across are: Avco; Beneficial Trust; Boston Moneyshops; Chartered Trust; Citibank; Forward Trust; HFC; and Western Trust and Savings.

Very often the parent is an American company. Money shops are better established in the United States and American banks are keen to export their expertise over here.

The loans available from money shops are very similar to those offered by the high street banks but the interest rates will be higher. There is a choice of unsecured personal loans, secured personal loans (usually a second mortgage) and revolving credit accounts which can include a cheque book and a cheque guarantee card.

The interest rate charged will vary from place to place but do watch the APR.

There will probably be a minimum amount you can borrow, say £1000, and a maximum. For very large loans you can negotiate the terms. Some money shops will also offer revolving credit schemes similar to those run by the big banks.

So, why should you borrow from a money shop when you can obtain cheaper loans from a bank? One advantage is that they are open all day Saturday and normal office hours during the week. Then, money shops specialise in dealing with individual customers only; they have no other business.

Many customers of money shops already have a bank account but choose to spread their borrowing further afield.

MONEY LENDERS

Someone who is having difficulty borrowing money may well consider going to a money lender. These people often place small advertisements in local newspapers and work within a limited geographical area.

The true interest rate will be high because he assumes the recognised lenders have already turned you down. The only reason that this would have happened is because they consider you a bad risk.

Think twice or three times before borrowing from a money lender because the interest rate you will be charged reflects the risk they are taking.

MONEY BROKERS

A money broker may be able to negotiate a loan for you when you yourself have failed. Unlike a money lender, he will not be lending you his own money, but he will charge you commission for his work.

The commission will be included in the APR figure which will almost certainly be extremely high. If you approach a money broker but decide in the end not to take the loan, you can still be charged a fee of up to £3.

LIFE INSURANCE POLICY

A less well-known way of borrowing is through an existing life insurance policy. The amount you can borrow will be a percentage of the surrender value of the policy and, of course, you will pay interest on the loan.

You may be able to borrow up to 90 per cent of the cash-in value of an endowment or whole life policy. You are unlikely to be able to borrow against a unit-linked policy.

This kind of borrowing is often used for emergency top-up funds but the loan can run for the life of the policy. You pay back only the interest while you are borrowing the money, as the capital sum will be deducted from the amount repaid to you when the policy matures.

The rate of interest you pay will vary from company to company. But, because there are no extra charges and the interest is payable half yearly, the APR will not be very much higher than the flat rate; there will be less than ½ per cent difference.

This makes borrowing against a life insurance policy a cheap option and an even better deal because you are repaying only interest out of your income, and none of the capital. The capital is reclaimed from the proceeds when the policy matures.

CREDIT SCHEMES

As well as borrowing money to buy goods, another way you can possess them immediately is to shop on credit. You pay for the goods in instalments over a period of months or years.

Credit Cards

There are two kinds of credit cards: those run by the banks and credit cards run by individual stores.

Bank credit cards

For small borrowings, credit cards are the easiest form and can, if used correctly, be free of interest charges. The credit cards in this country fall into two camps: the Mastercard run as Access by Midland, Lloyds, National Westminster, Williams & Glyn's, Royal Bank of Scotland, Clydesdale, Bank of Ireland, Northern and Ulster banks. The other is the Visa card from Barclays (Barclaycard), the Trustee Savings Bank (Trustcard), Yorkshire Bank, Bank of Scotland, Allied Irish and the Co-op Bank.

The interest rate is quoted monthly and the APR works out like this:

monthly rate %	APR %
1·5	19·56
1·75	23·14
2	26·82
2·25	30·62

There is an interest-free period before the first payment is due so, by paying off the whole bill, there is no charge at all. On average you will get about six weeks' free credit after buying the goods.

The amount you are allowed to borrow will depend on how much you can negotiate with the credit card company. If you really want to borrow up to the hilt, you could have both an Access and a Visa card. The individual limits range from £250 to over £1000 for most customers though the very rich are allowed to borrow tens of thousands of pounds. If you pay for goods or services by credit card and the goods are faulty or the service failed, the credit card company is jointly liable with the trader if the cost is between £100 and £30,000.

Stores' credit cards

The disadvantage of using a particular store's own card is that you are restricted to buying in that chain of shops. The shopkeepers love this. They claim that shoppers benefit by hearing about special promotions and they welcome the chance of tying customers to their stores.

The terms are more expensive than a bank's personal loan but about the same as Access or Barclaycard's APR. However, you do not have the advantage of a period of free credit.

Shop's revolving credit

This operates in a similar way to bank schemes. You pay a fixed amount each month and, in return, you can buy goods to the value of 20 or 30 times the monthly sum. As you pay off the debt you can buy more items and the retailer hopes that you will keep topping up your loan with new purchases.

There are also straightforward charge account loans and hire purchase or extended credit accounts.

OTHER WAYS TO BORROW

Hire purchase

If a store does not provide its own credit facilities, you can apply to a hire purchase company for a loan though it is more usual for the retailer selling the goods to arrange the HP loan for you.

The trader will be paid commission by the finance company for any loan signed up; garages often offer HP agreements. But you should make sure you know exactly how much the money is costing you: the terms of HP deals can range from being a reasonable way of borrowing to being extremely expensive.

Any goods you buy on HP do not legally become yours until you have finished paying for them. As the name suggests, legally you 'hire' the goods while you are repaying the loan.

You will have to pay a deposit and then make regular monthly repayments which include the interest charge. To be covered by law, the amount you borrow must be below £7500 rising to £15,000 in May 1985.

If you do not keep up the repayments, the HP company can repossess the item because, legally, it still belongs to them. But, once you have paid more than one-third of the full HP price, they have to obtain a court order to do so.

Mail order

This is a very well-advertised area of buying on credit. No interest is charged on purchases and repayments are spread over 20, 38 or 50 weeks. For expensive goods, you can pay over 100 weeks but in this case you will pay interest at about 20 per cent APR.

The prices charged by the catalogue companies can be higher than you would find in the shops but you receive the goods before you have to pay for them.

The advantages of buying by mail order are that you have the opportunity to choose goods in your own home which are then delivered to your front door. There is no delivery charge. Mail order agents are paid commission, even on their own purchases. The rate is about 10 per cent if they take the commission in cash or 12½ per cent if they take the value in goods. This cuts down the cost of the goods they buy. Also, when hire purchase restrictions are in force and credit is difficult to obtain, it is still easy to buy on mail order. Mail order repayments are sometimes made weekly though the trend is towards monthly settlement.

Trading checks

For those who can manage only weekly repayments, trading checks are available. This is a service aimed at people who can budget on a weekly timescale only. Agents call at your house on Thursday or Friday evenings, whichever is pay day, and collect the contribution.

In return, customers receive either a check or a voucher which they can spend in any shop accepting that particular company's scheme.

Checks are issued for small amounts of money, typically £20 and £50 and the money is repayable over 23 weeks. Trading vouchers are issued in specific amounts to buy an individual item at a named shop. The maximum is £1000 repayable over two years and the APR is about 50 per cent.

It is also possible to borrow sums of up to £1000 in cash from check traders. This is an expensive way of borrowing because of the high cost of collecting repayments.

The most expensive of all is a short-term loan. Often customers borrow over 13 weeks to pay the gas or electricity bill. **The APR for this sort of loan is over 100 per cent.**

Check trading is an expensive form of borrowing because of the cost of employing an agent to call every week; other lenders simply receive your cheque through the post or by banker's standing order. It is aimed at people who do not have bank accounts and who are unable to budget other than weekly.

Credit unions

These are groups of individuals who set up and organise their own savings and borrowing schemes. To form a credit union, you must have a common link, such as the area in which you live, your place of work, or some other association.

The weekly savings are pooled in a common fund, out of which members can borrow. The rate of interest is fixed at 1 per cent a month, an APR of 12·68 per cent, which means that monthly repayments work out at £6.50 for every £100 that you borrow for one year.

At the end of the credit union's year, 20 per cent of any surplus goes into reserves and the remainder is distributed to savers in proportion to their savings. The maximum that unions are allowed to distribute is 8 per cent but in practice the amount varies between 4½ and 6½ per cent. Until April 1985 this is tax free.

The most that you can save in a credit union is £2000 and this would entitle you to the maximum borrowings of £4000. You can use the loan for whatever purpose you wish, and it is used most frequently for buying household goods.

There are two associations which help people set up credit unions: the Credit Union League of Great Britain and the National Federation of Credit Unions. See p. 249 for addresses.

YOUR RIGHTS

Credit scoring

This is an increasingly popular method of assessing someone's ability to repay a loan. It is in widespread use in the United States and fast catching on here. Retailers, banks or anyone else involved in lending are likely to use it.

But, you will not know if this is the way your request for a loan has been treated and if you are rejected you will not be told why.

Credit scoring takes the human element out of judging loan requests. You will fill out a questionnaire, just as you would anyway, but the questions are weighted. Depending on your answers, each question is awarded a certain number of points. At the end, the totals are added together: you pass if they are above a certain figure and fail if they are below another. If you fall between the two and you are asking for a bank loan you may be given another chance – that means someone will look into your case. But if you have applied for credit in a shop, there is unlikely to be an override system to give you a second chance.

It is not possible to get the better of credit scoring. It is more complicated than guessing which is obviously the 'best' way to answer the questions. Each company will have its own credit scoring system specially devised for that particular type of business.

Companies using the system love it. As well as being far cheaper in salary terms, they claim that the results are less fallible and quicker.

If your request for credit is turned down, you can try asking if you have been assessed this way but you have no right of appeal.

Credit reference agency

These are independent companies who keep files on individuals' credit-worthiness. When you approach someone for a loan they might refer your file to a credit reference agency who will check you out.

But this system is not infallible and, if the information about you is incorrect, you are unlikely to find out. However, if someone has used an agency and rejected you, they must, if you ask, tell you.

You then have the right, for a fee of £1, to see your file and, if you find incorrect information, you can amend it. You are entitled to know what information a credit reference agency holds about you even if you have never applied for credit. See p. 250 for addresses.

Consumer Credit Act

Borrowers' rights are protected by law under the Consumer Credit Act. This covers hire purchase agreements, credit card purchases, bank loans and loans arranged through an intermediary. But only loans between £100 and £10,000 rising to £30,000 in May 1985 come within the terms of this Act.

When the Consumer Credit Act comes fully in force, in 1985, shoppers will legally have a slight breathing space after signing an application in which to change their minds. The contract will not become legally binding until the lender has approved your application, which will probably be a few days after your first approach. Also, if you sign the form in your own home, you will have a 'cooling off' period during which you will be able to change your mind about a loan, even if you have signed a document.

Except for a mortgage and a commitment made entirely by post or telephone, you will be able to back out of a deal within five days of signing an agreement and receiving the lender's copy which he has also signed.

Problems repaying

If you have any difficulty repaying a loan, you should tell the lender immediately. If it is a bank loan, it is in the bank's best interest as well as your own to help you through a difficult patch and the manager may be willing to negotiate a new, slower way of repaying the debt.

If you have bought the goods on credit, then all the company can do to get its money back is to sue you. But, if it is an HP agreement, the HP company can repossess the goods because, legally, they belong to him until you have paid for them completely.

If you have paid more than one-third of the total price, then the HP company will have to obtain a court order to repossess. If you have repaid less than one-third, he does not, though this still does not mean that he can enter your home without your permission.

5/Buying Your Home

Where to start • How much can you afford to pay? • The cost of borrowing • Tax relief • *gazumping* • Where to find the money • *guaranteed mortgages / Homeloan scheme / first-time buyers* • Shared ownership • *how it works* • When you might have difficulties • What type of mortgage • *topping-up a loan / joint mortgages / single people / difficulties / paying off the mortgage early* • What to look for in the house you buy • *do-it-yourself conveyancing / cut-price conveyancing* • The solicitor • *building society's solicitor / searches / choosing a solicitor* • Other costs you will have to face • *stamp duty / land registry fee* • The surveyor • *do you need a separate survey? / choosing a surveyor* • Making an offer • Buying a flat • *leasehold / ground rent / service charges / insurance* • Buying a council house • Mobile homes • Buying a house in Scotland • Letters

The process of buying a house is appalling: there are financial and legal hurdles to be overcome and you are unlikely to reach the finishing line without at least one stumble.

However, you can save yourself mishaps by going about the deal the right way and by being prepared for anything going wrong.

WHERE TO START

First, the two big decisions: determine how much you can afford and where you want to live. The choice of area may not be yours because of your work, or other commitments. But then again, you may have no restraints of any kind on where you live. Start by deciding as precisely as you can the area where you want to buy.

Whatever and however you are buying, do not rush into the process. There is rarely any need to make a hasty decision and you are far more likely to end up with the home of your dreams if you have thought through every aspect of choosing a house or flat with care.

Even if house prices appear to be rising every day, you will be better off taking a considered view. After all, the average person stays ten years in a house before moving and you could be there for 20 years: a long time to live with a mistake for the sake of believing you will save a few hundred pounds at the beginning.

HOW MUCH CAN YOU AFFORD TO PAY?

Once you have an idea of house prices in the area of your choice, you can start to define the type of house you are looking for. There is always a gap between what you want and what you can afford, invariably you must scale down the first to meet the second.

You will have to take out a mortgage to raise the money and as a rough guide to how much you will be able to borrow, multiply your gross earnings by 2·5. If you are buying jointly with someone else, the second salary can be taken into account. This applies whether it is husband and wife buying, or two friends.

At times when money is easily available, you can hope to borrow more than this. When money is tight, you may have to look longer to find it.

You should be able to borrow 85 to 95 per cent of the purchase price. On occasions when the banks and building societies have plenty of money to lend, you may be able to negotiate a 100 per cent mortgage. But you cannot rely on this happening because, as soon as their funds dwindle, this is the first facility to disappear.

One reason why building societies are usually reluctant to lend you all the money for the house is that you need show no commitment to the deal. If you have not put a penny of your own money into the transaction, they argue, then you are more likely to default on the repayments because you have nothing of your own to lose. If you had put down a 10 per cent deposit you would think twice before jeopardising that money.

Another reason is that, when building societies are short of funds, it is a way of forcing you to invest with them first.

You will have to pay a 10 per cent deposit on the day you exchange contracts. Be extremely careful who you pay this money to. It is safe to hand the deposit to a solicitor, or an estate agent if he is a member of one of the professional associations. But never pay deposits to anyone else or you may not get your money back if the deal falls through before you complete.

If you do not have enough saved up for the deposit, try asking a generous relative, or the bank manager. You may be able to borrow it, but it will be expensive money. Alternatively, ask if you can pay a deposit of only 5 per cent instead.

Is it wise to commit yourself to every penny you have in the world to buy a house? To a degree this depends on your temperament. Some people are quite happy to forgo holidays and clothes to buy a house while for others this would be too great a sacrifice.

But do remember that the mortgage repayments are only one element in the cost of buying a house. Before you can move in you may have to pay a valuation fee, a solicitor, removal firm, stamp duty and land registry fee.

Once you have settled in, there will be rates, redecorations, gas and electricity bills. You will soon discover how expensive houses are to maintain in good order. See p. 11 for details of how to budget.

THE COST OF BORROWING

Monthly repayments on a £10,000 loan with Mortgage Interest Relief at Source (MIRAS)

Mortgage rate %	20-year loan £	25-year loan £	30-year loan £
9	74.50	67.10	62.50
9·5	76.60	69.30	64.90
10	78.70	71.60	67.20
10·5	80.90	73.80	69.60
11	83.00	76.10	72.00
11·5	85.20	78.40	74.40
12	87.50	80.80	76.90
12·5	89.70	83.20	79.40
13	92.00	85.60	81.90
13·5	94.30	88.00	84.40
14	96.60	90.40	87.00
14·5	98.90	92.90	89.60
15	101.30	95.40	92.20

TAX RELIEF

The compensation for paying out large sums of money to buy a house is the tax relief you receive on the interest payments, up to a £30,000 loan. At present, for every pound you pay in interest charges, you receive tax relief at the highest tax rate you pay, which for most people is the basic rate of 30 per cent. When you move house, if you are stuck with two mortgages for up to a year you can claim tax relief on both subject to the £30,000 limit. Also, with the same proviso, you will get tax relief on a loan to buy a house for an elderly relative. Two people living together but not married can both claim up to the £30,000 maximum.

Since April 1983, tax relief at 30 per cent has automatically been deducted from the majority of repayments made to building societies. This is called Mortgage Interest Relief at Source (MIRAS).

Those with larger than £30,000 mortgages still receive tax relief on the first £30,000 through their Inland Revenue bill. Higher rate tax-payers have only 30 per cent tax relief deducted by the lender; they have to negotiate with the taxman for the balance.

Gazumping

You may be unlucky and discover that, even if you have had an offer accepted by the vendor (seller), someone else comes along and makes a higher offer which is accepted. This practice is called gazumping, and it particularly happens when house prices are rising quickly.

There is nothing legally to stop anyone gazumping and even if contracts have been exchanged you cannot reclaim any expenses you have incurred. You can hope only that your vendor is someone with more integrity. The practice cannot happen in Scotland because of the tender system.

WHERE TO FIND THE MONEY

The main source of home loans is the building societies. The banks grant some mortgages but their enthusiasm waxes and wanes. There is a Government Homeloan scheme for first-time buyers (see p. 67), though its terms are fairly rigid (you must register and save with it for at least two years) and it has almost disappeared.

You can ask an insurance company directly for an endowment mortgage but they prefer to work through a middle man, usually an insurance broker or estate agent.

Be prepared to put in some solid groundwork at this point. There is no need to accept the first offer of a mortgage you receive; you can thank the AB Building Society very much but then go and see what the XY Building Society can offer and compare the terms. It depends on how easily available money is at the time.

There is less scope for picking and choosing when mortages are harder to find, but you need never feel overly grateful for the loan. No one is doing you a favour. Banks and building societies are in the business of lending and you, the customer, are essential to this. Unfortunately too many large institutions have lost sight of the fact and treat the customer almost as if they are doing him a favour instead of providing a service.

If you already have a building society savings account, then that society is the best place to ask for the loan first. You stand a much better chance of obtaining a mortgage from one that already holds your money. In fact, if you have enough savings you would do well to spread them around with several societies to improve your options.

Try asking your bank manager (you will need to be an existing customer) if he will grant you a mortgage. You may be able to borrow more from a bank.

Guaranteed mortgages

Some building societies and banks run schemes whereby, if you save a minimum amount of money for a period of, usually, two years, they guarantee to give you a mortgage when you want one. The amount they will lend is related to the sum you have saved.

Anyone who knows that they will be saving for a fixed time with the sole intention of buying a house could put at least some of their cash in one of these schemes, or register under the Government Homeloan scheme. When you come to buy, mortgages may be in short supply and a guaranteed loan invaluable.

But always check the rate of interest you are offered on your savings, it could be unacceptably lower than you would get elsewhere. Make sure you ask the building society precisely what rate of interest it will charge you. Building societies charge higher rates for borrowing large sums of money. The exact differentials, and the practice, vary from time to time but do not assume you will pay the publicised mortgage rate. On the other hand, banks do not charge more however much you borrow.

Homeloan scheme

The Government has a scheme for first-time buyers called the Homeloan scheme. If you save at least £600 over two years with a building society or some other acceptable institution, you will get an interest-free loan of £600 and a tax-free bonus up to a maximum of £110.

To qualify you must fill out a form HPA1 from the building society notifying it that you are joining this scheme. Also, the house you are buying must cost less than a fairly low maximum.

First-time buyers

First-time buyers might not think so at the time, but you are in a highly favoured position. Most lenders court the first-time buyer: one reason is that once they have you, you are more likely to go back to them for your next mortgage (and always remember that *they* make money out of *you*).

Builders, particularly those building estates, sometimes run promotions for first-time buyers, especially if the houses are not selling too well. They may offer to arrange a 100 per cent mortgage, or perhaps give you free kitchen equipment, or pay your conveyancing fees.

Some of the larger building firms have sales offices which will take the whole burden of buying off your shoulders. All you need to do is sign your name and the builder looks after the mortgage and the legal work. If you are not a first-time buyer, the builder may offer to buy your existing house from you. If he does, make sure he gives you the full market price, otherwise it is no bargain.

But, above all, remember that you get what you pay for and, while 'special offers' may seem attractive, the goods may have attractive packaging and little else. You will have paid for these extras in the price of the house but these elements, perhaps a fitted kitchen, a cooker or a refrigerator, will not rise in value as your house price increases. In fact they become worthless and so the overall value of your house does not improve as much as you may expect.

SHARED OWNERSHIP

Two fairly recent plans to help first-time buyers with insufficient monies to own a house are 'shared ownership' and 'do it yourself shared ownership' (DIYSO). These schemes are run by some local councils, new town development corporations and housing associations.

To find out if there is a shared ownership scheme in your area, ask at your town hall, or if you live in a new town, write to the development corporation or contact the Housing Corporation, address on p. 249.

How it works

Shared ownership means that you own a portion of your house and rent the remainder. The scheme is designed for those who cannot afford to buy a house outright in the first place. Later you have the opportunity to buy the rest of the house in tranches of, say, 10 per cent.

In the beginning you pay for a proportion of your house. This is commonly 50 per cent but can be any agreed amount, say 25 or 75 per cent. You take out a lease on the remaining proportion from the landlord which is the housing association or local authority.

You pay rent on the leased portion, just as you would if you were in a straightforward rented house. The rent can, as anywhere, rise over the years.

As the value of your house goes up, so the value of your share increases. Then, at any time you wish, you can either buy a further share of your house or buy all the remainder in one go. You will pay the market price operating at the time.

Do-it-yourself shared ownership (DIYSO)

Because shared ownership houses were not available all over the country, the Government introduced a trial do-it-yourself shared ownership. Home buyers could choose their own house and acquire it under a DIYSO scheme; the balance that they cannot afford to buy will be held by a housing association in the area which has been nominated by the Housing Corporation. The Government is keen to encourage this scheme and it will soon become more easily available.

FOR MORE INFORMATION

There are many places where you can find information about buying a house. All the building societies will have their own printed leaflets while The Building Societies Association has various useful free booklets and the Royal Institution of Chartered Surveyors, the National House Building Council and the House Building Advisory Bureau give free advice. Addresses on pp. 248–9.

WHEN YOU MIGHT HAVE DIFFICULTIES

A brand new house on an estate is a straightforward mortgage proposition. However, if this is not what you have in mind, there are some houses that can be difficult to mortgage.

For instance, if you have an urge to buy a derelict windmill standing on the edge of a cliff for conversion, you might have some difficulty finding someone foolish enough to lend money on it. The building society is not bothered that your square-edged furniture will not fit; but they do worry about being able to get their money back if you default.

Some societies will not lend on sub-standard older property and this has contributed to the decline of residential areas in many inner cities. Now the fashion is to revitalise these areas so you stand a better chance of being able to borrow on a run-down Victorian terraced house. Extremely old property in bad order is still hard to mortgage.

Similarly if the house has a preservation order on it, this could cause you problems when it comes to finding a mortgage. Also, if you want to buy a flat with a short lease, or a house with a sitting tenant in part of it, you will have difficulty getting a mortgage.

WHAT TYPE OF MORTGAGE?
With the preliminaries out of the way, the next decision is: what sort of mortgage do I need? The basic choice is between a repayment and an endowment. Which is best for you depends on your circumstances.

Here is what to look for:

Repayment
This is the most straightforward kind of mortgage. You borrow so many thousand pounds at the going mortgage rate over a set number of years; each month you are repaying part of the capital you have borrowed and some of the interest.

You will probably repay the loan over 20 to 25 years for your first house. But there is no automatic life insurance cover to pay off the loan if you die early. If you have dependants who would suffer financially you can arrange this separately.

Since the introduction of Mortgage Interest Relief at Source (MIRAS), tax relief is granted at source through lower repayments to the building society. This is mostly done using a constant repayment system which means that your repayments stay the same (assuming there is no change in the interest rate) throughout the life of the loan.

The alternative method is increasing net repayments. By this method you will repay in the same way as under the old system when you received tax relief through your PAYE payments. Tax relief is allowed on the interest element of the payments only and, because in the early years you are repaying more interest than capital, you benefit from higher tax relief.

Increasing net repayments allow you to pay less in the early years of the mortgage. With constant repayments you will pay the same all the way through.

Endowment
Under this system you take out a life insurance policy which will mature on the same day as the mortgage is due for repayment and for exactly the right amount to meet the bill. If you die before the term is up, the mortgage will automatically be paid off.

Each month you pay the interest on the loan to the building society or bank and the premiums on the insurance policy to the insurance company. There is more than one kind of endowment mortgage. You can take out a low cost, a with-profits or a without-profits. If you have taken out a with-profits policy you will receive an additional cash lump sum at the end as well. One disadvantage of endowment mortgages is that, when interest rates rise, you do not have the option of extending the length of the loan as you do with a repayment mortgage; you must pay more.

Another problem can arise if you want to pay off the loan early. Endowment policies, like other insurance policies, have a poor early surrender value and you can lose heavily.

However, you can choose to keep the policy going, even though you no longer have a mortgage. And when you move house, you can transfer the same policy to your new home.

If you took out an endowment mortgage before the March 1984 Budget, you will be getting tax relief on the premiums you pay. This advantage was abolished in the Budget.

Low cost endowment mortgage
These were introduced when endowment mortgages were unpopular because of their expense. They work on the principle that, when the with-profits policy finally matures, there will be more than enough money to repay the loan.

So, you take out a policy for less than you will eventually need because, when the policy matures, it will have grown large enough with the profits added on to repay the debt. And, naturally, you are meanwhile paying smaller premiums because the amount insured is lower.

If, in the end, there is more than enough money, you will receive the bonuses as well. But, if there is not enough, then you will have to find the outstanding balance.

With-profits endowment mortgage
The premiums are higher for a with-profits policy, but at the end you will receive hopefully a large sum of money; exactly how much depends on how well your insurance company has invested.

If you have the money to spare, this is one way of saving but, if you are down to your last halfpennies, it will not be worth the struggle as you are trying to save at the same time as repaying the mortgage.

It may sound like a small fortune when you are promised £20,000 or whatever in bonuses, but, by the time the policy matures in 20 or 25 years, this will not be such a grand sum of money.

Without-profits endowment mortgage
The premiums for this policy are cheaper because the policy will mature with exactly enough money to pay off the loan, leaving no excess to pay you a lump sum.

Topping-up a loan
Even with a 10 per cent deposit saved up and a loan from the building

society, you may still be short of the total amount you need to buy your house. These last few hundred pounds are going to be the most difficult, and the most expensive, to raise.

But you can do it. Start with the family; a rich relative may be able to help with a short-term problem. Then, ask your bank manager for a loan or, failing that, if your mortgage is a repayment kind ask an insurance company for an endowment policy against which to borrow the remainder.

If you already have an endowment, you may be able to take out another. If you wish you can take out an insurance policy for more than you exactly need to buy the house, the excess will be a bonus for you.

Joint mortgages

A husband and wife taking out a mortgage together should always register the property in both their names. If they do not, and the husband (or wife if it is in her name) dies, the spouse should automatically inherit the home, but this way there can be no possible doubt.

If you are unmarried but living together, however permanently, the woman can lose her right to the house if she does not have a financial stake in it. So in this situation it is crucial that she legally owns half the house.

Today, it is quite common for people, whether unmarried couples or two or three friends, to buy jointly. This is a good way for people to launch themselves on the house market, or to buy a more expensive property than they could afford by themselves.

The most important factor is that everyone involved is aware of, and agreeable to, the conditions. These will usually say that, if one partner wants to sell, the other will have the opportunity to buy that share, or else the property will be put up for sale on the open market.

It is important for the two of you to agree the terms of occupation beforehand and draw up a proper legal document to provide for any later changes.

Single people

Building societies recognise that single people want, and are serious about, buying a home. In fact, they are enthusiastic about lending to single people.

Difficulties

Even with a high level of unemployment very few people fail to meet their mortgage repayments. Payments to the building society take priority over any other commitment in most people's budgeting.

Anyone who finds himself in difficulty with mortgage payments should go and see the building society (or bank) manager straightaway. They will nearly always be understanding but, if you are unlucky enough to have an unhelpful manager, go straight to the head office.

If necessary, the building society, or bank, can make arrangements for you to pay only the interest and not the capital part of what you owe for a time. You will catch up with the repayments later.

The manager would far rather do this than take possession proceedings if you totally fail to make repayments.

If you are receiving supplementary benefit, you may have the interest on the mortgage paid for you. You cannot have the capital paid by supplementary benefit but that is the part you can ask the lender to postpone.

Paying off the mortgage early

You may have to pay a penalty if you pay off the mortgage earlier than you have agreed, particularly if it is in the first five years. No one will stop you doing this but it may cost you, for example, three months' extra interest.

If you wish, you can pay off lump sums every now and then to reduce the overall cost and amount of interest you will pay in the long run.

WHAT TO LOOK FOR IN THE HOUSE YOU BUY

How do you go about choosing exactly the right house for you to buy? Especially with a first home, it is difficult to know just what will suit you.

People go about buying houses in a ridiculous fashion: you spend a couple of hours pouring over the estate agent's handout, or simply read a newspaper advertisement, which give you only a general idea of what the house is really like; then you spend maybe half an hour looking over a house, to which you are about to commit every penny you have in the world.

If you were buying a new car, you would at the very least go for a drive in it. But you cannot live in a house for a few weeks to make sure it suits you before deciding whether or not to buy.

To help make up your mind ask yourself these questions:
- is it freehold or leasehold?
- if it is leasehold, will there still be a reasonably long lease left for you to sell in a few years' time and will it be mortgagable?
- are there any restrictions in the lease that might be an irritation?
- is it new or second hand? new houses tend to be further away from town centres but there is no risk of being caught in a chain of sellers.
- does the house have enough room for your future use?
- is there a garden and is it large enough? or too large?
- is there a garage large enough for your car?
- does the sun come into the house? if it is a gloomy house, the direction of the sun is one thing you cannot change.

- do you have to share a driveway with a neighbour?
- is there room to build an extension should you need to?
- are the boundaries clearly defined?
- will the house be expensive to heat?
- how much are the rates?
- does the house have main drainage?
- are there likely to be any unusual costs involved with this particular house, such as the upkeep of a thatched roof?
- does it need rewiring or replumbing?
- can you, and visitors, park your car easily?
- does a neighbour's tree overhang, and overshadow, your property?
- is the street very busy or noisy?
- is there water nearby that could be a hazard to your children?
- are there other children around for yours to play with?
- what are the neighbours like? as far as you can tell, are they likely to be compatible?
- are there schools nearby?
- are the shops conveniently close?
- is there a bus stop or railway station close by?
- will you be able to find work in the area?
- can you commute fairly easily?
- is it close to a factory which might throw out noxious fumes?
- is there a noisy playground nearby?
- is the view likely to change?
- the house may have eccentricities that appeal to you, but will it be difficult to sell?
- is the area safe for your animals? and what about the neighbours' animals?
- does the house feel comfortable?
- are there any building works or road building planned for the area?
- if it is a flat, who is responsible for the maintenance of the structure of the building?

Do-it-yourself conveyancing

If you sold one house for £30,000 and bought another for exactly the same amount, the move could cost you £2000. You can save a great deal of that money by doing the legal work yourself. It is quite feasible to do your own conveyancing. Solicitors reckon it is about eight hours' work.

Conveyancing simply means transferring a property from one ownership to another. And there are just two basic premises that are important: if you are selling, you want to be sure you get the money; if you are buying, you want to be sure you can move in.

There are two types of conveyancing: one for registered land and another for unregistered land. To find out which you have, contact your local land registry office.

If you do decide to have a go at conveyancing yourself, buy a good guidebook. You can buy the forms you need for about £5. See the letters on p. 91.

Cut-price conveyancing
You can save on the expense of using a solicitor by going to a cut-price conveyancing firm. But, be careful who you use. See p. 244.

THE SOLICITOR
A solicitor will charge you around 1 per cent of the purchase price for conveyancing if you are buying and a further 1 per cent if you are selling as well. There is a minimum charge of around £150.

For this, he will:
- draw up a draft contract
- act as stakeholder for the deposit (he keeps any interest that accrues on the money)
- send a list of questions for the seller to answer
- conduct local authority searches
- conduct bankruptcy searches
- check that the property is registered
- check the lease if there is one
- can act for the building society as well and draw up the mortgage deed
- make sure any stamp duty is paid
- make sure the money arrives on completion day

Building society's solicitor
The solicitor who acts for the building society can charge according to a set scale of fees. But, whatever it is, you have to pay.

Your own solicitor can act for the building society.

The scale, to which VAT must be added, is:

Mortgage	Fee
£5000 or less	£40
£5000 to £10,000	£40 plus £2.50 for each £1000 above £5000
£10,000 to £15,000	£52.50 plus £2 for each £1000 above £10,000
£15,000 to £25,000	£62.50 plus £1 for each £1000 above £15,000
£25,000 to £30,000	£72.50 plus 50p for each £1000 above £25,000
£30,000 to £35,000	£75 plus 25p for each £1000 above £30,000
above £35,000	£76.25 plus 50p for each £5000 above £35,000

This is what you will pay, before VAT:

Mortgage	Fee
£5000	£40
£7000	£47.50
£10,000	£52.50
£15,000	£62.50
£20,000	£67.50
£25,000	£72.50
£30,000	£75
£35,000	£76.25

Searches
The solicitor writes to the local authority to ask if a motorway or any other nasty is planned in the vicinity. This takes many weeks and can hold up the sale. If this is happening to you, telephone the local authority yourself, explain the problem and they may give your application priority.

Choosing a solicitor
● ask friends, neighbours and colleagues for recommendations
● ask your building society or bank manager for suggestions
● the Law Society keeps a list of solicitors in each locality
● Citizens Advice Bureaux have lists
● ask for an estimate of the bill; there is no set scale of charges for conveyancing. Remember you will have to pay VAT on top.

OTHER COSTS YOU WILL HAVE TO FACE

Stamp duty
On any house you buy costing more than £30,000, you will have to pay a tax called stamp duty. The rate is 1 per cent of the price of a house over £30,000.

Under a new Act of Parliament due to be passed about 1985–86, the building societies will be allowed to arrange all this for you. It should make housebuying simpler and even, possibly, cheaper.

You pay stamp duty only on the price you pay for the house itself; if the money includes carpets and curtains, or any other fitments, you do not pay duty on those.

Land registry fee
When property changes hands, in some parts of the country, mainly urban areas, it is recorded on a land registry.

If the land is already registered, you will pay:
- £8 for a house up to £4000
and a further £5 for each £2000 or part of £2000 above that with a maximum of £703.

If the land is being registered for the first time, you will pay:
- £3 for every £2000 or part of £2000 on houses costing up to £100,000.
- over £100,000 the scale is £150 for the first £100,000 and £2 for every £10,000 over that with a maximum of £332.

This is what you will have to pay; there is no VAT to add:

Purchase price £	First registration £	Subsequent registrations £
10,000	15	23
12,000	18	28
14,000	21	33
16,000	24	38
18,000	27	43
20,000	30	48
25,000	39	63
30,000	45	73
35,000	54	88
40,000	60	98

THE SURVEYOR

Whether or not you employ your own surveyor to look over the house, you will have to pay the building society's valuer. He inspects the house you are buying to make sure it is adequate security for the building society. This is called a valuation inspection.

It is not his worry if you are paying twice as much as he thinks the house is worth, though his report will show what he considers a fair market value.

This is a rough guide to what the building society's valuation report will cost. You will need to add on VAT.

Purchase price £	Fee £
Under 12,000	25
12,000 to 15,000	30
15,000 to 20,000	35
20,000 to 25,000	40
25,000 to 30,000	45
35,000 to 40,000	50
40,000 to 50,000	55

It is not safe to rely on a valuation inspection only because this will not tell you about every defect in the property. You can pay for your own separate surveyor to provide you with a full structural survey and this will cost about £150 to £200.

Building societies have recently relaxed their rules on their valuation reports. They now allow you to see a copy of their valuer's report (previously they would not, even though you were the one who had to pay for it). Some societies will now give you the choice of a valuation survey or, more expensive, a structural survey which you can keep. This saves duplication of effort.

Many societies offer 'half and half' surveys which are combined valuation and structural surveys. The Royal Institution of Chartered Surveyors has a prepared form which provides a reasonably-priced survey and valuation for both house and flat buyers. This is called the 'report and valuation scheme' and gives a concise report on the state of the property you are buying and a valuation.

Do you need a separate survey?

If you are buying a brand new house, it will be covered by the National House Building Council's ten-year guarantee. However, there would have to be a major structural fault for you to be able to claim anything after the first two years.

During those two years, the builder has to put right any defects; after that it is the NHBC's responsibility but only for serious faults.

With older property it is advisable to pay for a survey. If you do, and the house falls down from dry rot the day you move in, and the surveyor had failed to notice it, you could sue the surveyor for negligence. But in less severe cases this would not be worth while. A good surveyor should pick up both existing problems and potential ones to warn you about. He will give you an idea of how much it is going to cost to put right.

Do not expect a clean bill of health from a surveyor. You are paying him to find out what is wrong and you want to know the worst. It is not his job to tell you the good points about the house. You may be horrified to hear of rot and woodworm and leaking roofs but these defects are quite common in older properties.

And, whatever you do, **do not ask the estate agent who is selling you the house to survey it for you**. His responsibility is to the person paying him to sell the house, not to you.

If you are having a full survey, the surveyor will give an opinion on the price you are paying; inspect the surface areas; and lift the floorboards if they are loose. But he will not look at anything that is fixed, covered, unexposed or inaccessible; he will look only at exposed woodwork.

If you ask (and pay extra) he will undertake a drains test.

His report is confidential to you: it will not be shown to the vendor.

The report should include comments on:
- roof structure (as far as he can see it)
- gutters
- pipes
- damp-proof course
- walls
- brickwork
- pointing
- rendering
- dampness
- water tanks
- insulation
- partitions
- floor boards where he can see them
- plaster work
- windows
- doors
- fittings
- chimneys
- fireplaces
- ventilation
- plumbing
- gas and central heating

Choosing a surveyor
- ask your building society if its surveyor can do the work
- ring the Information Centre at the Royal Institution of Chartered Surveyors for names of qualified surveyors in your area
- ask your solicitor or bank manager to recommend one
- ask for an estimate of the fee – there is no set scale
- ask if the surveyor carries indemnity insurance

MAKING AN OFFER
1. If the house is being sold through an estate agent, make the offer through him. This saves the embarrassment of bargaining.
2. Decide in your own mind exactly how much you are prepared to offer.
3. Offer less than this. If you are not sure how much, 10 per cent is a reasonable starting point.
4. If the offer is rejected, the seller may indicate what he will accept. Otherwise, make a slightly higher offer.
5. The point comes when you must either agree a price or forget the whole thing.
6. Ask whether carpets, curtains and any other accessories are included in the price.

7. It is advisable to get an inventory of exactly what will be left behind, whether it is included in the price or you are buying separately.

8. Once the price is agreed, instruct a surveyor.

9. If your offer is accepted, ask the vendor if he will take the house off the market for a few weeks at least, to avoid your being gazumped. A vendor is under no obligation to do so, but it will show goodwill on his part. It is particularly worth while when the vendor has instructed two agents to act for him; the one who has not made the provisional sale will be tempted to find an alternative buyer, at a higher price, to earn his fee.

If you are not dealing through an estate agent, the same basic rules apply but be sure, when you are making any offer, whether written or verbal, that you say it is 'subject to contract'.

You may be asked by the estate agent to put down a small deposit at this stage to 'show good faith'. This will be returned if the deal does not go through. There is no need to pay this deposit, unless the agent threatens you will lose the house to someone else and you believe him. This practice is not allowed in Scotland.

This deposit is held by the estate agent as 'stakeholder' and he will put it on deposit somewhere to earn interest. If the deal falls through and your money is returned, you will not be given the interest: the estate agent keeps it.

When contracts are exchanged you will have to pay the vendor a deposit of 10 per cent of the purchase price. This sum should be held by his solicitor as stakeholder.

BUYING A FLAT

There are different and extra problems to bear in mind if you are buying a flat. It is essential to be aware of these.

Leasehold

Invariably any flat you buy will be leasehold: you buy a lease which has a certain number of years left to expire and at the end of that period your right to live in the property also runs out.

By law, if this happens you must be given the opportunity to take out another lease, but this will involve spending a large sum of money, almost equivalent to the freehold price, all over again. In some cases, the right to a new lease might be opposed by the freeholder, or it might be offered subject to new conditions.

So, do look carefully at the length of lease left to run. Generally, building societies will not give you a mortgage if the lease would have less than 20 years to run after you have paid off the mortgage. So, to get a 25-year mortgage, the lease must have at least 45 years left to run.

You might think that a 60-year lease is quite long enough when you buy. But think what will happen when you come to sell. Will any prospective buyers be able to get a mortgage then?

Even leases of only three years are marketable – but at a price. The price by then will be very deeply discounted and open to cash buyers only. As with any other cash deal, the buyer will expect to knock you down.

Sometimes houses are sold leasehold rather than freehold, in which case the same terms apply. But usually you will buy the freehold of a house, which means that it is yours forever.

There are some freehold flats around, but be wary of these and do not buy one without detailed advice.

Ground rent

You will have to pay this to the landlord. This could be a small sum, say £5 a year, or it may be more, around £500. You pay it to the landlord so that he retains his right to the freehold.

Service charges

The biggest bugbear of a leasehold property is the service charge. You must be sure that you understand exactly what you are getting for your money.

It could be very little or it could include cleaning communal areas, hot water and porterage. You may find you have to pay extra every time the outside needs repainting. Or the service charge may include a provision for a 'sinking fund' which builds up to meet the large exceptional bills.

As all flats in a block pay an equal service charge, depending on the size of your flat, the expense works out fairly. The person in the basement contributes to a new roof and the person on the top floor pays towards flood damage down below; the person on the ground floor contributes to the maintenance of the lift.

You have no control over the service charges, which can rise every year, and you will have to pay the bill. Make sure you know who is responsible for paying for what.

Insurance

The building should be insured by the landlord. See p. 123. But you will still need to insure your personal possessions separately.

BUYING A COUNCIL HOUSE

If you are a council tenant, you may have the right to buy the house you live in. If you can, you will be able to do so at a discount of the market price. This was originally up to a maximum of 50 per cent if you have been there more than 20 years, but later changed to 60 per cent after 30 years.

Anyone who has been a council tenant for three years has the right to buy and the discount increases depending on how long you have lived in the house.

The first thing to do is to ask the landlord, that is the local authority or housing association, for a Right to Buy claim and read the Department of the Environment's Housing Booklet form.

If you live in a house you can buy the freehold; if it is a flat you can buy a lease. You can borrow money towards the cost of buying from a building society the same way as you would if you were buying any other house.

MOBILE HOMES

'Mobile homes' is a misnomer. The one thing they do not do is move, although by definition they must be capable of being moved. But, if you own a mobile home or caravan and rent the pitch from a landlord, you are protected by recent legislation, which gives greater security and safety.

To start with, anyone living in a mobile home must have a written agreement with the owner of the site. In this, the owner must tell the resident:

- the name and address of the site owner
- the name and address of the resident
- the date the agreement begins
- a description of the pitch
- how permanent his interest in the land is
- the terms of the agreement

He must also give details of the pitch fees and any other charges.

A resident is entitled to stay on the site as long as he wants, unless the written agreement specifies that the owner's planning permission will run out. A resident can end the agreement by giving four weeks' notice to the landlord, but the site owner has to apply to a court to remove a resident. Even then he can do so only if:

- the mobile home is not the main residence of the occupier
- the condition of the mobile home is detrimental to the site
- the resident has refused to comply with the terms of the agreement

You can sell a mobile home that you own and pass the agreement on to the new occupier, but the site owner can claim a commission, up to a maximum of 10 per cent of the price. But if you transfer the home to a member of your family, no commission is payable.

If a resident dies, the widow, widower, or any member of the family who was living there at the time of death can inherit. People living together but who are unmarried count as husband and wife.

The site owner must have a licence and must obey the rules about the number of homes on a site, the landscaping, fire precautions, and health and safety.

Anyone who rents a mobile home is not covered by the Mobile Homes Act 1983 but will have the same protection as other tenants under the Rent Acts. The Mobile Homes Act does not apply to people who use the caravan for holidays only.

BUYING A HOUSE IN SCOTLAND

The Scottish system of buying a house is quite different from the English and Welsh. If you want to buy a house in Scotland, you put in a tender and, once this has been accepted, then both you as the buyer and the seller are legally bound to go ahead with the deal. You know that the house is yours so you cannot be gazumped or let down at the last minute.

The process starts off the same way: you see a house advertised that you think you might like, you arrange to view it and, if you decide you are interested, you instruct a surveyor to check it over.

At this stage, if ten people are interested in buying the same property, there will be ten surveyors' reports. Meanwhile, you instruct a solicitor who satisfies himself that you will have the funds to buy the place should your offer be successful.

At the same time, the building society sends its own surveyor round. If, after seeing the surveyor's report you want to buy the house, you write down how much you are willing to pay and hand this to your solicitor.

The vendor's solicitor then announces the closing date on which all offers will be opened and the vendor chooses which offer he or she finds most acceptable. This is usually the highest but, if that one is hedged about with unacceptable conditions the vendor may choose another.

At this point the two sides agree the completion date, usually two months' hence, which in Scotland is called the entry date, and both sides are committed to going ahead with the transaction.

However, the practice in Scotland is slipping more towards the English system: for example, you can agree with someone privately that you will accept a certain offer.

THE COST OF SELLING A £30,000 HOUSE IN THE UK

	£		£
Estate agent's fee	600	plus VAT	690
Solicitor's fee	300	plus VAT	345
			£1035

The average selling cost will be between 3 and 4 per cent of the price of the house.

THE COST OF BUYING A £30,000 HOUSE WITH A £20,000 MORTGAGE

	£		£
Mortgage arrangement fee (only to a bank)	75	plus VAT	86.25
Solicitor's bill	300	plus VAT	345.00
Land registry fee	73	no VAT	73.00
Surveyor	150	plus VAT	172.50
Building society's surveyor	45	plus VAT	51.75
Building society's solicitor	67.50	plus VAT	77.62
Mortgage indemnity insurance	80	no VAT	80.00
Building insurance premium	45	no VAT	45.00
			£931.12

The average buying cost will range from 2·5 per cent to nearly 4 per cent of the price of the house.

LETTERS

Q. I have read a great deal about repayment and endowment mortgages. But the more I read, the less clear I am about it all. Which one really is best?

A. *The 'best' for you might not necessarily be the 'best' for your next-door-neighbour. You need to weigh up the pros and cons as you see them.*

You can pay off a repayment mortgage at any time you wish and, if interest rates go up, you will quite likely be able to extend the period of the loan instead of making higher repayments.

With an endowment, you will have life insurance cover and a lump sum payment at the end. The difference in actual monthly payments between the two fluctuates but there is not much to choose.

Q. My building society was very enthusiastic for me to switch from a repayment mortgage to an endowment. How much money would they have made out of this?

A. *It varies, but generally they get £2 for every £100 you borrow under an endowment policy. So, if your loan is £20,000, the building society earns commission of £400.*

6/How to Sell a House

Estate agents • Selling the house yourself • *making your house attractive / the extras / your responsibilities / bargaining / fixtures and fittings / diy conveyancing / cut-price conveyancing firms* • The contract • Bridging loans • How to sell a house with an estate agent • The stages of selling a house without an estate agent • Moving house • Hiring a removal firm • Before you move – details to remember • Letters

Selling a £40,000 house could cost you £1000 in estate agent's and solicitor's fees. Or you could do the whole job yourself. You will find yourself involved in much of the work anyway.

When you are selling and buying a house at the same time, you have to perform a balancing act requiring delicate timing. To complete both transactions on the same day so that (a) you have the money to buy your new house and (b) are not homeless, will seem impossible, especially if you have been caught up in a long chain of buyers and sellers all trying to stay on the same tightrope.

But once you have decided to move, you will want to know if you should try to sell the old house first, or commit yourself to buying a new one and then start selling? This chicken and egg question really depends on the house market at the time, and on the sheer chance of finding the right house and the right buyer.

You can go about selling in two ways. You can simply put the whole matter into the hands of an estate agent (or several), or you can sell your house yourself.

ESTATE AGENTS

You do not need an estate agent to sell a house for you, but you may not have the time to do the job yourself. What the estate agent offers is a list of names of people looking for a house like yours. He will advise you on the price you should be asking but if you do a little research on local prices yourself, you will get a pretty good idea of the value.

He may show prospective buyers round the house for you or he may just arrange the appointment and leave you to take them round. He should also conduct the embarrassing haggling over price, though often you will find it more efficient to talk directly with the buyer yourself.

Estate agents charge around 2 per cent (plus VAT) of the selling price. The range is from 1½ to 3 per cent varying around the country. You might pay 1½ per cent plus the cost of advertising in the North and 3 per cent for an expensive property in London. **The fee is negotiable and you can bargain with an agent before giving him the contract.**

So to sell a £35,000 house you would pay the estate agent £805, including VAT.

An estate agent should:
- put a market value on the house; you can ask a number of different agents to do this without committing yourself
- provide particulars and photographs of the property
- keep tracks on all offers that are made
- make enquiries about the buyer's finances, for example, to find out if he has a mortgage arranged
- offer advice on the buyer's survey report and renegotiate price
- show prospective buyers around if vendor at work during the day
- can help arrange mortgage if necessary
- advise on repairs that may be necessary before the property is sold.

If you give the estate agent 'sole agency', he will charge you a lower commission. Sole agency means that he is the only person who can sell your house for you. But make sure you do not give him 'sole selling rights'. With sole agency, if, in the end you sold the house to a friend without going through the estate agent, he has lost his fee. But if he has sole selling rights, he could claim the fee even if you sold the house to your mother.

Often he will ask for sole agency for a limited period of time. The fee will then be about ½ per cent lower. After about six weeks, he sub-contracts the particulars to other local agents who will receive an even lower fee from him if they sell it for you. These secondary agents will not be terribly enthusiastic about putting much effort into selling your house.

He may charge you for advertising in local newspapers, but you should be told that this will happen before agreeing terms. If the fee is high to start with, you should challenge any extra payments, or shop around.

There are private house selling agencies springing up around the country. You pay a fixed fee (about £100) to the company which puts details of your house provided by you on to a computer. The details are matched up with potential buyers and the two of you sort out the deal. Your house details stay on the file, at no extra cost, until your house is sold. You will find the agencies advertising in local newspapers.

SELLING THE HOUSE YOURSELF

If you want to sell the house yourself, first you can put up a notice board outside inviting buyers to look around. But be careful who you allow to come in if you are alone in the house. Then put a postcard in the local newsagent's window which is a minimal cost. Finally, put an advertisement in the local newspaper. You may need to advertise for several weeks and the cost of this will mount up.

If you are not sure what price tag to put on your house, look around the local estate agents to see what they are asking for similar properties and check the local newspaper. You can soon get a feel for local prices and, if you are having difficulty selling the house, you can always reduce the asking price.

Making your house attractive

Silly as it seems, prospective buyers are vastly impressed by a neat and tidy house. In winter make sure the house is comfortably warm and in summer, fresh and airy. By putting a lot of hard work into maintaining an unnatural tidiness (and bribing the children to do the same) you can give the appearance of living in an easy to run, effortless, house.

If the house and garden are full of mess and rubbish, a buyer will think this is a very difficult house to look after. An American tip is to place a vanilla pod or coffee beans under the grill just before the viewers arrive. They will smell a delicious aroma of home cooking but see no sign of dirty pans and dishes. Their subconscious will tell them that this is a happy, contented, down to earth, home requiring no effort. Anyway, that is the theory.

The extras

You may be tempted to install double glazing or central heating to add to the value of your house. These extra refinements will not necessarily increase the value of your home, though they might make it easier to sell if the market is slow. But, if you are just on the point of moving, it is a bit late to start home improvements – even worse is to have the house in a mess while people are looking around.

Remember the importance of first impressions: it could be worth painting the front door a bright cheerful colour to entice viewers inside.

Your responsibilities

You do not have to volunteer any information to prospective buyers. You may be moving out because the next-door-neighbours have noisy parties every night, but you do not have to say so, unless asked.

You must answer truthfully any questions you are asked, for example about the state of the roof, the condition of the drains or whatever. You can be a little less categoric about the neighbours and to the straight question 'why are you moving?', you will, honestly, be able to give several answers. **The less said the better.**

Bargaining

You will be lucky if someone offers you exactly the price you are asking unless you have priced the property too low. Buyers naturally want to pay as little as possible. From the outset, have a figure in mind that you know you will accept and below which you will not go. Then you can go ahead and bargain confidently.

Fixtures and fittings

There are grey areas here and you should not leave any doubt about what you are taking and what you are leaving behind. Prepare a typed list and see that your solicitor includes it in the contract. If you intend leaving the carpets and curtains behind, this is a good selling point. Or if you do not mention them in the first place, you can use them as a bargaining point later.

When you have reached a final agreement with a buyer, write down exactly what you intend to take with you. Among the items that could be in doubt are shelves, wall lights, and shower curtains. You can negotiate separately about selling items such as window blinds, which are usually more nuisance than they are worth to take with you.

In any communications you have with the buyer, always state that the deal is 'subject to contract'. This is very important. Otherwise, you can find yourself committed to handing over the house on terms that do not suit you. But 'subject to contract' means that neither side is committed to anything until you sign the contract.

DIY conveyancing

It is easier to do your own conveyancing when you are selling a house than if you are buying. Even so, it is still time consuming and involves many paper transactions.

If you were to begin your own conveyancing and then found that an unexpected complication made it too difficult, you could still pass the work over to a solicitor at that stage.

Cut-price conveyancing firms

There are a number of these around the country: they will do the conveyancing for you at a lower price than solicitors charge.

If you decide to use one be sure that he is a member of the National Association of Conveyancers and carries negligence insurance otherwise you have no control over them. By law only a barrister, solicitor, or notary public can convey title to land for gain.

THE CONTRACT

Once you and the buyer have agreed the finer points you can draw up a contract. If you are using a solicitor he will do this for you. When you, the seller, have signed the contract and sent a copy to the buyer's solicitor, then you are bound to go ahead with the transaction on the completion day stated in the contract. This is usually one month after the date of exchange.

If either side is not willing to move on completion day, he is liable to pay compensation. If the buyer is delaying, he will have to pay interest on the amount owed, the rate for which will be stated in the contract. If the seller is delaying, the buyer is in a weaker position; he cannot claim any interest, he can serve a 'notice to complete' only and if this has no effect, he can go to court.

At exchange of contracts the buyer will pay a 10 per cent deposit which is usually held by the seller's solicitor as 'stakeholder'.

There are two standard forms of contract: one is 'national conditions of sale' and the other is the Law Society's conditions of sale. You can buy these from Oyez Publishing or the Law Society. They are known as draft contracts and you can make amendments to them to suit your circumstances.

BRIDGING LOANS
You may have to commit yourself to paying for a new house before you have received the money from the old. In this case, you can ask your bank manager for a 'bridging loan'. These are expensive, about 5 per cent above base rate, so you will want to have a clear idea of how long you are likely to need the money for. The bank manager is unlikely to grant a bridging loan for an indefinite period, anyway.

HOW TO SELL A HOUSE WITH AN ESTATE AGENT
1. Ask neighbours for their opinion of local estate agents.
2. Check that the agent is a member of the Royal Institution of Chartered Surveyors or Incorporated Society of Valuers and Auctioneers or National Association of Estate Agents.
3. Ask three agents to value your house before agreeing to give one the business. Remember that the agent recommending the highest price is not necessarily the best or the most reliable.
4. You can give one agent 'sole agency' in which case the fee will be lower.
5. Otherwise you can give multiple agency to as many as you want, but check the terms carefully otherwise you might have to pay a fee to more than one of them.
6. Negotiate the fee. You can argue, but expect to pay 1½ to 2½ per cent or even 3 per cent in Central London. The agent has a statutory duty to agree his charges with you when you first instruct him to sell.
7. Check whether the agent will charge you for any newspaper advertisements.
8. Check that, if you manage to sell privately, you are not still liable to pay his fee.

9. You can have the estate agent's 'For Sale' board outside your house, but you do not have to if you do not want it. You are mostly giving him free advertising.

THE STAGES OF SELLING A HOUSE WITHOUT AN ESTATE AGENT
1. Look round locally to get an idea of the price you should ask.
2. Erect a sign outside the house saying it is for sale.
3. Place a card in the newsagent's window.
4. Advertise in the local paper.
5. Make the house look clean and tidy.
6. List the items you will leave behind.
7. Make sure potential buyers can contact you easily.

when you have a buyer
1. Agree the price 'subject to contract'.
2. Agree any items you are selling separately.
3. Agree what you are leaving behind.
4. Tell your solicitor (if you are using one).
5. Otherwise buy a guide to DIY conveyancing.

MOVING HOUSE
There is very little difference in cost between moving 500 yards and 500 miles.

HIRING A REMOVAL FIRM
The choice is between paying someone to do it for you and doing it yourself. If you go the whole hog and pay a removal firm to pack everything for you and then unpack at the other end, it will cost several hundred pounds for an average size family.

If you are moving because of your job, you may be able to persuade the company to foot the bill, in which case you may as well make it as easy for yourself as you can.

Whatever you do, ask for at least three quotations – they will vary enormously. The dearest could be three times the cheapest, but do not assume that the cheapest is necessarily the best.

The price you pay depends on which day of the week you want to move (Fridays and Saturdays are more expensive); whether it is a one- or two-day job; the time of year (peak holiday period is more expensive); how keen the remover is to have your business.

To choose a removal firm, ask anyone you know who has moved recently who they used and what they thought; check if the firm is a member of an association, which will have a code of practice; do not use a specialised firm (unless you need to) because they will be more expensive.

But if you do not fit into the average mould, find a specialist firm which can cope with your requirements: you may be moving overseas; or have valuable antiques; or you may be moving to a high block of flats.

Most complaints about removers arise because the van is late, followed by complaints about breakages leading to arguments over insurance. Another cause of complaint is unexpected expenses often arising because the customer has forgotten to mention that there are parking meter restrictions in the road, or that the lift is too small to take the furniture so the removal men have to carry everything by the stairs. The removal firm will be able to give you a leaflet of helpful hints.

Make sure you know whether the quotation includes insurance. You should have remembered to transfer your house contents insurance to the new address on the precise day and you may find that your insurance policy will cover you for the transfer as well. If not, make sure that you are covered one way or the other, either by the removal firm or on your own policy.

If you are not moving very many possessions, you can hire a van and packing crates and do it all yourself. Look for advertisements in the local paper. It will be a very tiring day and you will need as many strong friends to help as you can find.

BEFORE YOU MOVE – DETAILS TO REMEMBER
This is a busy time and there are many things to do.
- arrange for the electricity board to read the meter on the day you move out
- do the same with the gas board
- make sure this has been done in the house you are moving to
- inform the electricity and gas boards in the new area that you are now responsible for the bills
- arrange to have any gas appliances disconnected and reconnected when you arrive in the new house
- ask for a final bill for the telephone
- ask your buyer if he wants the telephone left on or disconnected and tell British Telecom
- inform British Telecom in the area you are moving to that you will be taking over the existing telephone making sure the outgoing owner also contacts them; or arrange to have a telephone installed
- hire a removal firm, or van and packing cases if you are doing it yourself
- tell the local authority that you are moving out and will no longer be responsible for the rates. They will arrange any rebate due to you. If you use a solicitor, he will do this
- tell the local authority when you are moving in
- if you want your letters redirected, ask the post office for a redirection form. This will cost £2.25 for one month
- have your name put on the new electoral roll
- inform everyone who needs to know of your new address

As well as friends and neighbours, remember to include: bank/building society savings accounts/ driving licence centre/ television licence/television rental/credit card company/any HP or credit agreements/all insurance policies: house, life, car/doctor/dentist/club memberships/ subscriptions to magazines and charities/road fund licence/cancel the milk and newspapers.

As soon as you arrive in the new house, check that everything is as you expected it to be: that nothing has been taken which should have been left behind. Lastly, hope for a fine day.

LETTERS

Q. I am wondering whether to do my own conveyancing on the houses I am selling and buying. Do you think this is a good idea?

A. *You really will have to make your own mind up about this one. You will certainly save yourself a great deal of money and you do not need years of legal experience.*
   There is no reason why anyone of normal intelligence should not be able to do their own conveyancing; it just requires a little concentration and effort and a guide to follow. If you do come across an intractable legal problem, you can always swallow your pride and go to a solicitor at that point.

Q. Where can I find more information about DIY conveyancing? Obviously I am going to need a little help and guidance to do it myself.

A. *There are several books on the market although you should need to buy only one. Try:* The Legal Side of Buying a House *from the Consumers' Association, Castlemead, Gascoyne Way, Hertford SG14 1LH;* Bradshaw's Guide to DIY House Buying, Selling and Conveyancing *from Castle Books, 1 Blackdown, Leamington Spa CV32 6RA; or* The Conveyancing Fraud *published by Michael Joseph, 27 Occupation Lane, London SE18.*

Q. I would like to have a look at the file which my solicitor has compiled on my house purchase. Can I do this?

A. *Yes. You paid him to do this work so, by rights, the file is yours. You can ask him to hand it over to you for keeps if you like.*

7/Renting Accommodation

Fair rent / reasonable rent / eviction / family's right of tenure / deposits / advance rent / rent book • Service charges • *gas and electricity meters* • Housing Associations • *co-ownership schemes / repairs / council housing / insurance* • Renting out a property • *sitting tenants* • Letters

Private rented accommodation is nowadays very difficult to find. House owners today are very reluctant to rent out flats because they fear it is impossible to be rid of bad tenants. This is not strictly true, but it is nonetheless difficult to evict unwanted tenants.

There are different categories of tenancies and your rights differ according to which you belong to: full or restricted protection.

You will have full protection if the tenancy started after 14 August 1974 and the landlord does not live in the same house. If you were a tenant before that date, the position is more complicated but basically, if the landlord does not live in the same flat or house and does not provide any services such as changing the sheets, cleaning the flat or house, or providing meals, you have full protection.

So restricted protection applies mainly to tenants who have a resident landlord. Your rent can be registered by the rent tribunal but you will have little security.

If you have full protection, you could be in either a regulated or shorthold tenancy. A regulated tenancy's rent has been registered by the rent officer and is totally secure from eviction except in a few, very specific circumstances.

A shorthold tenancy is one that you know from the outset has a limited life of between one and five years. In London the rent must have been registered by the rent officer at the outset although this is not necessary outside London. For the fixed period of the tenancy, you have total security unless you are in breach of the covenant of the lease but none after that, as long as you were given proper notice. Before granting the tenancy the landlord must give proper (or valid) notice that the tenancy is to be a protected shorthold tenancy.

Whatever sort of tenancy you have you should be sure that it comes within the Rent Acts. **You could be just a licensee which means you have very little security**.

Licences mainly apply to rented rooms such as student hostels, but some unscrupulous landlords have tried to draw up contracts which leave the tenant a licensee and not a regulated tenant.

A recent category is assured tenancy which started in 1980 and applies to property built after August 1980. The rent for these is not controlled by the rent officer but it will be at the market rate, that is what the market can stand.

But before anyone can grant an assured tenancy, the landlord must be approved by the Government as someone with integrity, such as a building society. You will have full protection.

Fair rent

A tenant with full protection can apply to the rent officer to determine the amount of rent the landlord can charge. Once a fair rent has been registered, this is the most the tenant need pay.

Of course, it may be that this is in fact higher than the tenant was paying previously. The only occasions when you will have to pay more than the fixed rent are if the rates go up, or, if you have a variable service charge.

If the rent officer does say that you should pay a higher rent, you do not have to pay it all at once. You pay half of the increase straightaway and the remainder 12 months later.

When fixing a fair rent, the rent officer takes into account the position of the property, its age, size and state of repair. He does not take notice of any changes in the condition of the property (for better or worse) nor of the financial status of either landlord or tenant.

Neither does he put a scarcity value on the rent, however few properties there are to rent in the area. This can make a 'fair' rent seem very low in some situations.

If you move into a flat that has a registered fair rent, it will apply to you just as it did to the previous tenant.

Reasonable rent

A tenant with restricted protection can apply to the rent assessment committee for a 'reasonable rent': once this is agreed, that will be the maximum the landlord can charge.

Eviction

A landlord must obtain a court order before evicting anyone, whatever sort of tenancy it is. In certain situations tenants can be evicted.

You may be evicted if:
- you fall very far behind paying the rent
- the landlord now needs the space for himself and would be in a worse position than you without it
- you are a nuisance to the neighbours
- you use the flat for illegal or immoral purposes
- you damage the property
- you sublet the property without the landlord's permission
- the landlord finds you alternative and comparable accommodation
- you rented the flat as an employee and no longer work for the company

You will certainly be evicted if:
- the landlord told you before you moved in that he had lived in the accommodation himself and will need it back
- the landlord wants to retire to your accommodation
- you signed a shorthold tenancy agreement which has ended
- the property is a holiday home and you have no more than an eight-month agreement

A tenant with restricted protection cannot be evicted if he has a contract unless he breaks the terms of the contract (and then he can still be evicted only with a court order).

Even after the contract has ended, he can stay there until a court orders him to leave.

Family's right of tenure
When a tenant dies, his family can continue living in the rented house. His wife can take over the tenancy and, on her death, she can pass it on to a child. But the tenancy can be passed on only twice.

Deposits
The old practice of charging 'key' money, that is asking you to pay a lump sum before you move in, is now illegal. If you feel you have been forced to pay this, you can claim it back by applying to the local authority.

However, reasonable deposits are permissible with furnished or unfurnished lettings. The deposit must not be greater than one-sixth of the annual rent. The deposit will be returned to you when you move out. You can also be asked to buy the fixtures and fittings in a flat. But this must be an appropriate sum for the items involved; if you think you have paid more than the fixtures and fittings are really worth, claim the excess back again through the local authority.

Advance rent
You can be asked to pay rent in advance when you first move in. You do not need to pay more than two months' rent in advance.

Rent book

Only tenants who pay rent weekly need a rent book but it is a good idea to ask for one anyway so you have a record of your payments.

The rent book will tell you your rights, the amount of rent to pay, and give the name and address of the landlord.

SERVICE CHARGES

These can be disturbingly high so it is important to understand your position. If you are protected by the Rent Act, a charge for services will probably be included in your rent. This must be explained in your contract.

Unless your contract specifically allows it, no increase in the cost of services can be passed on to you. However, if you are living in a flat with a long lease, then the service charge can rise from year to year because you pay the actual cost of the services.

If your contract does permit increases, you have a right to know how the charge has been calculated before you pay the bill and the landlord must tell you how the charges have been arrived at.

If you think the charges are too high, or you have been charged for a service you did not receive, you should complain to the landlord or managing agent. If you cannot come to an agreement you can take the landlord to court.

One way out of this dispute is to pay the amount you think is fair and then leave it to the landlord to sue you for the balance. You may have to pay some of the money for service charges in advance if the contract has stipulated this.

For any large-scale expense the landlord must consult the tenants first; but this applies only to work and not to services. He must obtain at least two estimates and you, the tenant, can obtain a separate estimate too if you wish.

However, this does not apply to small blocks of four flats or less.

Gas and electricity meters

A landlord can charge more than it costs him for reselling gas and electricity to you through a meter. But there is a maximum price he can charge and also a maximum charge for renting the meter.

But, be careful. Meters are sometimes faulty and you may be paying for more energy than you use. See p. 105.

HOUSING ASSOCIATIONS

More and more housing associations are being set up around the country as groups of people get together to buy and restore houses or to build new ones. If the Government accepts the association's scheme, it will receive help with the building costs through grants from the Housing Corporation.

The housing association charges the tenants a rent which is assessed and controlled as a fair rent by the rent officer, just like any other protected tenant. Housing Association tenants have security of tenure under the Housing Act 1980 rather than the Rent Act.

Co-ownership schemes

These are similar to housing associations but the members buy the property rather than rent it. Co-ownership schemes can apply to the Housing Corporation for grants. After five years, the members will receive a share of any profit when they sell out of the scheme.

Repairs

Generally, as a private or housing association tenant, your landlord is responsible for carrying out any necessary repairs. He is also required to provide standard amenities such as hot and cold water and a bath or shower.

However, check the terms of your agreement. Particularly with older tenancies or leases longer than seven years, the responsibility for repairs may be different.

As a tenant you can carry out some improvements yourself and get a grant towards the cost of work. But you will have to pay the balance of the cost yourself, you cannot claim it back from the landlord if you received the grant. It is more advisable to try and persuade the landlord to undertake the work and claim the grant for himself.

And remember that the rent officer will ignore the value of any work which the tenant has paid for when calculating a fair rent.

Council housing

Most rented accommodation is now council housing. The amount of rent you have to pay is fixed by the local authority and you cannot argue against paying it.

Moreover, the local authority can raise the rent whenever it wants, the only stipulation being that the amount demanded is 'reasonable'.

When a council tenant dies, the tenancy can be passed on to the husband or wife, or to any member of the family who has been living there for 12 months and regards it as their main home. The tenancy can be passed on once again.

Most council tenants have a secure tenancy which means that they can be evicted only if they have seriously broken the terms of their lease and then only by court order.

Tenants now have the right to buy their council house. See p. 80.

Insurance

Lastly, remember to insure your possessions. Even in rented property, it is up to you to take responsibility for your valuables. For more details, see p. 116.

RENTING OUT A PROPERTY

If you are renting out part of your home or a separate property you will have to go to court to evict a tenant who is not paying the rent.

When the tenancy comes to an end, you are entitled to have possession of your property again. But, if the tenant does not move out, you cannot force him out. You will have to go to court for an eviction order; you do not have the right to break into the house or to harrass the tenant in the hope of persuading him to move.

If you are providing bed and breakfast, or other services, and you live in the house yourself, the tenant will have restricted protection only. But you will still need a court order to make him leave.

A landlord has the same right to apply for a fair rent as the tenant. And, again, once this has been registered then no one can reapply for an amendment for two years.

Sitting tenants

Like council tenants, if you are a sitting tenant you may have the right to buy your home. If you are renting privately you may be able to persuade your landlord to sell the house to you.

In that case, you go about buying the house in which you are living in just the same way as you would buy any other property.

If you buy a house that already has a sitting tenant in it, you will be bound to honour the agreement. You will be able to buy the house cheaper than you would if you had vacant possession but you may have a little difficulty finding a mortgage.

LETTERS

Q.   I am going to work abroad for two years and I would like to rent out my house while I am away. But I am nervous about not being able to regain possession when I return. How can I make sure there will be no problem in getting the tenants out?

A.   *You should have no problem as long as you follow the correct procedure. Any home owner can regain possession of his property if:*
(a) he lived there before he moved out
(b) he told the tenant before the tenancy started that he would be returning
(c) he gives the proper notice to quit
(d) he, or a relative, needs to live there, or he needs to sell with vacant
    possession.

Q.   I have moved into my boyfriend's flat. Am I right in assuming that I'll be able to stay there if anything happened to him?

A.   *If you have his children, then you will be regarded as his 'family' and you will be able to take over the tenancy. But if not, then you are unlikely to inherit until you have lived there for a very long time.*

8/In Your Home

Rates • *rate reduction* • Housing benefit • *for people not on supplementary benefit / if you are on supplementary benefit* • Water rates • Home improvements • *home improvement grants / is it worth it? / decorating* • Security • *false pretences* • Heating costs • *insulation / pipes and tank lagging / cavity wall insulation / double glazing / temperature / separate heaters / electricity / gas / oil / paraffin / solid fuel / electricity costs / gas and electricity meters* • Extended guarantees or service contracts • Home income plans

Moving into your house will have taken much time, trouble and fretting. Unfortunately the problems and expenses do not end once you have closed the front door. Many are just beginning.

To start with, you will find the largest, perpetual, bill to face is for the rates. Under the housing benefit rules, if you are on a low income you may be able to get help with the rates bill and, if you are in rented accommodation perhaps a rent rebate as well.

RATES
These are a tax that you pay to your local authority for providing local services such as: the dustmen; sewers; street cleaning; libraries; parks; fire service; schools; social services.

Your bill is calculated according to the size and quality of your property and its surroundings, including the garage and any outbuildings, and it does not take into consideration how many people use the services.

When you buy a house, you will be told the 'rateable value' of the house and the 'rate in the pound' that the local authority is charging. To work out your rates bill, you multiply one figure by the other.

For example, if the rateable value of your house is £200 and the local authority charges a rate in the pound of £1.10, then your rates bill for the year is £220.

Even if you are renting property, you will pay rates though they may be included in your rent.

If you improve your house, maybe by adding an extension or a bathroom, you should inform the local rating authority because this could affect your rates bill. If you had to ask for planning permission, the local authority will in any case be aware of your building work.

You will have to pay any higher rates due either from the date the work is completed, or 1 April whichever is earlier. Rates are supposed to be reassessed every five years but there has not been a revaluation since 1973.

The rates bill falls due in April each year and that is when your local authority will tell you exactly how much you have to pay for the coming year.

The money is due in advance for the whole year though you can ask to spread the cost. You can pay in two half-yearly lump sums if you wish or, by far the best way is to pay in monthly instalments spread over ten months of the year. See p. 11.

Rate reduction

If you think the rates you are paying are too high, you can ask for a reassessment. You may feel, for example, that the late night noise from the gambling den next door warrants a lower bill.

Ask at your local valuation office (you will find its address in the telephone directory under 'Inland Revenue' or you can ask at the town hall) for a form 'proposal for the alteration of the valuation list'.

Complete this and try to persuade your neighbours to join in the fight. There is added strength in a united complaint. The appeal will be heard at a valuation court which you or your adviser will be required to attend to state your case for a reduction in rates.

After weighing the evidence, the court will give a ruling on what it considers fair. However, you do not have to settle for this if you are still dissatisfied; your next step is an appeal to the Lands Tribunal but you will probably need a surveyor or solicitor to help you and you will have to pay their costs unless these are awarded against the Valuation Office.

If a house is standing empty you do not have to pay rates to start with but the local authority can, after three months, start charging rates at the normal level.

HOUSING BENEFIT

New housing benefit rules started in 1983 with the result that rent and rate rebates became very confused. The new housing benefit system is meant to work as follows:

For people not on supplementary benefit

You can earn a fairly high income and still qualify for help with your housing costs. A single person paying £40 a week in rent and with earnings of around £143 a week can claim a rebate; a couple with one earner and three children can claim even if their income is as high as £203 a week.

A single person paying rates of £780 a year can apply for a rebate on earnings of £156 a week and the couple with three children at £216 a week.

To apply for a rent or rate rebate ask for an application form at your local housing department at the town hall.

A rent rebate can be claimed if you live in a council property or you are buying your home under a shared ownership scheme. If you are a private tenant you apply for a rent allowance; you can also ask for this if you live in a mobile home or on a houseboat.

A rate rebate is payable to anyone who pays rates on their home, whether a council property, an owner occupier, or a private rented tenant.

If you are on supplementary benefit

Previously you would have received your rent and rate rebates from the DHSS. Under the new housing benefit arrangements you will receive assistance from the local authority.

If you are receiving supplementary benefit, you are automatically entitled to housing benefit. The DHSS sends a certificate to the local authority confirming that you are on supplementary benefit and this becomes your claim for housing benefit.

WATER RATES

You will have to pay water rates in two half-yearly sums to the local water board. It is not possible to get a rebate for water. You are paying for the supply of water and sewerage collection, treatment and disposal.

The bill is calculated by multiplying the rateable value of your house by the water authority's charge. There is one charge for water and, a smaller one, for sewerage treatment, plus a standing charge for both.

You will pay a higher water rate than your neighbour if you have a swimming pool. You may have to pay more if you have a garden hose or sprinkler to water the plants or wash the car but most authorities do not charge extra.

HOME IMPROVEMENTS

People are improving their houses in preference to moving more than ever before. Around a third of building society lending is now for home improvements rather than for house purchase.

You can expand your living space in various ways: by adding rooms over the garage, or in the loft or by extending out into the garden. You will need planning permission from the local authority for any major changes you make. But, unless there are special local authority regulations you do not need permission for small extensions. So you can go ahead, unless you are raising the height of the roof or bringing the front of the house forward or increasing the overall size of a terraced house by more than 50 cubic metres or one tenth of the cubic capacity, whichever is the greater. Other than terraced houses can be enlarged by 70 cubic metres or 15 per cent of the cubic capacity, whichever is the greater, without permission.

Home improvement grants

You can obtain a grant from your local authority to help towards the cost of repairing an old house, providing a bathroom and, in some instances, installing proper kitchen facilities. If the house is in a very bad state, you may be able to get most of the money, on occasions up to 90 per cent, from the council.

This is not a loan – the local authority is giving you the money to improve the condition of your house, although there may be certain conditions about reselling.

To obtain a grant, you must follow the procedure demanded by the local authority. You cannot have the work done first and then ask for a grant towards the cost. The local authority must come along and inspect the property in its original state before giving you the go-ahead. You will need to produce several quotations from local builders.

There are three different types of grants to apply for: repair grants; improvement grants; and intermediate grants. The grants are discretionary, you are not entitled to the money by right, and different authorities have varying attitudes towards handing them out.

Householders can obtain improvement grants for insulating the loft, pipes and water tanks. The elderly and severely disabled on low incomes are entitled to larger grants for this.

Intermediate grants are for installing standard amenities such as hot and cold running water, an indoor toilet and bath. Repair grants are for substantial and structural repairs to pre-1919 houses, and will cover reroofing, repointing, and installation of a damp-proof course.

You cannot get a grant for rewiring a house alone but if you are having a larger job done, then rewiring will be included as part of it. It is worth asking your local authority if a grant is available for any job you have in mind.

To qualify for a grant you must own the house in question, though in some instances tenants can be allowed grants as long as the landlord approves the work being done. The rateable value of the property must not exceed £400 in Greater London or £225 elsewhere.

If you have to borrow money to top up the amount of the grant, it can be worth borrowing it rather than using your savings. This is because the money qualifies for tax relief, just like the mortgage you borrowed in the first place. The only stipulation is that your total borrowings on the house, the home loan plus improvement loan, do not total more than the tax relief ceiling of £30,000.

Is it worth it?

You will gain the extra space of course, but will an extension add to the value of your house? Small improvements like loft insulation and double glazing can make the house easier to sell, but you cannot necessarily add on £500 to the asking price to recover your outlay.

An extra bedroom or second bathroom will certainly increase the value of your house, possibly by more than it cost you to install. A shower, in particular, is a good selling point.

But the costs of substantial alterations are high. A good quality extension will cost about £450 a square metre to build and a loft conversion about £320 a square metre. Since July 1984, VAT at the rate of 15 per cent has become payable on all building extensions and home improvements.

Decorating

Whenever you buy a second-hand house, the chances of your liking the decorations already there, even if they are brand new, are a hundred to one against. But even if you are happy with your predecessor's colour schemes, you will at some stage have to redecorate.

Decorating is expensive, particularly if you pay someone else to do the work. But it is false economy to buy cheap materials. You have only the hassle of repeating the job the following year if the paint blisters or the wallpaper disintegrates.

SECURITY

You should be extremely aware of the necessity of keeping your house secure, particularly if you live in a city centre.

You should have secure locks on all your outside doors and also locks on the windows. If you have rooms where access from the outside is easy you can fix iron grilles over the windows.

Whether or not to install a burglar alarm is a more difficult decision. By having a little box on the outside wall you are telling the world that you think you have something inside worth stealing. And then these alarms tend to be over sensitive; they are often set off because of a fault rather than a burglar, and this has the same effect as crying wolf. A noisy (not necessarily large) dog might be a better deterrent.

Remember that if a burglar is determined to break in, he will succeed. So, your main concern is to dissuade him from even trying. If a light is on in the house, he will think twice about breaking in, so a time switch can be useful.

When you go away on holiday, obviously remember to cancel the milk and the newspapers but also ask a neighbour to call in from time to time to move the curtains around and switch the lights on and off. Then, do not leave anything valuable where it can be seen from the road. That is flaunting temptation.

And once you have fixed these security gadgets, do remember to use them. Otherwise they are a complete waste of money. To keep unwanted callers outside, fit a chain to the front door and a spy hole so you can see who is knocking. Again, remember to use the door chain.

You can ask the crime prevention officer at your local police station to come round and advise you; they are happy to do so.

If anyone calling himself an official turns up unexpectedly, ask to see his identity card. If you have any doubts at all, ask him to come back in half an hour while you telephone the authority he claims to represent to make sure he is genuine.

Do not be embarrassed about doing this. If he is genuine, he will understand. If he is not, he will not come back. And do not ever, ever, let anyone come into your house if you do not know who they are.

False pretences

If a dealer offers to look over any old 'junk' you may be interested in selling, tell him to come back in a week's time. Meanwhile, get an idea of the real value of the items from another source and when he returns keep an eye on him the whole time he is in the house. Even better, arrange to have someone else in the house with you.

HEATING COSTS

Always remember that hot air rises, so the air you are paying so expensively to heat is simply floating up and out through the roof. But there are quite a few steps you can take to help keep your heating costs down and it is worth investing in most of them.

Insulation

The first thing you should do is to insulate the loft. It will cost about £100 to insulate an average three-bedroomed semi yourself.

You may be able to obtain a grant to help with the cost of materials. See p. 101.

Pipes and tank lagging

Like loft insulation, this is an elementary (and inexpensive) job which should be done immediately if your pipes and hot water tank are not already lagged.

Cavity wall insulation

This is expensive. A three-bedroomed semi costs about £250 to insulate using foam or £350 with mineral fibre. So it will take longer to recoup the outlay in saved heating bills.

Double glazing

How much you will save on your heating bills by installing double glazing is debatable. It is obviously cheaper to do the job yourself if you are able but it will still take many years to recoup the expense.

Double glazing can shut out noise if you live in a busy area and can deter burglars because it takes longer to break two panes of glass.

Above all, do make sure that you can open the windows quickly in case a fire breaks out. It is easy to become trapped inside a secure house.

Temperature

To cut costs, try turning down the central heating thermostat a degree or two. Very likely you will not notice the difference but if you turn down the heat by 4°F (2°C) you can save 10 per cent on your electricity bill.

You can install separate thermostats in each room. This way you are not heating a little-used room unnecessarily. In any rooms that are unused turn the radiator off altogether.

Separate heaters

It may not be worth the cost of installing central heating. If you are out a great deal or have several rooms you do not use, it will be far cheaper to heat only those rooms as and when you need.

With electric fires, you can use a time clock which automatically turns on the fire and heats the room before you get up in the morning or arrive home at night.

The price will vary according to where you live. Not only do fuel prices differ around the country but in the colder parts of the country you will spend substantially more on heating bills than you would in the milder south-west. The figures given are for the south-east.

Electricity

An average family living in a three-bedroomed semi will spend about £400 a year using electricity for central heating and hot water.

Night storage heaters operate by building up and storing a reserve of electricity at night when the rate is cheaper and then releasing the heat during the day. It costs about £90 a year to heat one room using one night storage heater.

Gas

Gas heating is cheaper than either oil or electricity. Gas central heating and hot water will cost about £350 a year for the average family. An individual gas fire costs £100 a year to heat one main room.

Oil

Oil is expensive and needs space for a large storage tank. Oil central heating will cost about £500 to heat a three-bedroomed semi for a year, including hot water.

Paraffin

This is a cheap way of heating individual rooms. It costs about £80 a year to heat one room.

Solid fuel
Again this needs space for storage. It costs about £400 a year to heat and provide hot water for a three-bedroomed semi; £150 to heat one room.

Electricity costs
Here is how much use one unit of electricity gives:

3 KWH radiant heat	20 minutes
2 KWH fan heater	30 minutes
cooker	meals for one person for one day
kettle	12 pints of water
colour television	3–7 hours
black and white television	7–10 hours
iron	2 hours
fridge	one day
tumbler drier	half-an-hour
hair drier	3 hours
vacuum cleaner	2–4 hours
electric blanket (under)	7 evenings (**under**); 2 full nights (**over**)
spin drier	4 hours

One unit of electricity is equal to one kilowatt or 1000 watts, running for one hour. So, if you buy an electrical appliance marked 250 watts, you know you can use it continuously for four hours and you will burn one unit of electricity.

This is how much you will be using:

dishwasher	1–1½ units per load
freezer	1½–2 units per cubic foot a week
automatic washing machine	9 units to wash clothes of a family of four for a week
twin tub washing machine	12 units to wash clothes of a family of four for a week
bath	4–5 units if tank lagged
shower	2–2½ units

One unit of electricity heats three gallons of hot water from 10°C (50°F) to 60°C (140°F). A bath uses 25 gallons of water; a shower uses half the amount of water and moreover at a lower temperature.

Gas and electricity meters
Sometimes these meters are faulty and you may be paying for more energy than you are actually using. You can have a meter checked by asking the gas or electricity boards.

The gas board will charge around £11 to £21, depending on where you live, if the meter turns out to be working properly. However, if you are right and the meter is faulty, beyond a 2 per cent tolerance either way, you will not pay anything.

Different electricity boards have different policies about charging: some charge nothing, whatever the outcome. Others will demand, say £15, if the meter turns out to be accurate; they charge mainly to deter time wasters.

In the first instance the electricity board will come and look at your meter to see if there is anything obviously wrong. If you are not satisfied, they will conduct a timing test and, failing that, a check meter test.

If you still do not accept their findings, you can ask for the Government meter examiner to take the meter away. The examiner at the Department of Energy will strip the meter and check it thoroughly. His findings are final and legally binding.

The Electricity Consumers' Council has produced a leaflet which explains many reasons that you may have forgotten about which could have resulted in a higher bill than you expected.

They suggest:
- you check that the meter reading is right
- the price has gone up
- the last bill was paid late and that amount has been included in this bill
- the last bill was based on an estimate which was too low
- the bill includes other charges such as HP payments
- the weather was very cold
- there was someone at home ill
- there were more people at home than usual
- a new baby
- a new heating system
- new equipment such as a freezer or tumbler drier
- there have been workmen in the house using electricity
- the wiring or thermostat may be faulty

EXTENDED GUARANTEES OR SERVICE CONTRACTS

When you buy a new domestic appliance you will almost certainly be asked by the manufacturer if you would like to take out a service contract. They will explain to you just how worth while this is and how much peace of mind it provides. But does it?

Service contracts, or extended guarantees, cost about £35 for a washing machine down to £10 for a vacuum cleaner.

This will probably cover parts and labour for four years beyond the first-year guarantee which you are given anyway. About a quarter of washing machines sold need repairing in the first five years and about half of tumbler driers. Fridges and freezers rarely need repairing.

Like any form of insurance, you cannot tell in advance if you are going to get your money's worth out of the policy. If you want to know that you can call a mechanic out at no charge other than the premium, a service contract will be worth while. But if you do not like paying out any additional money and you think you can cope with minor repairs yourself anyway, then save the cost of the insurance.

HOME INCOME PLANS

Elderly home owners may be living in a house, already paid for, worth tens of thousands of pounds and yet not be able to afford simple repair jobs. There are several solutions, but none is ideal.

One option is to sell the house and move to a smaller and cheaper one, thereby releasing some of the capital. Another is to rent out rooms to lodgers. But there are likely to be many excellent reasons why you do not want to do either.

A further choice is a home income plan. The drawback here is that you need to be at least 70 years old before you can take out such a plan.

There are two schemes at present, one run by the Abbey National Building Society in conjunction with Royal Life Insurance Company and the other by Hambro Life.

The insurance company lends you money against the value of your house. You can borrow up to 65 per cent of its current market value with Abbey and 80 per cent with Hambro. This money is used to buy an annuity which provides you with an income for the rest of your life. The money is paid to you in monthly instalments. When you die, the amount you owe to the insurance company is repaid out of the proceeds of your house, which means that your heirs will receive a smaller inheritance than they otherwise would.

Although the capital is repaid out of your estate when you die, you have to pay interest on the money while you are still alive. Both the Hambro and the Abbey National plans work on a fixed rate of interest so from the very beginning you know exactly how much you will receive each month.

You are entitled to tax relief on the interest payments if the loan is no more than £30,000 just as you were when you had a mortgage. You may have to pay a small amount of tax on the income from the annuity, but a home income plan could reduce your capital transfer tax liability because, when you die, the value of your estate will not be so high.

An additional option is Capital Protection. This scheme is slightly more expensive but it means that if you die shortly after taking out the loan, only part of it has to be repaid. This way your beneficiaries do not feel that they have lost a large part of their inheritance for no reason.

If you die in the first year, only 25 per cent of the loan is repayable; in the second year it is 50 per cent; and in the third year, you need repay only 75 per cent. After that you have to repay in full.

Home income plans do not suit everyone; the stumbling block is the fact that many people still want to be able to pass on as much as they possibly can to their children.

There are many questions you should ask:

Q. Must I own the house before taking out a home income plan?

A. *Yes. However, if the house is not fully paid for, you can take money out of the annuity to pay off the mortgage up to 10 per cent of the loan.*

Q. Must I really be 70 years old?

A. *Yes. And if you are a married couple, your joint ages have to be at least 150. This is because the insurance companies cannot provide a worth while income until you reach this age.*

Q. How much can I borrow?

A. *Up to 65 per cent of the value of your house when you start the plan with Abbey National; 80 per cent with Hambro, with a maximum of £30,000.*

Q. Can I borrow more later when the value of my house increases?

A. *Yes. You go about it the same way as the original plan.*

Q. Will I receive the same amount each month?

A. *Yes. Hambro and Abbey National plans have a fixed rate of interest.*

Q. Can I cancel the home income plan after taking one out should I want to regain 100 per cent of my house?

A. *You can repay the loan at any time. And, even if you do, you will continue to receive money from the annuity. You cannot stop the annuity.*

Q. Does the scheme operate for a leasehold flat?

A. *Yes. But you might not be able to borrow as much.*

Q. Could my heirs pay off the loan themselves when I die rather than sell the house?

A. *Yes. All the insurance company wants is its money back.*

Q. Can I move house if I have a home income plan?

A. *Yes. The loan is repaid from the proceeds of the sale. You will nevertheless continue to receive the annuity. If you wish you can then take out another loan on the new house.*

Q. I receive supplementary benefit. Will this be affected by money from a home income plan?

A. *Yes. You will almost certainly lose the supplementary benefit. Your entitlement to a rate rebate might also be affected.*

Q. How can I get the most money from a home income plan?

A. *Only by waiting until you are even older. But you might as well go ahead as soon as you can because you are unlikely to make up the money you lose by waiting one or two years.*

Q. How do I receive the money?

A. *It is paid directly into your bank account or building society account.*

Q. Can I take a lump sum at the beginning?

A. *Yes, in some circumstances and up to a maximum of 10 per cent of the loan. But this will reduce the amount you then receive each month.*

Q. When do I repay the loan?

A. *When you die.*

Q. How will this affect my capital transfer tax liability?

A. *The value of your estate will be reduced by the amount of the loan so this could reduce your CTT bill.*

Q. What about my income tax?

A *If you pay tax at the basic rate, you will receive tax relief through MIRAS as you do on a mortgage. If you are a higher rate taxpayer, you will have a higher rate tax relief as well, but you will have to pay extra tax on part of the annuity.*

Q. Will it cost me anything to set up?

A. *Yes. You will have to pay a surveyor's fee for valuing the house and a solicitor. The Abbey National and Hambro help out with these expenses.*

Q. What happens if I have to sell my house and go into a home?

A. *The debt is repaid out of the proceeds of the sale. But you will continue to receive the annuity until you die.*

Here is an example:

A woman aged 75 paying basic rate tax owns a house worth £30,000. She borrows 65 per cent of this, which is £19,500. This buys an annuity worth £3149 a year. But, on the interest element of the annuity, she will have to pay tax at 30 per cent amounting to £404 a year. This leaves her with a net annuity of £2745 a year.

Now, she has to pay interest on the loan. If this is 10·25 per cent a year, on the loan of £19,500 the bill is £1998. Tax relief on these payments is £599 leaving a net bill of £1399.

So, by deducting the tax bill from the annuity income, she is £1346 a year better off.

The figures for a married couple who are both aged 75 look like this:

Value of house	£30,000
Loan (65 % of value of house)	£19,500

This £19,500 is multiplied by an annuity rate (given by the insurance company).

Gross annual annuity	£2705
of which interest is	£1245
tax on interest at 30%	£ 374
Net annual annuity	£2331

Interest is payable on the loan of £19,500:

Interest at 10¼%	£1998
Tax relief on interest at 30%	£ 599
Interest net of tax	£1399

By deducting the net interest of £1399 from the net annuity of £2331, the couple is left with an extra £932 to spend. This might not sound a great deal of money. But the alternative is to have nothing and you will receive this amount every year for the rest of your life. There are other schemes around, called home reversion plans, where you actually hand over all or a part share of your house in exchange for an income or a highly discounted cash sum. Think very carefully before committing yourself to one of these.

9/Telephones and the Post Office

Telephones ● *installation / charges / help with the cost / disconnection / stamps / the new telephones* ● Post ● *opening hours / letters / redirection / registered letters / parcels / compensation fee parcels / cash on delivery / datapost same day / datapost / Intelpost / stamps / Royal Mail Special Delivery / recorded delivery / postal orders / television licences / telemessage / Post Office Users' National Council* ● National Girobank ● *banking / Transcash*

The familiar post office is changing. It is offering some new services; other old ones have disappeared. And at British Telecom push button telephones have made dialling a thing of the past. But the basic service from these two separate organisations is still communications, and here is a guide to what is available.

TELEPHONES
Installation
To install a telephone in a private home costs £75 plus VAT regardless of where you live. There is now no charge if you move house and take over an existing telephone line. Although you must remember, before moving in, to write to British Telecom informing them of the change; and make sure the previous occupier does the same. If you are an existing customer moving into a house with no telephone, you will pay £55 to have one installed.

The cost includes a standard British Telecom telephone in a choice of colours with push button numbers. The old grey dial telephones are no longer made. You will have to pay extra only if you want something rather more fancy, perhaps a digital display and memory.

You can have more than one socket installed in your house to enable you to move the telephone from room to room. To convert an existing installation costs £15; to convert an existing installation and fit one extra socket costs £28; each additional socket costs £12; add VAT to all these prices.

To find out more about telephones, contact your local telephone sales office which is listed in the front of any telephone directory with a Freefone number.

Charges

The quarterly rental for a telephone is £14.15, or £13.15 for a shared line, plus VAT. You pay no extra for any additional telephone sockets.

Each unit you dial costs 4.4p plus VAT. You can talk for eight minutes for one unit on a local call in the cheap rate period; two minutes in the standard rate period; and one minute 30 seconds at peak periods.

A five-minute local cheap rate call costs approximately 5p; at standard rate 15p; and in the peak period 20p. Peak time runs from 9 a.m. to 1 p.m.; standard time from 1 p.m. to 6 p.m. and 8 a.m. to 9 a.m.; and the cheap rate from 6 p.m. to 8 a.m. and all day at weekends and on public holidays. If you telephone from a push-button payphone, the minimum charge is 8p.

If you want the person you are dialling to pay for the call, you can reverse the charges. This costs an extra 22p from a private telephone, or 25p in a call box, on top of the price of the call. The person at the other end pays all this.

Anyone who uses fewer than 120 units in a quarter will automatically receive a low user rebate. This is worth 3p for each unused unit below 120.

Help with the cost

Anyone who is chronically sick or disabled can ask the local authority to help towards the installation and rental charge of a telephone. But you will have to pay for the calls yourself. The allowance is entirely at the local authority's discretion. However, no one else, not even anyone on supplementary benefit, is entitled to any assistance with the cost.

Disconnection

If you are disconnected for not paying the bill, you will have to pay to be reconnected. The amount charged varies according to circumstances.

Stamps

You can buy telephone stamps to save towards the cost of the telephone bill, but see p. 13.

The new telephones

You are no longer only limited to renting the instrument from British Telecom. At the moment British Telecom is responsible for providing the first telephone, or 'private instrument', but extension telephones are liberalised. You can buy telephones from private companies and you will find them for sale in department stores, electrical retailers and specialist shops. Having one of these in no way affects the quarterly bill you pay to British Telecom.

But you need to watch what you are buying because you could have a problem with installation. You should buy an 'approved' instrument which will be clearly marked by a white label with a prominent green circle. A non-approved instrument should be labelled as such.

If you buy an approved telephone, you know that the plug will fit into an ordinary British Telecom socket. If you want your house wired with these plug-in sockets, ask British Telecom to do the work.

If you buy a non-approved telephone, it may still be satisfactory, but you do not have a guarantee. They are usually imported, cheaper to buy and could be difficult to have repaired if they go wrong.

An approved telephone will cost about £40 to £50 for a straightforward standard instrument and up to £100 for an 'intelligent' one.

POST
Opening hours
All post office services are mostly available between: 9 a.m. and 5·30 p.m. Monday to Friday, 9 a.m. to 12·30 or 1 p.m. on Saturdays.

Letters
There are two classes: first and second. The post office aims to deliver 90 per cent of first-class letters the following working day; second-class letters take about three working days.

The rate is 17p for a first-class letter and 13p for second class, both weighing up to 60 grams. There is no top weight limit on first-class letters, but second-class letters cannot weigh more than 750 grams. A 750 gram first-class letter costs £1.28 and a second class 98p.

You are forbidden to send through the post explosive or dangerous materials, obscene literature, counterfeit bank notes and messy objects, among other things. You are also forbidden to address letters or parcels in a way which will embarrass post office staff!

Redirection
If you move house and want your letters redirected to your new address by the post office, it costs £2.25 for one month, rising to £13 for 12 months.

Registered letters
You can register a first-class letter, and if you do, you may receive compensation if the letter is lost or damaged. The compensation you receive depends on how much you have paid.

£1.10 entitles you to compensation of £600
£1.25 entitles you to compensation of £1250
£1.40 entitles you to compensation of £1750

Parcels

You can send parcels through the post as long as they weigh no more than 25 kg and are no longer than 1·5 m (3 m length and circumference) and do not contain prohibited articles.

Compensation fee parcels

By completing a certificate of posting, you are entitled to compensation above the usual level if the post office loses or damages the article. Compensation fees payable are 27p for £60 of compensation; 37p for £125; 55p for £225 and 70p for £350.

Cash on delivery

You can ask for payment to be made when the parcel is delivered. The post office will collect the sum (known as the COD amount) and forward it to you by giro. The fee is 65p on top of postage charges.

Datapost same day (previously Expresspost)

In and between certain cities and large towns there is a fast post office same-day delivery service by messenger.

Datapost

This is an overnight courier delivery service with a money back guarantee. The price depends on weight: sending a parcel inland weighing 5 kg or below costs £9.50 and the heaviest allowed is 27.5 kg costing £28.90. There is also a fast courier delivery to 50 countries from £12.50.

Intelpost

This is a facsimile transmission service enabling you to send copies of documents between 117 UK post offices and the USA, Canada, Australia and Western Europe.

Stamps

You can buy books of stamps from 50p to £1.70.

A cheap way to send letters abroad is by using aerogrammes which cost 26p each to go anywhere in the world.

Royal Mail Special Delivery

If you have first-class letters and packets that are posted in time for the last collection but not in time for delivery in the morning, a post office messenger will deliver them for you. The cost is £1.50 on top of the first-class postage rate, but if for any reason the letter does not arrive the next day, the special fee is refunded.

Recorded delivery

This gives evidence of posting and obtains the signature of the recipient on delivery. The fee is 22p on top of the normal postage, first or second class. You can claim compensation up to £18 if the post office loses or damages a letter. You can ask for an advice of delivery note to be sent to you afterwards if you wish for an extra fee. This service is intended for documents, it is not suitable for money, jewellery or anything of intrinsic value.

Postal orders
You can buy postal orders in denominations of 25p to £1 at a cost of 20p each. More expensive postal orders from £2 to £10 cost 30p each. You can increase the value between these denominations by adding on one or two postage stamps up to 4½p on any one order.

Television licences
You can buy television licences at the post office and also savings stamps towards the cost. See p. 13. A black and white television licence costs £15 a year (£13.75 if you are blind) and colour costs £46 (£44.75 for the blind).

Telemessage
Telegrams no longer exist. The post office, through Intelpost, has a short message form which can be used with a greetings card for same day or next day delivery in the UK and certain overseas destinations. In the UK it costs £2.25 for messages and next day delivery; 45p for a choice of six cards; same day delivery costs extra. Now, if you want to send a message quickly, you must ask for a Telemessage. The message must be telephoned (dial 190) or telexed to British Telecom before 10 p.m. to arrive the following working morning. It costs £3 to send up to 50 words, but your money will be refunded if the message is late.

Centenarians will still be remembered by the Queen with a Royal Telemessage delivered with the morning mail.

Post Office Users' Councils
These are independent organisations which look after the interests of the consumer. Whenever the post office plans a major change to its services, it must first consult the Post Office Users' National Council (POUNC). See p. 250 for address.

NATIONAL GIROBANK
There are various services provided at post offices by the Girobank. Girobank is a separate organisation from the post office and it pays a fee to use post office counter services such as staff.

Banking
There is an ordinary banking service available from Girobank which includes cheque books, cashing facilities, easy household bill payments, travellers cheques and Postcheques.

This is a free cheque account as long as your account is in credit, but you cannot run up an overdraft. You can, however, ask for a personal loan and have a deposit account.

Transcash
Even if you do not have a Girobank account yourself, you can pay bills to anyone who does by Transcash. Just fill out a slip at the post office and hand it to the clerk with the money. There is normally a fee of 35p. You can send money abroad through Transcash; it costs £2.50 for each transaction. Using Transcash or Freepay you can order and pay for goods advertised on television, in the press or by direct mail, free of charge.

If you are not a Girobank customer you can pay your gas or electricity bills by Transcash at the post office, but you pay a 35p fee. If you are buying something on mail order, this could be through a Freepay account, in which case the company pays the fee.

10/Insurance

Your house ● House contents insurance ● *index-linking / all risks cover / how to do it* ● House contents to insure ● Household contents rates ● Personal all risks insurance premiums ● Buildings insurance ● Personal liability insurance ● Health insurance ● *permanent health insurance / personal accident insurance / hospital cash insurance / private health insurance* ● Life insurance ● *do you need life insurance? / how much cover will you need? / how it works / term insurance / family income policy / whole life insurance / endowment policy / with-profits policies / premiums / early surrender values / insurance as investment / unit-linked insurance / annuity / commission / tax* ● School fees ● Legal expenses insurance ● Insurance salesmen ● *how to choose an insurance adviser / how to beat the insurance salesman at his own game / life insurance policies / what insurance terms mean / life expectancy chart* ● Letters

It is an unnecessary expense to be over-insured; it is dangerous to be under-insured: you should aim for the happy medium. Insurance breaks down into two broad categories: insurance which offers recompense if your belongings are damaged or lost; and assurance which pays money to your dependants when you die.

You can insure almost anything in the world: your legs; your garden party against rain; a supertanker; a dog. The aim is to pay for no more insurance than you need and to be certain that you are clear about what the policy offers you.

Most disagreements between insurance companies and policyholders occur because of misunderstandings about the scope of the policy. Rule one is to make sure you are getting what you want before you sign the proposal form.

For information about motor and holiday insurance see Chapters 17 and 18.

YOUR HOUSE
You need two kinds of insurance policy if you own a house; one for the building and one for the contents, although some insurance companies will combine the two in one policy.

HOUSE CONTENTS INSURANCE
You will need this whether you own a house or rent one. The stolen goods are recovered in only one-third of all burglaries and the crime is

growing faster than the detection. It is foolhardy not to have insurance to replace the cost of your possessions.

With contents insurance policies there is a choice in the type of insurance you can take out. You can either have an 'indemnity' policy, which values your goods in their second-hand state, or more commonly now, a 'replacement as new' policy, which pays you the price the item costs today. Both of these can be index-linked.

Index-linking
Most policies today are automatically index-linked. That is, the amount you are covered for (and thereby the premium you pay), is increased by the insurance company every year in line with an index related to the consumer durable section of the retail prices index. However, if you think you are paying too much, tell the company. They may agree to leave you on last year's figure.

Remember that you may have increased the amount you have at risk one year, perhaps if you bought a new suite of furniture or a video recorder for example. Each time you renew the policy, think about what you are doing.

All risks cover
This is 'almost everything you could possibly think of' cover. It will be an extension to your household policy and it will cost more, but in return your insurance policy will cover you for many more situations. It is extremely frustrating to suffer a disaster, claim against your insurance policy and then be told: 'very sorry, your policy excludes this eventuality'.

Any ordinary policy will cover you for the risks specifically named in the policy; 'all risks' covers you for everything, including accidental damage, except for the situations stated to be excluded. For example, the all risks would cover the loss of a stone from a piece of jewellery even if you are out in the street; losing your camera; or it will provide a replacement if you drop a vase and smash it. An ordinary policy will not.

For a rough guide to the cost, the typical rate of an annual premium in a country area is around 50p for £100 of cover under an indemnity policy. London and other inner city areas will be more expensive than this, nearer £1 for £100 of full cover.

How to do it
To start, you should make a list of everything in your house that you will have to replace; you will be startled at just how much this adds up to. Walk round the house and list, room by room, everything you own. If you want to be totally covered, do not forget the suitcases stored in the attic, food in the kitchen, toys in the children's bedroom, pictures on the walls and the lawnmower in the garage. See p. 119 for a check list.

You will also be able to claim for any cash you might lose, probably up to a limit of £200. Mirrors and fixed glass which form part of the furniture are covered for accidental damage. If a heavy visitor sits carelessly on a glass-topped coffee table, you can recover the cost of the broken glass, if not the friendship.

You will wonder whether to include some items under 'contents' or 'buildings' insurance; shelves are the obvious example. The simplest guide is to regard anything you would take with you if you moved as coming under 'contents'; anything permanently fixed as 'buildings'.

Of course, you might not necessarily lose or damage something while you are at home. Most policies will provide an extension giving limited cover for possessions you have with you while you are away from home, or while you are in the process of moving house. But they will not automatically cover you when you are not at home. Again, the vital point is to find out exactly what your policy covers and ask for it to be changed if it does not meet your requirements.

A typical policy will exclude damage to cars, pets and documents. In the case of multiple occupancy, theft of certain items if the burglars have not forced an entry, will be excluded. Damage from war, sonic booms and contamination by radioactivity are excluded because, if you are still around to claim, the Government will take responsibility for paying out should the worst happen.

The policy will cover the same catastrophes as a buildings policy when your movable possessions are hit: storm; fire; flood; falling aeroplanes; lightning; escape of water; careering cows. The indemnity policy will make allowance for wear and tear, which is deducted before settling a claim. A replacement as new policy will pay out the current purchase price if something is destroyed or stolen, as long as the total sum assured matches current prices. If the item is slightly damaged, it may pay for repairs.

You can sometimes find a 'hybrid' policy which gives replacement as new cover on fairly recent items, such as furniture, carpets, electrical and household appliances and indemnity cover on everything else.

Valuables, such as antiques or jewellery, pose a different problem because the value is more arbitrary and may indeed increase rather than depreciate. It is advisable to obtain an expert valuation for anything you think might be worth £1000 or more. For values under £1000, the insurance company will probably pay up on an individual item, or if the claim for any one item is below 10 per cent of the total sum insured.

But a valuation, whether for an item of gold, silver, fur or diamonds, will become out of date after a couple of years. Remember to update the valuation from time to time. The first valuation will cost about 1 per cent of the valuation figure; you should be able to get a revision for less.

Remember, if you live in a rented flat, you will still need to insure your belongings. The landlord will not do it for you. Furthermore, the terms of your tenancy may make you responsible for fixtures and fittings, so find out if you need to insure these as well as your belongings.

Also, it is important to have your contents insured for their full value. If you are under-insured and have to claim, you may find the insurance company operates a practice known as 'averaging', particularly if you are insured with Lloyds. If the insurance company does not think you are fully insured, it will pay out less than the total amount you are claiming.

On some items you may want accidental damage cover both for when you are at home and when you are away. You can cover items, perhaps a camera, spectacles, guitar, by arranging an 'all risks' extension to the policy. Some all risk policies will cover your possessions while you are on holiday abroad.

HOUSE CONTENTS TO INSURE

	cost to replace	second-hand value
LIVING ROOM		
carpet, rugs		
curtains, blinds		
furniture: chairs		
tables		
sideboard		
books, records, tapes		
pictures, wall hangings		
television, radio, stereo		
ornaments and lights		
DINING ROOM		
carpet, rugs		
curtains, blinds		
sideboard		
table and chairs		
pictures		
alcohol		
china, glass, cutlery		
lights		
KITCHEN		
flooring		
curtains, blinds		
cooker		
fridge		
freezer		
washing machine/drier		
dishwasher		
cutlery, crockery, saucepans		
kitchen equipment, eg mixer, kettle		
tea towels		
food and drink		

	cost to replace	second-hand value

BEDROOMS
beds
mattresses
carpet, rugs
curtains, blinds
chairs
dressing tables, stools
chest of drawers
mirrors
bed linen
clothes
pictures
jewellery
children's belongings

BATHROOM/CLOAKROOMS
flooring
bathroom cabinet
toiletries
towels
bathroom scales
mirrors

HALLWAY AND HALL CUPBOARD
carpet, rugs
curtains, blinds
clothing, shoes
telephone table
cleaning equipment

LOFT
suitcases
items being stored

GARDEN SHED
lawn mower
garden tools
bicycle
ladders
diy equipment

GARAGE
garden furniture
freezer
ladders
items being stored

The value of the contents of your house could add up like this:

Two-bedroomed terraced house:

	£
living room	2000
bedroom 1	2500
bedroom 2	850
kitchen	900
bathroom	90
hall	100
garage	300
	£6740

Large three-bedroomed semi:

	£
living room	4200
bedroom 1	5000
bedroom 2	1300
bedroom 3	600
kitchen	1700
bathroom	230
hall	350
garage	450
	£13,830

Small three-bedroomed semi:

	£
living room	2600
bedroom 1	3400
bedroom 2	850
bedroom 3	500
kitchen	1300
bathroom	50
hall	250
garage	350
	£9300

Four-bedroomed detached house:

	£
living room	4200
dining room	1700
bedroom 1	7500
bedroom 2	1400
bedroom 3	750
bedroom 4	500
kitchen	2600
bathroom	300
hall	600
garage	520
	£20,070

HOUSEHOLD CONTENTS RATES*

COVER	Central London	Other London	London Suburbs	Country District
Sum insured £6750	£	£	£	£
New for old	64.13	57.38	40.50	23.62
Including accidental damage	74.25	70.88	57.37	33.75
Sum insured £9500				
New for old	90.25	80·75	57.00	33.25
Including accidental damage	104.50	99.75	80.75	47.50
Sum insured £13,750				
New for old	130.63	116.88	82.50	48.12
Including accidental damage	151.25	144.38	116.87	68.75

*The precise terms vary between policies; this is an average guide.

PERSONAL 'ALL RISKS' INSURANCE PREMIUMS

Sum insured £2500	£	£	£	£
Clothing and personal effects	31.25	31.25	31.25	31.25

Sum insured £5000				
Unspecified jewellery	110.00	110.00	80.00	62.50

BUILDING SOCIETY BUILDINGS AND CONTENTS LINKED INSURANCE SCHEMES

	Building sum insured £	Premium £
Mr A. lives in London	45,000	180.00
Miss B. lives in Romford	37,000	103.60
Mrs C. lives in Aberdeen	60,000	150.00
Ms D. lives in Newcastle	20,000	50.00

The cover is based on the building sum insured; the contents are not insured for a specified sum except this cannot be more than half the value of the buildings cover, often with an upper limit of £30,000.

BUILDINGS INSURANCE

If you have a mortgage on your home, then the building society or bank will insist that you insure the fabric of the building.

Moreover, they will probably strongly recommend a particular insurance company. Building societies have now been instructed to give borrowers a choice of several insurers and some allow you total freedom to name your own company. However, in these cases if you do not pick an insurer on the building society's list of contacts, the society will make a charge, usually about £5, to cover their extra administration costs.

The reason building societies like to handpick their insurance companies is because they receive commission from the insurer for every customer they pass on and they have negotiated special deals with some of them.

Many of these policies are now index-linked. The cover is increased annually according to a rebuilding cost index which takes account of the rising price of building. It is essential that you make sure your policy covers the full cost of repair.

The British Insurance Association issues a table of rebuilding costs which gives a rough guide as to how much cover you should have. The scale varies between £28.50 a square foot to rebuild a large semi-detached house built after 1945 in East Anglia and £52 for a medium-sized pre-1920 detached house in London. But it is very rare for a whole house to be destroyed and need rebuilding. Nearly all claims are for partial damage only. The figures do not include garages.

Building insurance will cover any damage to the structure of the house, including damage to permanent fixtures and fittings such as a weathervane on the roof. It also takes in the garage and any other outbuildings, sheds or stables. The cover will include a certain amount but not total cover for paths, drives, walls and swimming pools.

As a broad guide, anything that is fixed and which you would leave behind when you move, comes under the buildings policy. This includes kitchen units and loft insulation.

If you are renting, the owner of the building should pay for the building insurance and the lease should make it clear if this is not the case. Make sure you know, because sometimes the tenant is responsible for any internal damage and this might not be covered by your contents policy. If you have bought a leasehold flat, the landlord will insure the buildings and either reclaim a proportion of the premium from you or include it in the service charge.

There are various circumstances when the insurance company may refuse to pay out. For example, if the house or flat is left empty, or with insufficient furniture, for 30 days or more, the policy could become invalid. Or, if you have not maintained your house in a 'reasonable' state of repair, they can decide that the dilapidated condition rather than the storm was responsible for the damage.

If you claim for subsidence or landslip damage, you will have to pay more; this is spelled out in the policy. Some policies now include provision for 'heave' in the cover – that is an upward movement rather than the collapse of the ground which, like subsidence, became a serious problem after the 1976 drought.

If you let out part of your home, you can claim loss of rent if these rooms become uninhabitable. But the insurance company must be aware that you are renting and the cause of the damage must be an insured risk. You can claim the cost of having to rent alternative accommodation for yourself, if your own living quarters become uninhabitable.

Other events for which you can claim include accidental damage to underground pipes and cables, glass windows and doors, and bathroom fittings. If you suffer very serious damage, then you can claim for the cost of architects' and surveyors' fees, moving the rubbish and rubble, shoring up a building which is in danger of collapsing, and for any increased costs due to special requirements of the local authority.

But take care if your house has a special construction which might increase a risk – say it has wooden walls or a thatched roof. Any especially vulnerable or non-standard building will cost more in premiums.

Two types of building policy are available: an 'indemnity' and a 'reinstatement' policy. The indemnity policy will cover the cost of restoring the house to its state before the damage.

Today nearly all building insurance policies work on the 'new for old' basis. The 'reinstatement' or 'new for old' policy makes no deduction for wear and tear and, as long as the house has been maintained in good repair, the company will pay out the full amount to restore the house.

If you have been in any way responsible for the accident, say you dropped a burning cigarette which set fire to the carpet, the insurance company will still pay out. Insurance covers you for the cost of damage, it does not apportion blame. That is what is meant by 'indemnity'.

How to claim
If you need to claim on a building insurance policy, you should contact the insurance company as soon as practicable. But if you have to make immediate repairs to prevent further damage, maybe a water pipe burst at the weekend, then emergency work will be paid for by the insurance company without quibble. Make sure you keep a record of the cost of emergency repairs.

PERSONAL LIABILITY INSURANCE
The variety of accidents that can occur are as varied as human nature. For example, someone walking innocently past your house could be struck on the head by a slate falling off the roof.

Many contents and buildings insurance policies automatically include cover for this sort of eventuality, should you be legally liable. If the cover is not there already, you will be able to add liability insurance cover into your policies as an optional extra. In any case, check your policies now.

The insurance pays any compensation you might be liable for if you, or one of your family, accidentally damage someone else's property, or injure them. If the accident involves a car, it will be covered under the car insurance policy. But if your house was the cause (the front wall collapses on a neighbour's feet), then the buildings' policy should cover it.

If an accident happens around the home, say a friend's child trips over a frayed carpet at a party, or if you let your dog run across the road and cause an accident, look at your contents policy to see if it covers you for personal liability insurance.

HEALTH INSURANCE
Because the National Health Service exists in Britain, paying separately to insure your health should be unnecessary. But sickness benefit is no higher than unemployment benefit and many people, particularly the self-employed, would find themselves in desperate straits if they were out-of-work through illness for a long time.

There are several forms of insurance against hardship following sickness: sick pay insurance, which insurance companies call permanent health insurance; personal accident insurance; and hospital cash insurance. You can also take out insurance to cover the cost of dentists' and opticians' bills.

Permanent health insurance (PHI)

This pays you an income if, through ill health, you are unable to continue working and your earnings stop. Under a permanent health policy, the money is payable for as long as you are off work until you reach the age of 65 for men, or 60 for women. The cost depends on the terms you choose; how much you want to receive; how long you decide to wait before payments start (three, six or twelve months); and whether you want the insurance to stop when you are 60 or 65.

For example, a man aged 35 who wants to receive £100 a week benefit, after a 26-week deferment period, will pay £87 a year in premiums until he is 65. Insurance terms for women always work out differently and the same policy for a woman until the age of 60 will cost £81 a year.

It is up to you to decide how long a deferment period you want. The decision will depend on how long your employer is prepared to pay you. If the deferment period is only four weeks, the same policy will cost a man £168 a year but more for a woman at £199.

The terms are different for women because actuarial statistics, on which insurance companies base their premiums, show that women are more susceptible to frequent illness that men. One theory is that, because men die younger, women survive longer to be ill, or take what the insurers euphemistically call 'morbidity time'.

Any permanent health insurance plan will have exclusions, and pregnancy is one. If you are still unable to work three months after the delivery of the baby, then you are 'ill' and can claim on the policy. But otherwise pregnancy is not an illness. Illnesses which are self-inflicted or relate to drink or drugs will also be excluded.

There is no way you can insure yourself against illness for an enormous amount of money, become 'ill', and live in luxury for the rest of your life. If you decide you want health insurance, then the best advice is to take out as much as you can. But there is a limiting factor and the insurance companies will place a maximum figure on the amount they will pay out.

The generally-used formula is this: the amount you receive from the policy, or policies if you have more than one, plus certain state benefits, should add up to no more than three-quarters of your average income over the past year.

The insurance company takes various factors into account when working out how much you will pay; as well as the waiting period and amounts paid out, your age, health record, occupation and sex determine the size of your premium.

Insurance companies do not wish to encourage idlers, so they also define just how ill you must be to claim on the policy. You are likely to come across two definitions: the most restrictive says you must be unable to do any kind of work for which you are 'reasonably' qualified. That means that if you are unable to do your old job, you must try and find another, different one, more suited to your changed abilities. A more relaxed policy will pay out if, because of sickness or injury, you cannot perform your own usual job.

It is important to choose a permanent health insurance policy which is index-linked. After you have taken out the policy, the pay-out will not automatically increase as your earnings go up. It will rise only in line with the terms of the policy. With some policies the amount paid out remains the same through the life of that policy and so inflation, even at low levels, will soon make a nonsense of it.

If you want a policy where the benefit rises by 5 per cent a year, you will have to pay a 15 per cent higher premium; for an extra 7½ per cent each year, the additional cost to the premium is 27½ per cent.

At present, if you are in a job and fall ill but are not covered by a company scheme or insurance policy, the only amount you can claim is Statutory Sickness Benefit (see p. 141). If you are self-employed, you get nothing.

There are enormous advantages in joining a group scheme and a group need comprise only three or four people. The reason is that when a company pays the premiums, the employer is able to claim tax relief on the expenditure whereas an individual cannot. If you want to start one in your company, talk to the personnel officer and ask for details from an insurance broker or insurance company.

If the permanent health insurance is paid for by your employer, you have to start paying tax immediately you receive any benefit. But a permanent health policy taken out by an individual has a tax advantage: you do not have to pay tax on any benefit until you have received it for a full tax year; so if the payment begins in May, you can receive the benefit for 23 months before paying any tax – that is, until the following April to April tax year has been completed.

Permanent health cover is a long-term contract which cannot be cancelled by the insurer even if the policyholder's health deteriorates.

Personal accident insurance
This differs from permanent health insurance in that it is a short-term contract and is renewed annually. A personal accident policy will make payments for a specified period if you are unable to work because of an accident. This sort of policy could be of particular interest if you are in a high-risk job, maybe a window cleaner.

The policy will also pay out a lump sum if you die. The policyholder chooses the cover he wants; either for temporary or permanent disablement and pays accordingly.

Hospital cash insurance
This will pay out a set sum of money, say £10 or £20 a day, while you are in hospital. When you come out, even if to convalesce, the money stops.

Private health insurance
The cost of this is now very high. The main reasons people give for wanting private health schemes is to have a room to themselves, the ability to choose when they have an operation, to have a choice of specialist, and to avoid a queue. If these reasons are sufficiently important to you, you may consider paying for private health treatment.

The three companies which dominate this market are British: United Provident Association (BUPA), Private Patients Plan (PPP), and Western Provident Association (WPA).

As an example of the costs, a married man in his thirties with two children living in London can expect to pay around £540 (discounted net) a year, for a full refund of hospital charges and a full refund of all other necessary hospital treatment expenses up to a maximum of £40,000 each for all the family. Outside London hospitals, the same man would pay £345.

Because of rising costs and flagging interest, cut-price benefit schemes are cropping up. For example, one company has introduced a policy which pays up only if you cannot get into a NHS hospital within six weeks. The annual premium for this is about £250 for benefits of £45,000 plus the cost of the room and surgeon. **Always ask for a discount when you apply: nearly everyone gets it.**

LIFE INSURANCE
There is a saying in the insurance business: 'Life insurance has to be sold', meaning that if salesmen did not persuade you, you would never take out a life policy. This is probably true and it has created a huge force of professional salesmen in which the sharpest are the most successful.

In order to be able to deal with these salesmen, who are carefully trained to sell, it helps to know just what is available and what suits you best and also to understand how you are being handled. If you have decided you want life insurance, even if you go to see an insurance broker, you are far more likely to end up with the right policy for you if you have a very good and detailed idea of what you need before you ask. On any policies taken out before the March 1984 Budget you received tax relief on the premiums; this is not available on new policies.

Do you need life insurance?
A very basic question, and one to which the salesmen will answer 'yes'. But really, if you are young, with no commitments or dependants, then you do not. However, it is a good idea once you get married, or if you are

supporting an elderly relative. In other words, if anyone would suffer financially by your death, you should take out life insurance.

The definition of life insurance is a contract which will pay out a specified sum of money on the date when a particular event occurs, for example your death or your retirement. To become entitled to a pay-out, you pay one single premium, or a series of regular ones.

There are various different types of life insurance, but what they all do is to provide money at a time when it is likely to be needed.

How much cover will you need?

The more you want, the more it will cost you, of course. And the later in life you join a scheme, the more you will have to pay. You should base your calculations on how much your dependants need without you. And remember that this will increase as time goes by. Also, ask yourself if they will need a lump sum to pay off any particular debts, like the mortgage, when you die.

How it works

The money that life insurance companies collect in premiums from their policyholders is put into a life fund. Because companies know what they are going to have to pay out, they can make sure that they have sufficient funds. This is the work of the actuary, whose job is to study statistics. He balances the risk of death by assessing a person's age, state of health and job to determine how much premium you must pay.

Insurance companies, sometimes called life offices, offer a range of different policies. These are known as: term; family income; whole life; endowment; unit-linked; and annuity.

Term insurance

This is also known as temporary insurance and is a policy covering a fixed and limited period of time. If the policyholder dies within the period, the dependants get the benefit. If the policyholder survives, then no money is paid out.

This policy can be level term, which means the amount paid out stays the same all the time. Or it can be increasing, when the amount rises from year to year; or decreasing when it falls. Decreasing term insurance is used for mortgage protection policies.

More subdivisions include: convertible temporary insurance (a policy which has the option to convert a policy into something different); and renewable term where, at the end of the term, you can buy the same cover again.

Term insurance can be used to cover you on a journey and is the kind of insurance sold at airports. It is a comparatively cheap, flexible form of insurance but the policyholder is not given any cash when the policy ends.

Family income policy

A family income policy pays the policyholder's dependants an agreed sum at regular intervals for a set period of time, if the policyholder dies within the term of the policy. It is cheap insurance, paid in regular instalments, but you or your dependants receive nothing if you survive the said term.

Whole life insurance

This means that your beneficiaries will collect the money when you die. The policy lasts for the life of the insured. It is more expensive than term insurance, but assuming the policy is kept going, your beneficiaries will always receive the money when you die. They can have either a lump sum or regular payments. Policies come either with- or without-profits (see below).

If you want to discontinue paying towards a policy, the insurance company will give a surrender value, as long as the policy has by this time acquired one.

Surrender values are not guaranteed. When you take out the policy, you are sometimes given a projected value which is an intelligent guess but you may get more, or less, than forecast. This will not be in direct proportion to the number of years' premiums you have paid in. If you cash in a policy very soon after taking it out you will receive nothing. And for the first few years you will receive very little.

Indeed, you may very well get back less than you have paid in premiums. This is because nearly all the costs and expenses of setting up a policy, including commission, have to be met in the early years. This is called front end loading.

Whatever the costs involved in the policy, remember it is the policyholder who pays them, even if he is not aware of it.

Endowment policy

With an endowment policy, you are certain of getting the money back at an agreed date, say 10, 15 or 20 years hence. If you die before then, the money is paid immediately to your dependants.

An endowment policy is more expensive than term insurance or whole life, but either you or your family are certain of receiving some money. You can time the end of the policy to coincide with a particular, perhaps expensive, event: a future wedding or a round-the-world retirement cruise.

Endowment policies, like whole life policies, can be either with-profits or without. Premiums for with-profits policies are costlier than for non-profit policies because you get a higher pay-out at the end of the policy.

With-profits policies

These have become increasingly popular in recent years. The basic amount you receive at the end is guaranteed but, in addition, you will receive bonuses, depending on how well the company has performed. These will be 'reversionary', which means they are added at the end of the year, or maybe every three years. In addition there could be a terminal bonus, which is added at the very end of the policy.

Premiums

There are two ways of paying your premiums: either in one lump sum (for a single premium policy) or in regular premiums throughout the life of the policy. These can be paid monthly, quarterly, half yearly or annually.

Early surrender values

For a low-cost endowment mortgage for £10,000, over 25 years, a man aged 40 next birthday will be given this sort of estimate:

	£
Monthly premium	19
Value at maturity, excluding terminal bonus	12,000
Value at maturity, including terminal bonus	17,000
SURRENDER VALUE AFTER 6 YEARS	£1000

Insurance as investment

For more about insurance as a method of saving, see pp. 47 to 50.

Unit-linked insurance

A unit-linked insurance policy is one in which most of the premium buys an allocation of units in an investment fund and part of the premium goes towards life insurance cover. The proportions vary according to company – some obtain a higher amount of life cover and less in units; others the opposite. You should decide how much life insurance you want, or whether you want a policy as an investment, and find a scheme accordingly.

Some of the premium also goes in charges and, again, this varies from company to company. You can keep an eye on how well the fund is doing by looking in the *Financial Times* unit prices under Insurances. You can either buy a policy in one lump sum (a single premium bond) or through a regular savings plan.

Annuity

Annuities provide an income in old age. The older you are when the policy starts paying out, the higher the income you then receive. Annuities provide a pension, starting at an agreed age, and they generally pay out for as long as the policyholder lives. The premiums can be paid in one lump sum or in annual instalments before retirement. Because you stand to gain a considerable income from this policy, the premiums are high. See also Home Income Plans p. 107.

Friendly societies

Tax-exempt friendly societies are doing very little business now. In the March 1984 Budget, the size of the policies they could write was cut drastically and since then they have been prevented from introducing new schemes.

Tax-exempt friendly societies do not have to pay any tax on their investments but they are allowed to invest only in banks, building societies, local authorities, gilts and national savings.

Commission

Most people selling life insurance earn their living by being paid commission. Only two insurance companies do not pay any commission. They are Equitable Life Assurance Society and London Life Association.

It is written in the registered insurance brokers' code of conduct that salesmen's advice must not, in any way, be influenced by the amount of commission they receive, regardless of which company pays most. But the fact remains; **a salesman can earn more money by selling you one policy rather than another.**

Tax

Until March 1984, one of the advantages about taking out a life insurance policy was tax relief. On every pound you paid in premiums, the taxman allowed you 15 per cent back. This tax relief has now been abolished but existing policies were not affected.

Money that is paid out under a life insurance policy, either to the policyholder or his heirs if he dies, is free of income tax.

SCHOOL FEES

The cost of sending an 11-year-old child to private school is somewhere around £1000 a term. For an idea of the total cost, multiply that by three terms, ten years and two or three children and add on the extra expenses (items like uniforms, sports equipment, food, travel). To send two children to a modest private school for ten years, if they are non-boarders, will cost about £75,000 in fees alone.

In the past, people often borrowed the money to pay school fees as they arose, and spent the rest of their lives repaying the debt. But when tax relief on interest payments (other than mortgages) was scrapped, there was little attraction in funding school fees that way.

Not so many people today are in a strong enough financial position to pay school fees out of their current income. There are many ways to spread the cost and the overriding advice is to plan as far ahead as possible.

If you are lucky, your child may win a scholarship or grant. But, for the majority, the best way is to take out an insurance scheme: the choice is between capital and income schemes.

Under the capital scheme you pay out a substantial lump sum. Many private schools operate their own capital scheme, in which case the money is known as a 'composition fee'. The fee is paid in advance directly to the school.

The amount you will have to put down depends on how expensive the fees are and also how far in advance you pay. As a rough guide, a lump sum paid when the child starts school to cover all the expected fees could be worth 15 per cent off the bill. But a lump sum deposited four years before the child enters school could knock as much as 40 per cent off the cost. If the parents pay the capital sum, they will not be liable to capital transfer tax.

An insurance policy bought in advance can be used to pay school fees. This is an income scheme. You need an insurance policy that is an investment rather than one providing life cover, though this life element means that, if you die, the sum insured will be paid out and will meet the school fees. Also, if for any reason you do not eventually need the money to pay school fees, you will receive a lump sum anyway.

You should start a policy at least four years before the child starts school. What you do is to take out one policy to mature in each year that the child is at school. So, if your child will be at a fee-paying school for eight years starting in five years' time, you should take out eight life insurance policies now, one of which will mature each year starting five years from today.

LEGAL EXPENSES INSURANCE

A more recent type of insurance enables you to cover yourself for any legal costs you may incur. The policy will pay the costs involved in fighting a case and, if you lose the case and have to pay the other side's legal expenses, the policy will meet these. But it will not cover any damages or fines you are ordered to pay. Some policies may pay for divorce cases but others will not, so if you think this might be an area you want cover for, make sure you have the appropriate policy.

Legal expenses cover only cases that are fought in court, or settled out of court. You cannot cover yourself for conveyancing costs or making out a will. Neither will they pay out if you are defending a criminal charge. Premiums cost around £60 to £80 a year.

PROTECTION

Insurance companies are supervised by the Department of Trade and Industry which can intervene if it is unhappy about the way a company is operating. Insurance policies issued by companies authorised by the DTI are safe-guarded by the Policyholders' Protection Act.

If an insurance company collapses, policyholders will receive up to 90 per cent of the money they were entitled to.

There is one proviso: if the Policyholders' Protection Board thinks you have been promised an 'excessive' amount, they will pay you less.

This is to prevent companies deliberately making extravagant promises and going bankrupt on purpose, leaving the Policyholders' Protection scheme to pick up the tab and keep policyholders happy.

Alternatively, the failed insurance company may be kept going either by being taken over by another company, or by other life insurance companies paying a levy towards its salvation. If this happens policyholders may get lower benefits than under the original company, but at least the policy will continue.

INSURANCE SALESMEN

People who earn a living by selling insurance call themselves by a variety of different titles. Only in specific circumstances can they describe themselves as 'insurance brokers' (see below) but other than that they can use any fancy name they think sounds suitably dignified.

Impressive-sounding names which have no practical meaning whatsoever include: financial consultant; insurance adviser; insurance consultant; financial management consultant. They all boil down to the same thing – selling insurance.

The various terms for insurance agents have a specific meaning and you can learn about the salesman's scope or limitations by understanding them.

Insurance brokers

Before anyone can be called an insurance broker today, they must register with the Insurance Brokers Registration Council and agree to abide by a statutory code of conduct. They make a living by earning commission on what they sell; there is no charge to you.

If you ask, they must disclose the amount of commission they are receiving. They pledge themselves always to act in the best interests of the client and with the utmost good faith and integrity. Advisers such as bank managers, accountants and solicitors also earn commission if they sell you life insurance.

They will work with a limited number of insurance companies, though they must show the Registration Council that they are not unduly dependent on any one. They limit themselves because it is far too complicated to keep full details of all insurance policies offered by every company. Rather they will stick with the ones they like.

Most insurance brokers belong to the British Insurance Brokers Association (BIBA). The Association monitors members' activities and lays down additional guidelines for behaviour.

Collecting agents

They are the people who come round door-to-door selling insurance and collecting the premiums. They offer a 'home service' and the companies they are employed by are 'industrial life' insurance offices.

The salesmen will work for one company only, they earn a salary and will visit once a week or once a month to collect the money. This is the only way of buying insurance if you do not have a bank account.

Insurance agents

These people work for themselves, are paid commission and will have negotiated agencies with any number of different insurance companies. They are not tied to one company and they could hold agencies for as many as 40 different companies. This means they can offer a wide choice of policies.

Part-time agents

They are called part-time because their main job is doing something quite unconnected with insurance. They are usually solicitors, accountants, building societies or banks. Because they do not devote much time to selling insurance they will be connected with only, perhaps, two or three companies. They will earn commission on any life insurance policy they sell you.

Tied agents

These people are restricted to selling through one company only for each type of business they do. But, if they are selling different categories of insurance, for example both life and motor, they can be tied to more than one company.

Various companies will have different definitions of what a tied agent is allowed to do. It could be that the agent is free to use another company to obtain a particular policy (maybe a pension) that his main company cannot offer.

He will most probably earn a living solely from commission though this is not always the case. He could be earning a combination of salary and commission.

Associate

This person will have a connection with one particular company but he will be self-employed and will earn a living from commission. The company he works for will help out with some of his expenses and provide a free telephone, office facilities and notepaper.

Inspector

His job is to generate new business for one particular company. He is unlikely to be selling to you directly; he spends his time visiting insurance salesmen and intermediaries recommending his company's products.

How to choose an insurance adviser
Ask:
1. Is he a registered broker?

If he is, he should have a certificate hanging on the wall.

2. Is he a member of the British Insurance Brokers Association and is he on their Life and Pensions Directory? It is preferable that he should be.

3. How much commission will he make from selling me this life insurance policy?

4. How good is the investment policy of the company he is recommending?

5. Does he specialise in any particular type of insurance?

Ask yourself:

1. How much time has this broker spent with me?
   A good broker will spend a couple of hours with you to sort out your life insurance and investment problems.

2. What was his first question to me?
   If it was: 'This is the policy we have on offer', run out of the office. He should ask you many questions covering your tax position and rate of tax, marital status, commitments, expectations and needs.

How to beat the insurance salesman at his own game

Remember that he (or she) has been trained with the sole aim of persuading you to sign up for an insurance policy. The questions he asks are not haphazard or spontaneous: they are carefully rehearsed and designed to put you in a position where you cannot say no.

Even the neat suit and the polite, deferential smile are practised. Notice that, even in very hot weather, an insurance salesman will not take off his jacket in your home. This would be regarded as too informal. Neither will he sit down before you: that is not good manners, it is good training.

His questions are designed to make you feel that you are failing in your duty and are a disaster as a person if you do not take out a life insurance policy (or a second or third policy if you already have one).

Do not be fooled by this. And do not sign anything on the spot. He will always come back after you have had a few days to think it over if he senses that he has a chance of selling you a policy. You are worth money to him. You are not an individual that needs help; you are hundreds of one pound notes.

If you are pestered by an insurance salesman, rehearse your own patter. He will often start with a telephone call – that avoids having the door slammed in his face. He will suggest at least two possible dates for an appointment, preferably in your home, and has a rehearsed answer for any objection you can raise, even if you say that you already have plenty of insurance cover thank you very much.

Let him know that you understand what the game is all about. Throw back at him non-standard replies that are unlikely to have been covered in his training manual. If you have to, embarrass him.

Try some of these answers:
- you're not still using that approach, are you? My company improved on that old one ages ago.
- you can only come if my husband/wife is here. He/she is a hang glider, wall of death motorcycler, boxer.
- Oh yes. I've already had such good value out of life insurance. My three previous wives/husbands died very soon after I took out policies.
- you can come round only if my husband/wife is out. I'm just looking for a nice boy like you.
- my doctor has told me to take out life insurance urgently – he's not too confident about the pacemaker.

What insurance terms mean:

ACTUARY	The person who does the sums to decide how much you pay in premiums.
ALL RISKS	Comprehensive insurance that covers almost anything you can think of.
AVERAGING	If you are not fully covered when you make a claim, the insurance company may pay out a proportion of the total claim only.
COVER	The eventualities the insurance policy provides for.
INDEMNITY	Compensation for loss or injury.
INDEX-LINKED	The cover and premiums go up each year in line with inflation.
LLOYD'S	Lloyd's of London is an organisation through which underwriters act as go-betweens for those seeking insurance and private investors with the money to provide the cover.
NEW FOR OLD	Replacement as new: insurance that pays the current price for an old item.
REINSTATEMENT	Same as new for old.
SURRENDER - VALUE	This is how much the policy is worth if you cash it in early.
THIRD PARTY	The person you injure. The insurance company is the first party, you are the second party and anyone else involved is the third party.
UNDERWRITER	The person who takes the risk of insurance; the one responsible for having the money to pay up.

Life insurance policies

Name	What it covers	Cost
term	cover if you die within a fixed period	cheap
family income	payment if you die within a set period	cheap
whole life	payment whenever you die	more expensive
endowment	payment on a given date or if you die sooner	even more expensive
unit-linked	for long-term saving	variable depending on charges
annuity	regular income starting on certain date until you die	very expensive

Life expectancy

AGE	YEARS TO LIVE			
	MEN		WOMEN	
	years	months	years	months
20	53	4	57	6
25	48	7	52	10
30	43	11	48	1
35	39	3	43	6
40	34	6	38	10
45	30	0	34	3
50	25	7	29	9
55	21	6	25	5
60	17	6	21	2
65	13	11	17	2
70	10	9	13	6
75	8	1	10	5
80	5	11	7	7
85	4	3	5	6
90	3	0	3	10
95	2	2	2	9
99	1	9	2	1

LETTERS

Q. My insurance company is refusing to pay up on a claim which I think is totally justified. What can I do about it?

A. *There are two arbitration schemes for insurance companies: the Insurance Ombudsman Bureau and Personal Insurance Arbitration Service. See p. 249 for addresses. They can help you only if your company is a member of one of them; if it is they will look into your complaint. If it is not, you can try the appropriate insurance association which may be able to explain why the company is acting as it is.*

Q. I am about to take out an endowment mortgage policy and I thought I would need a medical examination for the insurance. But I don't. Have I signed up with a spurious company that is about to go bust?

A. *Probably not. Insurance companies will ask you to undergo a medical examination only if you are past 55 years or taking out a policy for a very large sum of money. Or if an answer to one of the medical questions worries them.*

Q. My wife and I think we should both have life insurance. Are there any special deals?

A. *You can take out a joint life policy. This can be a first joint life (or last survivor) policy which means that when one of you dies, the policy pays out to the other. This can be used as a mortgage protection.*

Or it can be 'last death' and pay out when the second of you dies, perhaps to provide money to pay CTT.

But you may find it more flexible (and not very much more expensive) to take out two separate policies.

If you had an endowment mortgage, you could make this a joint life one as well, so that when the first of you dies the other receives the money. Indeed, joint life policies need not be restricted to married couples.

11/At Work

Contract of employment ● *your pay packet / deductions / payment by cheque or cash / tax / sick pay* ● Unemployment ● *how much? / registering for unemployment benefit / short-time and part-time working* ● Redundancy ● *how much? / period of notice for unfair dismissal / reasons for fair dismissal* ● Wrongful dismissal ● *calculating compensation for unfair dismissal / successful cases* ● Equal pay ● Sex discrimination ● National insurance contributions ● *class 1 / class 2 / class 3 / class 4 / contribution credits / home responsibility protection / benefits for which you must fulfil two conditions* ● Married women ● Fringe benefits ● *profit sharing / share option schemes / SAYE share option schemes / bonuses / commuting costs* ● Self-employed ● Working at home ● Letters

If your employer sacks you, could you claim unfair dismissal? Your rights at work are protected by law but you need to know what they are.

Your entitlements and conditions of work will be set out in a contract of employment but this is not necessarily a very comprehensive document.

CONTRACT OF EMPLOYMENT
The whole contract does not have to be put in writing but the main terms of employment must be, and naturally it is clearer for both sides should you come to a dispute to have a written agreement.

The written statement must include these details:
● the name of both employer and employee
● job title
● the date you start working
● how much you will be paid and how regularly
● normal hours of work and any compulsory overtime
● annual holidays and holiday pay
● details of the pension scheme or statement saying that there is not one
● what happens if you are ill
● period of notice on both sides
● disciplinary rules
● complaints procedure

In addition, a thoughtful employer will make sure you have the following information:
- the requirements of the job and to whom you are responsible
- the circumstances which can lead to suspension or dismissal and disciplinary rules and procedures
- opportunities for promotion and the necessary training required
- welfare and social facilities
- health and safety rules and fire regulations
- any suggestion schemes
  Ideally you should also be told:
- whether you may be expected to move house
- whether you may be asked to perform different duties at any time
- whether this job will place any restrictions on your future work for other employers

Your pay packet

Your employer must give you a payslip with your wages showing exactly what you have earned, how much of this you are actually being paid, and what has been deducted. It makes no difference if you are paid weekly or monthly, by cheque, direct into your bank account or in cash.

Deductions

Before he hands over the money, your employer will deduct:
- tax, under the PAYE system
- national insurance contributions
- company pension contributions
- union subscriptions, if you have agreed to their deduction

Payment by cheque or cash

About 40 per cent of workers are still paid in cash but both employers and trade unions are in favour of encouraging everyone to have their wages paid directly into a bank account.

The advantage is mainly that of security – neither you nor your employer is handling large amounts of cash. Also, from your point of view you will find it easier to ask for a bank loan if the manager knows you have a regular pay cheque.

Under legislation known as the Truck Acts, only manual workers have the right to insist on being paid in cash.

Tax

For more detailed information about tax, see Chapter 15. After deducting all allowances, you are liable to pay tax at the following rates on your salary: *(Autumn 1984 figures)*

£	tax %	£	tax %	£	tax %
0 to 15,400	30	18,201 to 23,100	45	30,601 to 38,100	55
15,401 to 18,200	40	23,101 to 30,600	50	over £38,100	60

By looking at your PAYE code (see p. 197) which is assessed by the Inland Revenue your employer knows how much tax to deduct each week or month. You have to pay tax only on the amount that is left after taking away your personal allowance and pension contributions.

Once a year, in April, you will be handed a P60 by your employer which tells you exactly how much money you received and how much you paid in tax for the past financial year. It is important to keep this safely as proof of the tax you have paid.

SICK PAY

Under arrangements which started on 6 April 1983, whenever an employee goes sick, his employer may have to pay sick pay (called Statutory Sick Pay or SSP) for up to eight weeks' sick absence in any one tax year.

You will not be paid SSP until you have been off work for at least four days in a row; then you are in a 'period of incapacity for work' or PIW.

Your national insurance contributions entitle you to SSP and neither you nor your employer can opt out of the scheme.

After eight weeks, the DHSS may pay state sickness benefit and later still invalidity benefit.

Exactly how much SSP you are entitled to receive depends on your average pay, including bonuses and overtime. The rate is divided into three bands (November 1984 figures):

if you earn	you will receive
£68+ a week	£42.75
£50.50 to £67.99	£35.45
£34 to £50.49	£28.55

The employer then recovers these payments from the Inland Revenue. You will not be given SSP if your average earnings are below £34 a week.

The change means that the employer is required to take responsibility for paying workers when they are ill and also for deciding that the worker is genuinely off sick.

It also means that Statutory Sick Pay is now taxable, whereas the old sickness benefit was not. Married women who are still paying the reduced national insurance contributions are entitled to receive SSP although they are still not eligible for sickness benefit.

UNEMPLOYMENT

If you are out of work, you can receive unemployment benefit if you fulfil certain conditions:
- you must satisfy the contribution conditions
- you must be unemployed and unable to find a job
- you must be capable of, and available for, work and free from any other disqualification or disallowance

You can find out more information from leaflet NI 12 on unemployment benefit, obtainable from unemployment benefit offices.

Unemployment benefit is not paid for the first three days of unemployment and then it can be paid for one year excepting Sundays, or more exactly 312 days. After that you must work for an employer for at least 13 weeks for a minimum of 16 hours a week to qualify for benefit again. If you are unable to find work, you will have to claim supplementary benefit.

Immediately you become unemployed, you should claim at your nearest unemployment benefit office, the address of which you can find at the post office. Benefit will be paid by Girobank cheque which will be posted to you on the day after you sign and claim benefit.

Benefit is usually claimed, and paid, every two weeks and you can cash the Girobank cheque at the post office of your choice. You can also pay the cheque into your own bank account.

If you are unemployed, you should also claim supplementary benefit (then you will automatically receive the associated benefits) because unemployment benefit is fairly low.

How much?
The standard rate of unemployment benefit for those under pension age, from November 1984, is:

personal rate	£28.45
wife	£17.55

If you are over pension age, it is:

personal rate	£35.80
wife	£21.50

If your national insurance contributions record is insufficient, you will get less than this. Apart from the amounts payable for children, the benefit is taxable, though tax is not deducted before you receive it. The tax will be assessed by the Inland Revenue at the end of the tax year.

Registering for unemployment benefit
It is now voluntary to register at an employment office or local job centre. If you do you have to call in person, unless you live more than ten miles away, in which case you can register by post.

After the first visit, you will probably have to attend once a week, or once a fortnight to sign on. However, if you are suspected of secretly working and still claiming, you can be asked to attend every day.

Short-time and part-time working
You may be able to claim unemployment benefit if you are on short-time working. You would claim benefit for the days you are not working. You can also claim if you have been working part-time.

REDUNDANCY

Should you lose your job through redundancy, you are entitled to compensation from your employer. Only in the following circumstances do you not possess an automatic right:

● when you have worked for less than two years in the job
● if you have passed retirement age
● if you work part-time (less than 16 hours a week)
● if it is a fixed-term contract
● if you usually work outside the United Kingdom
● if you are offered a comparable job by the same employer

How much?

The legal minimum for redundancy pay for each complete year you have worked full time is calculated as follows:

18 to 21	half a week's pay
21 to 40	1 week's pay
40 to 65 (men)	1½ weeks' pay
40 to 60 (women) (see over)	1½ weeks' pay

The most you will receive if your firm has no special scheme is £145 a week and for no more than 20 years. This works out at £2900 and it is tax free.

Period of notice for redundancy

Assuming you have no better agreement with your employer, the minimum period of notice you must be given is:

4 weeks' to 2 years' unemployment	1 week
2 to 12 years' employment	1 week for each year
over 12 years' employment	at least 12 weeks

Proving redundancy

It is important that your employer admits that he is dismissing you because you are redundant. Otherwise, you are not entitled to any compensation.

Sometimes employers sack workers when they are, in effect, redundant to avoid paying out large sums.

If you think this is happening to you, you can appeal to an industrial tribunal (the address is in your local telephone directory, or ask at a Citizens Advice Bureau for help). You should take action immediately as you might forfeit your rights if you wait longer than six months.

Golden handshakes

Your employer may offer you a large lump sum when you are made redundant. These are unofficially called 'golden handshakes'.

The first £25,000 you receive is tax free. Larger amounts are taxed on a sliding scale until £75,000 which is taxed as full income for the year.

UNFAIR OR WRONGFUL DISMISSAL

Provided you have been in the job for more than 26 weeks, you can take action against your employer if you feel you have been sacked without good reason.

Unfair dismissal claims are made to win compensation and they are handled by an industrial tribunal. Wrongful dismissal claims seek to recoup wages owed and are heard in civil courts.

Unfair dismissal

Anyone who feels he has been unfairly dismissed, or is not receiving the redundancy money he is entitled to, can appeal to an industrial tribunal for compensation. This should be done within six months of losing your job or you might not be able to claim.

Reasons for fair dismissal

If your employer can prove any of the following against you, you could lose your unfair dismissal claim:

- misconduct, which includes:
  drunkenness
  violence
  dishonesty
  disobeying orders
  poor timekeeping
  non co-operation
- incompetence or lack of qualifications
- it is illegal for you to continue working (eg a driver who has lost his licence)
- striking, as long as all the other strikers were dismissed
- some other 'substantial' reason: this is not defined by the courts and, for example, can be used against someone who simply upsets his colleagues.

WRONGFUL DISMISSAL

Even if the dismissal is 'fair' you can claim 'wrongful' dismissal if you feel the contract of employment has been broken. For example, you were given insufficient notice or dismissed before the end of a fixed-term contract.

Calculating compensation for unfair dismissal

This is calculated in the same way as redundancy payments and the maximum basic award is £4350. On top of this you can claim compensation for loss of earnings and benefits such as pension rights up to a maximum of £7500.

Successful cases
These are instances where employees have won claims for unfair dismissal:
● someone sacked without being given the opportunity to defend complaints or improve his behaviour
● someone sacked for alleged stealing who was given no opportunity to clear his name
● someone whose job was changed and the most interesting element taken away
● someone sacked on the grounds of ill health without a full medical report being obtained.

If you win an unfair dismissal claim, the tribunal can award you either:
● your old job back, that is reinstatement
● re-employment but in a different job, which is re-engagement
● a cash sum

EQUAL PAY
Both men and women must now receive the same money and same conditions as their colleagues in the same job, or if a woman's job has the same value as a man's under a job evaluation scheme.
For details of maternity benefits see p. 154.

SEX DISCRIMINATION
You can claim discrimination on these grounds:
● you are passed over for promotion because of your sex
● the job you apply for has an unreasonable sex-biased qualification, like insisting that you can have babies
● you are treated less favourably because you are married
● the conditions of the job make it difficult for married people
● you are treated less favourably because you have already claimed unfair treatment

If you feel you have been unfairly treated, appeal to your employer, or the industrial tribunal, or failing that, the Equal Opportunities Commission.

NATIONAL INSURANCE CONTRIBUTIONS
Your national insurance contributions entitle you to sick pay, an old age pension, unemployment benefit as well as various other benefits and allowances.
There are four categories of contributions:

Class 1
You and your employer will pay at this level if you are employed; earn more than the lower earnings limit; are over 16 but have not reached

retirement age. In this context, company directors count as employees. See DHSS leaflet NI 35.

Just how much you pay depends on whether you are contracted in or out of the earnings-related pension scheme. For more information on pensions see Chapter 16.

Contracted in	
employee:	9 per cent of your salary up to the upper earnings limit (UEL)
employer:	10·45 per cent of your salary up to the UEL

Contracted out	
employee:	9 per cent of your salary up to the lower earnings limit (LEL) *plus* 6·85 per cent of your salary between the LEL and the UEL
employer:	10·45 per cent of earnings up to the LEL *plus* 6·35 per cent of earnings between the LEL and the UEL

Married women who are still paying the reduced contributions pay: 3·85 per cent of all earnings up to the UEL

In 1984–85, the lower earnings limit (LEL) is £34 a week and the upper earnings limit (UEL) is £250.

Class 2
This applies to the self-employed, who may have to pay Class 4 contributions as well. The rate is £4.60 a week unless your earnings are below £1850 a year (1984–85).

If you work as an employee, and also have a self-employed job, you may have to pay both Class 1 and Class 2 contributions.

Class 3
These payments are voluntary and will maintain your contribution record for a few entitlements if you do not pay Class 1 or Class 2 contributions. Ask the DHSS for advice if you come into this category but it is rarely worth-while paying. The amount is £4.50 a week.

Class 4
This class again is for the self-employed who have to contribute unless they are under 16 or over retirement age. The rate is 6·3 per cent of annual profit between £3950 and £13,000 in 1984–85.

Contribution credits
If you are out of work through no fault of your own, you will receive credit contributions for Class 1 or Class 3. But married women paying the reduced contributions cannot be credited.

Home responsibility protection

While you are looking after a child or an invalid, and not paying contributions, you are covered by home responsibility protection which means you will not lose the widowed mother's allowance, widow's pension or retirement pension. However, no year before April 1978 will count.

Before you receive a benefit, your contributions' record must fulfil one or two conditions. If you only partially fulfil the requirements, you may be allowed a reduced benefit.

The classes of contributions qualify as follows:
- *Class 1:* all contributory benefits
- *Class 2:* all contributory benefits except unemployment
- *Class 3:* all contributory widows' benefits; retirement pension; death grant; child's special allowance
- *Class 4:* no benefits

Benefits for which you must fulfil one condition

- widow's allowance
- death grant
- child's special allowance

The condition is that you must have paid 26 contributions (50 for child's special allowance) in any one year before the death which necessitates the claim.

Benefits for which you must fulfil two conditions

Short-term benefits:
- unemployment benefit
- sick pay
- maternity allowance

You should:
1) have paid 26 contributions in any one contribution year
2) have paid, or been credited with, in the relevant contribution years, an earnings factor equal to at least 50 times that year's lower earnings limit.

Long-term benefits:
- widowed mother's allowance
- widow's pension
- retirement pension

You should:
1) have paid 50 contributions in one year
2) have paid, or been credited with, sufficient contributions to produce an earnings factor of 52 times that year's lower earnings limit.

MARRIED WOMEN

If you pay reduced national insurance contributions, you will not receive:

- invalidity benefit
- maternity allowance
- sickness benefit (unless your incapacity for work results from an industrial accident or prescribed disease)

but based on your husband's contributions you may be entitled to:

- death grant
- retirement pension

You need only your late husband's contributions to receive:

- child's special allowance
- widow's benefits

Even if you are not paying national insurance contributions, you may be eligible for:

- attendance allowance
- child benefit
- family income supplement
- guardian's allowance
- sickness benefit (if you work and your incapacity to work results from an industrial accident or prescribed disease)
- invalid car allowance
- maternity grant
- mobility allowance
- non-contributory invalidity pension
- one-parent benefit
- supplementary benefit

FRINGE BENEFITS

As well as tempting you with a salary, some employers will offer various fringe benefits on top of your normal salary. These range from luncheon vouchers to private education for the children. In some cases the benefit will be completely tax free; in others you will pay full tax. See p. 190.

The sort of perks that are offered, and which you may be able to negotiate, if you are in a strong position, are:

- luncheon vouchers
- season ticket (or interest-free loan to buy one)
- car
- petrol
- private medicine
- living accommodation
- board and lodging
- television
- television rental or licence

- telephone rental
- cheap rate mortgage
- life insurance and death in service cover
- working clothes
- meals in canteen
- professional fees and subscriptions
- hairdressing expenses
- entertainment expenses
- shares or participation in share option scheme

Profit sharing

You may work for an employer who allocates you shares in the company. There are tax advantages in taking these up. The company provides the money to buy the shares, which are held by trustees.

You cannot sell the shares for two years but then you will be taxed on the value of the shares (either the original value or the sale price, whichever is lower). After that, the tax gradually decreases until, if you hold the shares for more than seven years, you pay no tax on the benefit.

Share option schemes

Your company may run a share option scheme which gives you the right to buy an agreed number of shares at a fixed price. You pay nothing at the time but you have the option to buy the shares, at the same fixed price, in three years' time when, hopefully, they will have risen in value. You do not have to buy the shares and pay no income tax if the scheme is approved by the Inland Revenue

SAYE share option schemes

Another way of investing in the company you work for is by a regular savings plan. See p. 33.

Bonuses

Any extra money your employer pays you is taxable at your top rate (the highest rate of tax you pay).

Commuting costs

These can be a very large element of your regular outgoings and it is worth finding any way you can to cut the costs.
- ask your employer for an interest-free loan
- if possible, travel in a cheap-rate period
- buy a long-term season ticket but time it so that you do not pay for holiday periods (see p. 13)
- share a car (see p. 222)
- walk or cycle short distances

SELF-EMPLOYED

The advantages and disadvantages of being self-employed are complex and personal. At one level, you may just be earning a few extra pounds knitting pullovers to supplement the housekeeping money.

In this instance you are entitled to earn up to your personal allowance each year before paying tax.

If you are a married woman, then your husband should declare your earnings on his tax return unless you are taxed separately. If you are otherwise unemployed, or a pensioner, you should inform the taxman even if your earnings are very small.

If you become self-employed in any larger way, you will need help and advice from professionals. There are various organisations which give guidance to small businesses: try the Government-sponsored Small Firms Advisory Centre listed in the telephone directory under Small Firms Information Service.

A helpful book is: *The Guardian Guide To Running A Small Business*. For other names and addresses, see p. 250.

If you enter the project wholeheartedly, you can set up a partnership; or if you become larger, a private company; or form a public limited company. Each has to be done formally and registered, with proper accounts kept.

WORKING AT HOME

If you work from home, this alters the tax position regarding your house. The advantage is that you can offset part of the costs of heating, lighting, and maintaining a telephone against the profit of the business. But the drawback is that you may have to pay capital gains tax when you sell on the proportion of the house you use as an office.

LETTERS

Q. I am receiving unemployment benefit but I have to go into hospital soon. Where do I stand?

A. *Unemployment benefit is not payable while you are in hospital but you will receive sickness benefit instead for the first eight weeks.*

Q. I am about to be made redundant and I have been told I do not have to register for work. How will my unemployment benefit be paid?

A. *You will receive it through the post. The unemployment benefit office will give you a postal claim form – they will also issue you with a postal claim form for supplementary benefit.*

Q. I have been paying the women's lower rate of national insurance contribution since I married. Is there a case for switching to the higher rate?

A. *First of all, anyone who married after May 1977 had no option but to pay the higher rate; and if you have since divorced then you should be paying the higher rate if you are earning.*

But if you are still on the lower rate, you are not building up the same pension rights as women on the full rate. If your husband is five years older than you, meaning that you will both retire on the same day, then you could claim on his national insurance contributions straightaway. Otherwise you will have to wait until he draws his pension before you will receive anything.

You will still be eligible for widow's benefits but you will not be able to claim other benefits, including unemployment benefit and maternity allowance.

12/**The Family**

Getting married • *registry office / Church of England* • When it's better to live together • When it's better to be married • Having a baby • *the cost of having a baby / maternity allowance / maternity grant / maternity pay / continuing work / returning to work / child benefit / one-parent benefit / child's special allowance / guardian's allowance / family income supplement / mobility allowance / Christmas bonus / attendance allowance* • Single parents • *maintenance / additional personal allowance* • School fees • Divorce • *cost / who pays / legal aid / children / separation* • Widowhood • *widow's allowance / widowed mother's allowance / widow's pension / death grant / funerals / costs / widowers* • Criminal injuries compensation board • Letters

Life is expensive. It costs money to get married, it costs money to have children and it costs money to bring them up. It costs money to get divorced, and it costs money to die.

Along the way you are entitled to certain help in the form of allowances and benefits and you can help yourself to minimise the costs.

GETTING MARRIED

The cost of weddings is as long as a piece of string. The decision whether you want a fanfare, trumpets and the cathedral choir, or prefer to slip round the corner to the registry office in a pair of jeans is a totally personal one.

However, there are certain minimum legal costs that you cannot avoid. In this country you can get married legally by a civil or a Church of England ceremony.

Registry office

You have to pay £6.50 for each notice of marriage which you must lodge 21 days before the wedding and £10 for the attendance of a registrar. If you are in a hurry, you can have a superintendent registrar's licence of marriage which costs an extra £23 and enables you to get married the day after you have lodged the notice. A copy of the marriage certificate costs £2.

Church of England

You pay £4 to have the banns called; if the two of you come from different churches you must pay £4 in each. The certificate to prove that the banns have been called costs £2 and the wedding service itself costs £33. This includes the vicar's fee but not the charge for music or choir. A certificate at the time costs £2, subsequently £5, or £10 by post.

So, if the cost of weddings can be so high, are there financial advantages in living together rather than getting married? In some instances you are better off; but on other occasions you would do better to get married. The pros and cons break down like this:

WHEN IT'S BETTER TO LIVE TOGETHER:

Living together	*Marriage*
woman's investment income is taxed as her own	woman's investment income always added to her husband's income
both can claim tax relief on mortgage payments; ie total of £60,000	can claim tax relief on £30,000 only
both of you can claim tax relief and capital gains tax exemption on a property	allowed tax relief on one property only, pay capital gains tax on second home
can take out an affiliation order against partner to claim extra tax relief	no tax relief for married men supporting their children
can make deed of covenant to partner (if non taxpayer) for extra tax relief	cannot covenant to each other
can claim single parent's allowance	no extra allowances

WHEN IT'S BETTER TO BE MARRIED:

Marriage	*Living together*
a woman can claim on her husband's national insurance contributions	she cannot
widow's benefits and pension when husband dies	no widow's benefits
will receive married man's tax allowance which is higher than the single person's	taxed separately
widow will inherit husband's property	unless he leaves a will, the woman will have to prove right to the estate and may not win
can claim maintenance for herself and child if partner leaves	can claim for child only, anyway more difficult

When it's better to be married (continued)

Marriage	*Living together*
can claim tax relief on insurance premiums on each other's lives	can insure own lives only for tax benefit
do not pay capital transfer tax or capital gains tax on gifts to each other	liable for capital taxes

HAVING A BABY

Apart from the emotional upheaval of having a baby, the change to your income can come as a serious shock at this time. If it is your first child and, until now, you have been working full time, then the reduction in income if you give up work will be sharply felt.

The cost of having a baby

To maintain a child for the next 18 years will cost around £35,000, ignoring inflation, and babies start as they mean to carry on. To kit out a new baby can cost more than £800.

You are entitled to money from the state when you are pregnant. One element is the maternity allowance, which is paid weekly for a few months only; and the other is the maternity grant which is a lump sum payment.

Maternity allowance

If you have been paying full rate national insurance contributions, you can claim £27.25 (November 1984) a week if you stop work to have the baby. If you have an adult dependant, you can claim a further £16. The money is not taxable.

If you do not have enough national insurance contributions to satisfy the conditions fully (see p. 147) you may be able to get the allowance at half or three-quarters the standard rate.

You can claim the allowance for 18 weeks from the eleventh week before the baby is due. Claim as soon as you can after the beginning of the fourteenth week before your baby is expected, even if you are still working. If you claim later than in the eighth week before your baby is expected, you may lose some benefit.

If you continue working after the eleventh week, you receive the allowance from the time you stop work but you will not receive it for any period in which you do paid work.

Should the baby arrive late, you can continue to receive the money until six weeks after the birth, but you will need to make an extra claim to receive it.

To claim the maternity allowance, you should obtain a certificate of expected confinement from your doctor or midwife, showing the expected date of birth, and send it with a complete claim form (BM4) to your local DHSS office. You can obtain form BM4 from your maternity or child health clinic or from your local DHSS office.

Maternity grant

You do not need to have made any national insurance contributions to receive the grant, but you must have been living in the UK for more than 182 days in the 52 weeks up to the date of birth. The amount is £25 and you will be paid the money even if the child is still-born. You can claim up to 14 weeks before you expect the baby and up to three months after the actual date of birth. However, the money will not be paid sooner than the eleventh week before the baby is due.

The payment is for each child; so if you have twins, you will receive £50. You do not pay tax on it. You can claim the grant on form BM4 supported by a certificate of expected confinement. The allowance can be claimed on the same form BM4. If you are in special need you can claim supplementary benefit. You should ask at your local DHSS office for help.

Maternity pay

Continuing work

If you have been in the same job for more than two years and work full-time, then your employer must keep your job open for you.

As long as you work at least until 11 weeks before the birth (if, in reality, you are off sick at that time, it still counts as 'working') and have been working there for at least two years by the eleventh week before the baby is due, you can claim maternity pay. You must give your employer at least three weeks' notice that you intend to stop working. You are then entitled to maternity pay which is six weeks' wages at the rate of 90 per cent of what you are earning.

Returning to work

If you have fulfilled the requirements for receiving maternity pay, and also told your employer when claiming the money that you intended to return to work after the birth, then your employer cannot sack you or make you redundant.

You should confirm your intention of returning to work seven weeks after the birth (in fact, this is the date of the expected birth, not the actual birth), and you must also give at least one week's written notice before you return to work. Also, you must return within 29 weeks of the actual birth.

If your employer refuses to take you back because you have had a baby, you can claim unfair dismissal.

The job you return to should be identical, in essence, to the one you left. But, you cannot insist on the self-same job. As long as the conditions are the same, your employer can ask you to take different job.

You will be entitled to any pay increases that occurred while you were away, but those missing weeks will not count towards length of service for pension rights. However, other benefits such as redundancy pay, will be calculated as though you had never been away.

You may be lucky enough to have an employer who agrees to pay you for the whole time you are away, if you say that you will return. But this is not a statutory right.

Child benefit

This is paid at a fixed rate for every child. It is paid regardless of income to the person who is responsible for bringing up the child, which is usually the mother. It is paid every four weeks in arrears.

The amount is £6.85 a week from November 1984 for each child and it is not taxable. 'Child' is defined as anyone under the age of 16, or 19 if they are still in full-time but not higher education.

To claim child benefit, pick up leaflet CH1 and forms CH2 and CH3 from a DHSS office. You should claim as soon as the child is born, but if you claim a little late, you can receive arrears.

One-parent benefit

If you are bringing up a child on your own, you can claim one-parent benefit of £4.25 a week from November 1984. This is a flat-rate sum and paid once however many children you may have. It is not taxable. Ask for form CH11 to claim.

You can get this in addition to the child benefit as long as you are not receiving any of the following allowances: child's special allowance; guardian's allowance; industrial death benefit for a child at the higher rate or an increase for the child with widow's benefit; war widows' pension; retirement pension; industrial disablement pension, which includes unemployability supplement; or invalid care allowance.

Child's special allowance

If you are divorced and your ex-husband dies after you get divorced, you are entitled to a child's special allowance of £7.65 a week (November 1984) for each child you have. This is not taxable.

Claim on form CS1. To be eligible your ex-husband must have been paying or been liable to pay at least a nominal 25p a week maintenance for the child and he must have paid sufficient national insurance contributions. You will lose this allowance if you remarry.

Guardian's allowance

This payment is for those bringing up children who are orphans or effectively orphans. It is normally paid only if both parents are dead, but it can also be paid in circumstances where the surviving parent cannot be traced, or is in prison for a long sentence, or where the parents were divorced and there is no liability for custody or maintenance. The amount is £7.65 a week (November 1984) and it is not taxable.

Family income supplement (FIS)

This is similar to supplementary benefit, but it goes to families where the man or woman is employed full-time (at least 30 hours a week) but on a low income. Someone in full-time employment would not be eligible for supplementary benefit. Like supplementary benefit it is means-tested. Single people and unmarried couples as well as married people can ask for FIS.

If you become entitled to FIS, you also become entitled to free school meals and other health benefits, so it is worth applying if you think you may be eligible.

If you are self-employed, you can claim as long as you work for more than 30 hours a week and earn a low income. To qualify, your gross earnings must be less than: £90 if you have one child, rising in stages to £120 for four children.

You can add another £10 a week for each additional child.

The maximum amount of FIS payable is £23 for a one-child family and £2 extra for each additional child. To claim, pick up form FIS 1 from a post office or DHSS office, though your initial claim is handled by a central office and not by the local one. Both the man and woman will have to sign the form.

Mobility allowance

If you are unable or virtually unable to walk, you can claim the £20-a-week mobility allowance. There are no contribution conditions but you must be aged between 5 and 65 when you first claim.

Christmas bonus

Pensioners are entitled to a bonus of £10 at Christmas. The bonus is also paid to anyone receiving invalid care allowance, widow's or widowed mother's allowance, or the attendance allowance.

Attendance allowance

This allowance is for people who need a great deal of care because they are severely disabled, either physically or mentally. No contributions are needed and you can claim on behalf of a child once it reaches the age of two.

There are two rates: the lower rate is £19.10 a week for someone needing care either during the day or at night; the higher rate of £28.60 is for people who need care both day and night.

SCHOOL FEES

If you want to pay for your child to be educated privately, you should start planning well before the infant is ready to go to school: the sooner you start paying, the less it will cost in the long run. The average fee at a boarding school today is easily £1000 a term just for a junior. Then you can start adding on the extras, such as books and meals, and you will see why so few people today pay for private education out of current earnings, or even borrow now to pay school fees.

Long-term planning is the most usual course, and there are two ways of approaching it: with either a capital or an income scheme. Neither is likely to satisfy the whole cost of the bill when it arrives, but will go a long way towards meeting it. See p. 131 for details.

SINGLE PARENTS

'Single' applies to anyone who is unmarried, widowed, separated or divorced.

Maintenance

If you are separated, your husband may have to pay you maintenance and he will certainly have to do so for your children. If you get divorced, then he is liable for the children only, as long as you have enough money of your own.

If the court does not order him to pay you money, you may need to contact your local DHSS office to ask for supplementary benefit if your income falls within their limits. They will try to contact him to force payment.

Make sure the payments are said to be payable TO the children; they are then counted as the children's income, not the wife's, and the children can receive up to the single person's allowance before they have to pay any tax. If the payments are made TO the wife FOR the children, it will be added to her other income and she will be taxed on the money.

If the payments made to a child are below £33 a week or £143 a month and made under court order, they are regarded as Small Maintenance Payments. In this case, the ex-husband makes the payments gross and can claim tax relief on them from the Inland Revenue. On larger amounts than this he deducts tax first.

If you are in a full-time job on a low salary, you may be able to claim family income supplement.

Additional personal allowance

You may also be able to claim an additional personal tax allowance for your children. This is for anyone who has no husband or wife to help bring up children and also includes a married man whose wife is totally incapacitated. The allowance is worth £1150 a year. See p. 183.

DIVORCE

In the year a woman becomes separated or divorced (or, in fact, widowed) she is entitled to claim the single person's allowance in her own right for the full year while her husband continues to receive the married man's allowance. Make sure the tax inspector has given you this. (A widow will also receive the widow's bereavement tax allowance.)

If you need help in any way you can contact several organisations which will help. They include: Child Poverty Action Group, Cruse National Widow's Association, National Council for One-Parent Families, Scottish Child Poverty Action Group, Gingerbread, and Families Need Fathers. See p. 248 for addresses.

Modern legislation has now made postal divorces possible and has helped to take some of the pain out of the process, but it will always be an unhappy experience. If you have been married for more than three years (new legislation will bring this down to one year) and the marriage has broken down irretrievably, you will be able to get a divorce. There are two stages – a decree nisi followed by a decree absolute. The time between the two is usually six weeks and is designed to ensure that each party is aware of what is happening.

Any financial matters or custody to be decided will be resolved between the decree nisi and decree absolute.

Cost

This is unquantifiable and depends on how complicated the case is. If both partners agree, have lived apart for more than two years and are childless, a postal divorce, using no solicitors, will cost £40.

The solicitor's fee for an undefended case could be about £150, but ask for some sort of estimate before you start. You will also have to pay £40 for filing the divorce in the court.

Who pays

If you cannot agree between yourselves how to split the costs, the judge will decide.

Legal aid

Legal aid is no longer allowed for undefended divorces since they can be carried out quite simply. Defended divorces, particularly if they turn into a bitter wrangle, can become very expensive and legal aid may be granted if you are eligible. Very broadly, if you have less than £4500 in disposable capital and a disposable income of less than £4925, you can apply. You may, however, be entitled to 'Legal Advice and Assistance' (the Green Form scheme), which can apply up to decree nisi (the actual processing of the divorce petition). This does not cover you for what is called Ancillary Relief, that is, the financial arrangements or maintenance or custody of any children. See also p. 244.

Children

If there are children involved, the judge will want to be sure that they are adequately provided for. This means agreeing which parent will have custody and who is to pay for the children's upkeep.

Separation

If you do not want to go all the way and get divorced, you can apply for a legal separation. It is advisable to have a properly drawn-up document and to take the advice of a solicitor. Otherwise you might lose out on the tax advantages of being separated and may have difficulty changing the maintenance terms of the deed later on.

For instance, if a wife is granted even a nominal sum of maintenance, however small, it is easier to have this amount subsequently increased when she might need it. It would be more difficult for her to start asking for maintenance afterwards.

WIDOWHOOD
To be classified as a widow and claim a widow's allowances, you must have been married to the man when he died: if you were divorced, unless the divorce had still to be made absolute, you will not be his widow.

In the year your husband dies, you can claim the single person's tax allowance for a full year, on top of the married man's allowance that your husband had been claiming up to the time of his death.

You will also be entitled to a widow's bereavement tax allowance of £1150 for both the year of death and the following year.

Widow's allowance
If your late husband had made sufficient national insurance contributions and you have not reached retirement age, you can claim £50.10 a week plus £7.65 for each dependent child (November 1984 figures). This continues for 26 weeks, provided you do not remarry, but you should claim within three months of becoming a widow. After 26 weeks, you can claim either the widow's pension or the widowed mother's allowance. This allowance is taxable, but the child's element is not.

Widowed mother's allowance
This is worth £35.80 plus £7.65 for each child if your late husband had made sufficient national insurance contributions (November 1984 figures).

This allowance is taxable but the child's portion is not. The allowance will continue for as long as you qualify and provided you do not remarry.

Widow's pension
If you are not entitled to the widowed mother's allowance and you are aged between 40 and 65 when your widow's allowance ceases, or you are in that age bracket when your widowed mother's allowance ceases, you will probably be able to claim a widow's pension.

For anyone aged 50 or over, the rate of pension is £35.80 a week but if you are between 40 and 49, an 'age related' widow's pension is payable.

The rate of this benefit depends on your actual age at the relevant time and is on a sliding scale with the lowest rate at age 40, the highest at age 49. You can find full details at your local DHSS office.

Your entitlement to the full amount depends on whether your husband made enough national insurance contributions. But, you might be entitled to an additional amount based on your late husband's salary if you were widowed after 5 April 1979. This entitlement will continue for as long as you qualify and provided you do not remarry.

Death grant
This is given to offset the cost of a funeral, although the sum nowadays is too paltry to be of much help. The amount is £30 for every adult who dies and who has paid sufficient national insurance contributions; less for children. You should claim within six months of the death; the money is usually paid to the executor if there is a will, or to whoever pays for the funeral.

Funerals
These are expensive. If there is no money and no one to pay for the funeral when you die, the local authority must take care of the body. If there is someone who might reasonably be expected to take responsibility for the funeral but does not have enough money, they can claim a grant towards the cost of the death certificate, a plain coffin, transport, flowers, undertaker's fee, and the cost of a simple burial or cremation.

Costs
Although this is a distressing time, if you are having to arrange a funeral, you really should ask for quotations before choosing an undertaker. The excuses for not doing this are that it is 'tasteless' to compare prices when a loved one has just died and 'penny pinching' to quibble about the cost afterwards.

The doctor will be able to give you advice and so will a solicitor. Or you can seek guidance from the National Association of Funeral Directors, address on p. 249. The standard death certificate costs £2 and a special death certificate, which you will need to claim on an insurance policy, costs £1.50. You will need two doctors' certificates for a cremation and they cost £16.80 each.

For a straightforward burial in a churchyard cemetery, fees vary widely and change from year to year. You may have to pay between £30 and £80 if you lived in the area, more if you did not. Additionally gravediggers might cost £50, a minister £20, embalming about £15. The fee in a crematorium can range from £25 to £90. If the body waits in a rest room, this can cost up to £2.50 a day. You will pay another £2.50 to have the ashes scattered. The other expenses you will incur are: the cost of a casket, moving the body; hearses and cars; a headstone.

The cheapest, most basic funeral will cost around £350, rising to £600. No VAT is payable. An elaborate coffin can cost £250 or more.

Widowers

Widows receive more financial assistance than widowers, but the Cruse National Widows Association and the National Association of Widows will give advice and guidance to men as well as women.

CRIMINAL INJURIES COMPENSATION BOARD

If you are injured as a result of a criminal act, you can claim compensation from the Criminal Injuries Compensation Board. This is a Government-funded committee set up to give money to victims of violent crimes.

You can claim from the board if you are injured as the result of a crime, or if you have been trying to prevent a crime, or while trying to apprehend someone you believe has committed a crime.

If you were to die as a result of your injuries, your husband or wife could claim a bereavement award which is fixed at £3500.

It does not matter if you do not know who committed the attack or whether or not the person is prosecuted. You can still claim.

LETTERS

Q. My eight-year-old claims that he can take his money out of the post office without my permission. Is he right?

A. *Yes. But if he tried taking out the whole lot, the post office staff should be sensible enough to question him to make sure he (and you) know what he is doing. These are the legal age limits:*

birth	*entitled to single person's allowance; bank, building society, national savings or post office accounts can be opened in your child's name*
3	*have to pay on public transport*
7	*can sign name to withdraw money from bank, post office or national savings accounts*
12	*some building societies make you wait to this age*
14	*can work part-time*
16	*can marry with parent's permission*
	can apply for supplementary benefit
	can join trade union
	can work full-time
	have to pay prescription charges
17	*can cash in Trustee Savings Bank account*
	can drive car or motorbike
18	*become adult*
	can obtain credit
	can vote
	can marry without parental consent
	can own house
	can make will
21	*can stand in general or local election*
	can drive lorry or bus

Q. I live, very happily, with my boyfriend and we have two children. I read somewhere that I should take out an affiliation order against him. This sounds unnecessarily hostile; what is the reasoning behind it?

A. *If you take out an affiliation order for the upkeep of the children, your boyfriend can claim tax relief on the money he pays you. So, the taxman is contributing another 30 per cent to your housekeeping. It must be worth while!*

13/Deeds of Covenants

Covenants • This is how you do it • Sample covenants

COVENANTS

Anyone who has to support children at university, or doting grand-parents who regularly give a child money, should, without exception, hand this money over under a Deed of Covenant. This way the taxman will donate another 30 per cent, that is basic rate of tax, on top.

The wording of a covenant must be acceptable to the Inland Revenue, and there are certain limitations, but there is nothing difficult about drawing up a covenant.

What happens is that the donor agrees to pay a set sum to the recipient every year for the next seven years. The donor hands over the amount he has agreed, but less 30 per cent. The recipient then goes along to his or her tax office and, providing the process has been followed correctly, the taxman will contribute the remaining 30 per cent.

The scheme takes advantage of the fact that children can earn up to the single person's allowance before they pay any tax.

Parents cannot covenant money to their own children until their offspring reach 18. Any other income a child has, from investment or earnings, must be included in working out the single person's allowance figure.

THIS IS HOW YOU DO IT
● write out a deed of covenant using the words shown
● insert the gross amount you wish to give (this is including the 30 per cent the taxman will contribute)

- insert the dates on which the money will be paid, the first payment must come after the date on the covenant
- stick a red seal, available from stationers, on the covenant
- date and sign the covenant and have it witnessed (but not by the beneficiary)
- hand over the net amount to the recipient – this can be done annually, once a term, quarterly or monthly
- make a copy for yourself, give one to the beneficiary and keep the top copy for the taxman
- pick up a copy of form R185(AP) from your tax office and complete it
- pass the form to the recipient to take to his own tax office
- he also completes tax claim form R40
- if the taxman is satisfied, he will hand over the extra 30 per cent to the beneficiary at the end of the year. If the beneficiary is under 18, the money is handed to the parent

The whole subject of covenants frequently confuses people and the following questions are often asked:

Q. Can I covenant money to my own children?

A. *Only after they reach the age of 18.*

Q. But could I covenant money to my grandchildren if they are under 18?

A. *Yes, indeed. This is commonly done. In fact anyone apart from the parents can covenant money to a child, as long as it would not bring the recipient's total income beyond the single person's allowance.*

Q. What is the significance of the single person's allowance?

A. *Everyone, even a newborn baby, is entitled to earn this much money before they have to pay tax. In effect you are providing someone with an income who would not otherwise have one and would, therefore, not be taking advantage of a tax allowance.*

Q. What can I do if I have covenanted the maximum single person's allowance, but then the allowance goes up the following year?

A. *You can insert wording like: 'I covenant such a sum as after tax shall amount to the equivalent of the single person's tax allowance' but every now and then some tax inspectors become awkward and may disallow this. Really, you are taking a risk. You would do better to make out an additional covenant for the extra amount. Alternatively, you could tear up the covenant and write out a new one inserting the higher figure.*

Q. Are there terrible consequences if I tear up a covenant or don't continue paying it for the full seven years?

A. *No. The child could, if it were so minded, sue you. But if you have stopped claiming tax relief, the inspector is not concerned that you have stopped handing over the money. And he will not ask you to repay the tax relief you have already received. However, there should be no pre-arranged decision to do this and you should ideally get the child's agreement in writing.*

Q. Why does it have to be for seven years anyway?

A. *This is what the law says. To be exact, the covenant must run for more than six years, so the seven year length is convenient. You can pay for longer if you wish. If you are giving money to a charity, the length of time need only be four years.*

Q. What would happen if I died before the seven years were up?

A. *If you use the suggested wording, the covenant automatically ceases. If you want the covenant to continue to be paid after your death, you could insert the words: 'and so as to bind my personal representatives and estate' instead of: 'during the remainder of the joint lives of myself'. But this will delay the winding up of your estate which will then be kept open until the covenant is completed.*

Q. I have only just learned about covenants and am making one out for my son who is just going to university. My daughter is already in her last year; can I make out a covenant to cover the years she has missed?

A. *No. Under no circumstances can a covenant be backdated.*

Q. My son is going abroad halfway through his degree course. How will the covenant be affected?

A. *You cannot stop paying while he is abroad and, using the same covenant, start again when he returns. If he earns any money while overseas, it could take his income above the single person's limit. It depends on the circumstances and where he is. You could always tear up the covenant and start a new one when he returns.*

Q. My daughter claims supplementary benefit during the long vacation. Will the income from a covenant affect her right to supplementary benefit?

A. *Yes, it can. But if you state on the covenant that the payments are only made during term time and preferably in monthly allowances, that should avoid the problem.*

Q. Can a husband and wife both covenant money to the same student, thus gaining twice the tax relief?

A. *No, it does not work that way. The tax relief is based on the student's personal allowance and regardless of how the parents split the payment, there is no advantage beyond that figure.*

Q. Can I transfer a covenant from my son to my daughter when she goes to university?

A. *No.*

Q. Can an 18-year-old use covenanted money to pay his own school fees?

A. *Yes. In fact, any money paid under covenant must be used solely for the benefit of the recipient.*

Q. My grandchildren live with their parents in West Germany. Can I covenant money to them there?

A. *You can if they are still subject to UK taxation. Otherwise you cannot.*

Q. I live in Jersey. Can I covenant money to my niece in Manchester?

A. *Only if you pay UK taxes.*

Q. My next-door-neighbour has two children the same age as mine. Is there anything to stop us covenanting money to each other's children?

A. *Yes. If the tax inspector suspects that you have agreed a* quid pro quo *arrangement with anyone else, whether friends, neighbours or relatives, he can declare the covenant invalid and refuse to give you tax relief. This is because, in these circumstances, you are attempting to evade paying tax.*

Q. If my mother were to covenant money to her grandchildren and I quietly reimbursed her, would I get away with this?

A. *You would for as long as the taxman did not find out. But if he did, you would have to repay the tax relief you have received and, if he turned nasty, he could fine you as well.*

Q. Where can I find a covenant form?

A. *You can use the wording shown on p. 169. Alternatively, the Inland Revenue produces its own form of Covenant, form IR47. This applies only to parents covenanting to student children and the Inland Revenue will not answer any detailed questions. For use in Scotland, form IR47 will have slightly different wording.*

Q. My husband is still studying. Can I covenant money to him for the extra tax gain?

A. *No. Married couples cannot covenant to each other.*

Q. My son receives a grant from the local authority to help him through university. Does this count as part of his income when working out what he earns?

A. *No. Grants and scholarships are not taxable and so do not count towards a student's total income for the year.*

Q. My son will be 18 in September. Can I covenant the full single person's allowance to him for the whole year?

A. *No. In the year that a child becomes 18, he starts paying tax separately from his parents on the day of his birthday. So, in that year, he can receive only a proportion of the single person's allowance, under covenant.*

Q. My daughter is only 17 but she is married. Could I covenant money to her now?

A. *Yes, but think first. Anyone under the age of 18 ceases to be a 'child' in the taxman's eyes if they marry. But your daughter and her husband presumably have some income to live on, so any money you covenant to her would be added to her husband's income and take them beyond the personal allowance limit.*

Q. Do I have to pay the money over once a year, or can I spread the payments throughout the year?

A. *You can hand the cash over how you like, though it should be done regularly. It could be done once a year, once a term, quarterly or monthly, but it should be paid in whatever way the covenant states.*

Q. My mother does not pay tax. Could she covenant a small amount of money to her grandchildren?

A. *No. The donor must be a taxpayer and the recipient must be a non-taxpayer, even after receiving the covenanted money.*

Q. Can anyone witness a covenant?

A. *Anyone except the beneficiary.*

Q. Must I really go to the bother of putting a red seal on the covenant form? I know someone who does not bother and has never had any problem.

A. *The Inland Revenue says you must and, while one inspector might turn a blind eye, another could invalidate the covenant if there is no red seal. Covenants can be refused simply because there was no red seal.*

Q. Where can I get these red seals?

A. *They are small red discs of paper which you can buy at most stationers. You can make your own, if you like, or use red wax.*

Q. I am covenanting as much as I can to my eldest son who is about to go to university. When his brother joins him in two years' time, I will be able to give the younger one more. So, to be fair, I shall want to increase the amount I give the first. Can I alter the figure on his covenant?

A. *No. Your best bet is to make out another one for the additional amount or tear it up and make out a new one when the time comes.*

Q. Which figure do I write on the deed of covenant and how much do I hand over?

A. *You insert the gross figure on the form, but you actually hand over the net amount, that is the gross sum less 30 per cent for tax.*

Q. I pay tax at the higher rate. Can I claim back higher rate tax?

A. *No. Only basic rate tax is allowed, whatever rate you yourself pay. The exception is if you are covenanting money to a charity, in which case you can claim higher tax relief.*

Q. Is the 30 per cent figure likely to change?

A. *Yes. The amount you get is whatever the basic rate of tax is at the time. So, if the Chancellor reduces this to 29 per cent, that is what the taxman will give you.*

Q. How will I know that my covenant is acceptable to the taxman?

A. *You will only find out if he has grounds for rejecting the covenant when the beneficiary comes to claim the tax relief.*

Q. My daughter needs the tax relief from the Inland Revenue urgently. How quickly can she get the money?

A. *There is no way of hurrying the taxman and sometimes it may take a while for the money to come through. Once the covenant is in operation it will not be paid until after the end of the tax year.*

Q. If I make out a covenant to my son at university, could this affect the grant he receives?

A. *No. But if he receives money under a covenant from anyone other than his parents, over a certain amount, it will.*

Q. I'm about to covenant money to my grandson. Can I appoint his parents as trustees, or should I nominate someone else?

A. *Certainly, you can name the parents. If, for any reason, you do not want his parents to be trustees, you can nominate anyone, perhaps a bank manager.*

Q. What does a trustee do?

A. *The trustee makes sure that the income from the covenant is used for the child's benefit. This can mean anything from spending it on school fees to investing it for the future. However, be careful that dividends from the investments do not take the child into a tax paying bracket.*

Q. I live in Scotland; is the procedure exactly the same here?

A. *No. If you make out the covenant in Scotland and have written it in your own handwriting, or written 'adopted as holograph' above your signature, then it is not necessary to have a witness. But if it is typed or printed, you will need two witnesses. This is the only difference. The tax laws are just the same.*

A covenant to be used by anyone other than a child's parents:

DEED OF COVENANT

I, ...

of ....

hereby covenant with .... ('the Beneficiary')

of ....

that for seven years from this date or during the remainder of our joint lives (whichever is the shortest period), I will pay the annual gross sum of £.................... out of the general fund of my taxed income. The annual sums are to be paid by equal instalments of £...

on ....

the first of such instalments to be paid on ....

Dated ....

Signed, sealed and delivered by ....

in the presence of:

....

....　　SEAL

....

A covenant to be used by anyone, other than parents, who wishes to name a trustee:

DEED OF COVENANT

I, ...

of ....

hereby covenant with .... ('the Trustee')

of ....

that for seven years from this date, or during the remainder of the joint lives of myself and .... ('the Beneficiary') (whichever is the shortest period), I will pay the Trustee the annual gross sum of £.................... out of the general fund of my taxed income. The Trustee shall hold all such annual sums upon trust for the absolute benefit of the Beneficiary with power to pay or apply them for the benefit of the Beneficiary as the Trustee thinks fit. The annual sums are to be paid by equal instalments of £.......... on .... the first of such instalments to be paid on ....

Dated ....

Signed, sealed and delivered by .... in the presence of:

....

....   SEAL

....

....

A covenant to be used by parents with student children:

DEED OF COVENANT

I, ...

of ....

hereby covenant with .... (the Beneficiary)

of ....

that for seven years from this date, or during the remainder of our joint
lives, or until .... ceases to be receiving full time education at any university, college, school or other educational establishment
(whichever is the shortest period), I will pay .... the annual
gross sum of £.................... out of the general fund of my taxed
income.

These payments are to be made on .... by equal instalments of £.................... the first of such payments to be made on

Dated ....

Signed, sealed and delivered by .... in the presence of:

....

....   SEAL

....

....

14/**Wills**

Printed forms / solicitors / making your own will / executors / witnesses / how can you leave your money? / what happens when you die / challenging a will / sample will / what happens if you die intestate / Scotland / trusts ● Letters

A solicitor will charge about £15 to £25 to draw up a will; if you die intestate, that is without having made a will, he will charge about £500 to sort out the mess. Even if you think you own nothing worth worrying about, your family might still squabble over your possessions after you die.

It is worth while for everyone to write out a will. By having a will you ensure that the people, or charities, that you want to receive your worldly goods will, and anyone you dislike who might otherwise be entitled to a share, is cut out. There are, however, a few circumstances in which a properly drawn-up will can be challenged.

You can, if you wish, write a will on any old scrap of paper. If it is correctly signed and witnessed, it will be perfectly legal. You must be confident, however, that your wording is completely clear. Of course, you know very well which is your 'favourite charity' and everyone else knows that you love cats. But this is not good enough to ensure that the money goes where you wanted. In these circumstances, lawyers can spend many expensive hours debating just what you had in mind.

Do not assume that once you have made out a will you can forget about it forever. Circumstances change and you should, if necessary, amend your will from time to time. You can do this by adding paragraphs, called codicils.

Printed forms
You can buy ready-printed will forms at many stationers or from

HMSO. They cost around £1.50 and include some guidance on making wills.

If your affairs are straightforward, you can save the cost of a solicitor by using a will form. Or, if you are confident that you can make your intentions completely clear, you can even save that cost and write out your own will.

Solicitors

If you have any doubts about what you want to say, use a solicitor. It is better to pay a few pounds now rather than run the risk of having much of your estate disappear into a larger bill later on when your beneficiaries start arguing over their inheritance.

A solicitor will charge about £15 to £25 to draw up a simple will, but you can telephone several to compare prices first. For advice on how to choose a solicitor see p. 244.

Making your own will

If you decide to do it yourself, these are the points to remember:
- keep it simple and absolutely clear:
  'I leave £500 to my children.' Does this mean £500 each or £500 between them?
- mention the people you wish to inherit by name:
  'I leave £500 to my sister-in-law.' Your brother might have divorced and remarried before you die and then both sisters-in-law could claim the £500.
- sign in front of two witnesses, who must not be beneficiaries.
- appoint two executors, who can be beneficiaries.
- date the will.
- say on the will that you are revoking all others. In any case, actually destroy any previous will when you make out a new one.
- keep it in a safe place: with your bank (which can charge), with a solicitor, or in a safe drawer and tell your executors where it is. The bank manager does not have to charge you, but it could cost you about £1.60 a quarter.

Executors

In your will, you must appoint executors who will be responsible for administering the estate when you die. You need, in fact, appoint only one executor, but people usually appoint two, or sometimes more, so that the work is not too great a burden for one person, and also as a precaution in case one of them dies before you. This also helps to ensure fair play and that there is no opportunity for bias.

Do check with the executors that they are prepared to take on the work before you commit them and remember, executors are fully entitled to inherit under the will.

You can ask a bank to act as executor. The banks gladly accept this work, but they charge steeply for it. The scale rises according to the value of the estate, regardless of how much work goes into it. The banks work to a fixed scale something like this: first £50,000, 5 per cent; next £50,000, 3 per cent; everything over £100,000, 2 per cent. There will be a minimum charge of about £500 but the bank manager can exercise a certain amount of discretion if the estate is extremely simple.

A £50,000 estate, which is not particularly wealthy these days if a house is involved, will cost around £2500 in bank fees. Neither do the banks have a reputation for being very efficient or speedy.

Solicitors will be cheaper than banks. You can appoint one as an executor in your will or your executors can decide after your death to go to a solicitor for help. A large firm of solicitors in the City of London will be very expensive, but a small firm in London, administering an estate worth £25,000 including no house, will charge between £500 and £750. In the provinces the cost will be less. The bill is assessed according to the value of the estate, the amount of time involved and the number of documents being handled.

Witnesses

Two witnesses must be present when you, and then each other, actually sign the will. It is not even enough for them simply to be in the house at the time. If they do not watch you sign it, then the will can be declared invalid. Unlike executors, neither witnesses nor their husbands or wives can benefit from a will.

How can you leave your money?

You can leave your money to whomever you wish, but you cannot tell them what to do with it. If your heirs wish to turn the money over to a cause of which you strongly disapprove, there is no way you can stop them.

But you do not have to leave your money outright. For example, you can bequeath just the interest being earned on a sum of money to one person for as long as they live. Then you can leave the capital sum itself to someone else after the death of the first person.

If any of your beneficiaries dies before you, unless it is your son or daughter, the bequest is cancelled and their share is divided between the others. If your son or daughter predeceases you, then that inheritance is passed on to their children.

You can, of course, bequeath individual items from your estate to specific people. These are called legacies. To avoid any misunderstandings it is worth listing the items, however many, and naming the recipients, with an alternative choice in case they die before you.

Whether you have made out your own will, or paid a solicitor to do it for you, make sure that several people know where you keep it. Then they can begin to administer your estate without delay.

What happens when you die

Before the money from your will can be shared out, your executors must obtain probate. This means that the will is valid. The executor adds together all the assets, values them and satisfies himself that he has missed nothing out. He then contacts the Probate Office in London. If the total falls below £2000 there is no need to ask for probate, though, of course, the process of winding up the estate will have to be followed by the executor. With a small estate, you simply contact those holding the deceased's money, whether it is in national savings, a building society, a bank, or an insurance company, and ask them to pass it on to you.

Certain charges are deducted from the final estate before the beneficiaries can receive the money. One of these, not surprisingly, is the solicitor's own fee; then the cost of the funeral and any bills that are left outstanding, such as gas and electricity bills, telephone, mortgage, etc.

If there is not enough money in the estate to meet these bills, then it is hard luck on the debtor. Your surviving family does not have to pick up the tab if your estate is insolvent.

Challenging a will

Usually, if a will has been properly drawn up, none of the beneficiaries or would-be beneficiaries, can challenge your wishes, however ridiculous or unfair others may find them.

But there are certain circumstances when a bona fide will can be challenged, and successfully.

One instance is when a dependant, usually a widow, is left insufficiently provided for. If a man dies and leaves all his money to his brothers and sisters and nothing, or very little, to his widow, then she has a right to more of the estate, providing she can prove she was dependent on her late husband. The court decides just how much. She can apply for legal aid to pay the cost of fighting, but she may find that if she wins a large sum of money she has to pay some of it back in legal fees.

The other instance when a legal will can be overturned is if anyone can show undue influence. It it can be proved that someone who benefited under the will used pressure to persuade the deceased to leave money to them, the right to the money can be rejected.

Writing out a will

Although you can make corrections to a will as long as they are initialled by you and witnessed, if you do make a mistake it is advisable to start again on a fresh sheet to avoid any possible queries later on. In the first place, draft the wording so you need copy it on the formal documents only. See next page for how to word a will.

A simple, straightforward will could be worded like this:

THIS IS THE WILL OF ....

I, Mary Elizabeth Jones, revoke all previous wills and codicils. I appoint to be my executors John Edward Jones of 1 Railway Cuttings, London NE6, and John Philip Brown of 2 Railway Cuttings, London NE6.

I leave everything to my husband, John Edward Jones. If he predeceases me, my estate is to be divided equally between, my sister, Susan Smith of 9 Green Park, London NE9 and, my brother, Peter Harold Smith of 46 Blue Street, London NE9.

Signed by Mary Elizabeth Jones ....
on the .... day of .... 19......

Witness's signature ....
Full name ....
Address ....

....

....
Occupation ....

Witness's signature ....
Full name ....
Address ....

....

....
Occupation ....

What happens if you die intestate

If you die without having made a will, there are strict guidelines about how your money is divided.

First, if you are married and have less than £40,000, everything goes to your husband or wife. It will not go to a divorced spouse. If you have more than £40,000, the spouse receives all the personal belongings and the first £40,000. Half the remainder is divided equally between the children (including adopted and illegitimate children) and the spouse receives the income on the remainder for the rest of his or her life. On the spouse's death, the capital is distributed equally among the children.

If there are no children, the spouse receives the personal belongings and the first £85,000 and the parents of the deceased share half the remainder. When there is no surviving spouse, or it is the estate of a single parent, the children share the estate equally. If the deceased was not married and had no children, the estate goes first to his or her parents; if they are no longer alive to brothers and sisters, or if they have died to their children; failing that to grandparents; and then to aunts and uncles.

If everyone who can benefit, whether or not a will was written, has already died, the estate then goes to the crown, that is, to public funds.

If a husband and wife die simultaneously, then the law assumes that the elder died first.

Scotland

The laws of testacy are different in Scotland. A surviving wife and children have an automatic right to part of the estate at least, regardless of what has been written in the will.

If there is no will, 'prior rights' apply which gives the widow or widower a large part of the estate, the house, contents and a large amount of cash. If there is a will, the widow or widower can either abide by the terms of the will or claim their legal rights. The spouse is legally entitled to one-third of the movable estate, the children to one-third and the remainder fulfils the terms of the will. If the spouse has claimed legal rights, he or she forfeits any further inheritance under the will.

In Scotland, if you have written the will in your own handwriting, it does not need to be witnessed. If it has been typed, you should have two witnesses; they do not need to see you sign it, or see the contents of the will, but they must hear you declare the signature to be yours. Alternatively, you could handwrite 'adopted as holograph' above your signature, which obviates the need for witnesses.

Also in Scotland, witnesses are able to benefit from a will, though the will could be challenged if the family thought a witness was inheriting unfairly.

If you made out a will while you were living in Scotland, but spent the next 30 years until you died living in England, the will is still valid. But it is advisable to write on the will that you want it administered under Scottish laws so that your executors are entirely clear about your intentions.

Trusts

When you are making your will, you could consider setting up a trust for the people who will benefit. This way you pass on the money before you die. You can avoid paying one level (that is one generation) of capital transfer tax by giving your money to your grandchildren, though you will need to have a lot of money to fall into the clutches of CTT at all.

If you think the children are too young to have control of the money, by setting up a trust, either you or another adult, can supervise what happens to the money. If a solicitor or accountant acts as a trustee, they will charge for their services. It will cost about £15 to £20 to set up an extremely simple trust, and the bill can run into thousands of pounds for a complex one.

A trust can be a fixed trust, where the named beneficiary automatically receives the money at a given age; or a discretionary trust, where the trustees can decide which of the named beneficiaries should benefit and what they should receive, either the income from the money, or the capital, or both. Normally the trustee will want to know how the beneficiary wishes to use the money (particularly the capital) when deciding how to allocate the funds.

LETTERS

Q. My wife and I are both in our mid-thirties and we have two children. The law seems very straightforward if one of us died, or even if we both died at the same time. Why should we bother to make out a will?

A. *One reason is that, if you both make out a will, then there is no possible chance of anything going wrong, and also it is far simpler (and when you are talking of lawyers that means cheaper) to execute a will than it is to sort out the affairs of someone who died intestate, however straightforward the inheritance.*

You may also wish to leave legacies, perhaps to your brothers and sisters, or nieces and nephews. Rather than just assuming that niece Susan will take the diamond brooch you always promised her, you can be quite sure that she will have it.

Q. I intend spending all my money before I die; that is the nearest I can get to taking it with me. If I leave nothing but debts, surely I do not need to have a will?

A. *You seem to be quite certain about the timing of your death. All our financial planning would be easier if we knew exactly when we were going to die. I hope you live as long as you think you will.*

15/**Tax**

To evade tax is an illegal offence: to avoid it is legitimate. There are no
options about tax; unless your income is very low indeed, you have to
pay.

Three main types of tax affect private individuals: income tax;
capital gains tax; and capital transfer tax. You pay income tax on money
you earn and income from investments; capital gains tax on any capital
profit you make when you dispose of an asset; and capital transfer tax
when you give away either money or property and when you die.

If you try to escape paying tax that you owe, the taxman can take you
to court. But you do not have to pay a penny more in tax than you
absolutely need and you should be aware of all your entitlements
because the taxman will not always award them to you automatically.

The Chancellor of the Exchequer announces how much tax you will
have to pay each year in his Budget every March or April, just before the
tax year starts on 6 April. Sometimes the Chancellor has an additional
'mini' Budget later in the year.

The tax year runs from 6 April to 5 April. This is the 'fiscal' year, or
year of assessment.

The amount of tax you pay varies depending on which income
bracket you fall into: the more you earn then the higher your rate of tax.
The Chancellor of the Exchequer can introduce whatever rates he feels
appropriate. At present, the basic rate of tax is 30 per cent and most
people pay tax at this level only.

But you do not pay tax on every penny you earn. Everyone is

entitled to various allowances and outgoings which are deducted before tax becomes payable.

INCOME TAX

Income tax is divided into separate schedules:

Schedule A: covers income from letting property

Schedule D: case I covers income from being self-employed

case III covers money from investments

cases IV and V cover income from overseas

case VI covers miscellaneous income

Schedule E: covers earned income and most pensions

Tax bands in tax year 1984-85

Taxable income	rate	Taxable income	rate
first £15,400	30%	£23,101 to £30,600	50%
£15,401 to £18,200	40%	£30,601 to £38,100	55%
£18,201 to £23,100	45%	over £38,100	60%

You pay tax on what is called your 'taxable income':

	£
Earned income	12,000
Investment income	6000
Less charges (eg maintenance payments and mortgage interest)	2000
Total income	16,000
Less allowances	2005
	13,995

So, your taxable income would be £13,995.

The calculation is broken down into:

● earned income
● unearned income
● charges (or outgoings) such as deeds of covenant
● allowances

Your income is split into earned income and unearned income (investment income). Your earned income is your salary or wages or, if you are self-employed, it is the profit from your business. If you receive a state pension, then that is also treated as earned income.

Your main source of unearned income will be dividends, bank and building society interest and maybe rental income if you let out a property.

One quirk of the tax system is that the amount on which you are taxed for a given year is not necessarily the amount that arose in that year. As far as your salary, or your wife's salary, is concerned, and also any investment income from the building society and dividends, then the amount taxable will be the amount that you received in the relevant year. It is called 'current year' basis taxation.

But for business profits and for investment income received gross such as National Savings Bank interest, you are taxed on the income received in the previous year of assessment. That is the 'preceding year' basis. Bank interest will be calculated this way until April 1985.

Your outgoings (or charges as they are known) consist of any actual payments out of income that you are contractually required to make. For most people, the main example will be mortgage interest but things like deeds of covenant and alimony, or maintenance payments provided they are made under a court order, also count as charges.

In the first instance, the charges are set against your investment income. Some charges, most notably deeds of covenant to individuals, are allowed only at the basic rate of tax. Others are allowed at your highest rate of tax.

Some payments you make net of tax and some you make gross. Under Mortgage Interest Relief at Source (MIRAS), your mortgage repayments are net of basic rate tax on the interest of a mortgage up to £30,000. All deeds of covenant are paid net.

In the end it is of no significance which way you pay because it all has to be accounted for to the taxman.

Giving to charity

If you give money to charity under covenant, you can claim tax relief at the highest rate you pay on the first £5000 you give, and at basic rate on larger donations.

Investment income

The investment income surcharge was abolished in the March 1984 Budget.

If a wife has a large element of investment income but little earned income, the couple cannot save tax by electing for separate taxation. Even if their earnings are taxed this way, a wife's investment income will always be included with her husband's earnings.

TAX ALLOWANCES

Allowances are the amounts you can subtract from your total income before working out the tax. Looking at it another way, your allowances represent the amount that you can earn before you have to pay any tax at all.

Allowances are not amounts of money which are handed over to you. At present (1984–85 tax year), these allowances are:

Single person's allowance

£2005. This is granted to everyone who is single, from the day you are born. Every child can earn the single person's allowance from either investments or working before paying tax.

If you are widowed, divorced or separated, both men and women will revert to claiming the single person's allowance. Also, if a husband and wife opt for the wife's earnings separate election, both will receive the single person's allowance.

Married personal allowance

£3155. A married couple will receive this allowance. The husband can also claim the allowance if they are separated but he is still wholly maintaining his wife.

In the year you get married, the wife continues to be treated as a single person and will receive the single person's allowance for the whole tax year.

The husband is also treated as a single person but he can increase his single personal allowance by one-twelfth of the difference between the single and married personal allowances for each complete or part tax month they are married.

So, if you marry in the middle of August, the husband will receive the single person's allowance plus eight-twelfths of the difference between the single and married personal allowances.

Wife's earned income allowance

£2005. In straight figures this is equal to the single person's allowance. But it can be offset against the wife's earned income only, and not her investment income. The normal single person's allowance can be set against total income, earned and investment.

Any investment income a wife receives (for example, from savings) is always, even if she has opted for wife's separate taxation, added to her husband's income for tax purposes.

Where you are entitled to a wife's earned income allowance, it is now given to the wife under the PAYE coding system which, effectively, puts her in the same position as a single person.

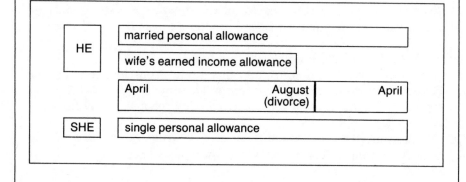

In the year that a couple are separated or get divorced, the husband is entitled to the full married personal allowance for the whole year and the couple are also entitled to the wife's earned income allowance in respect of her income before separation. In addition the wife is given the full single personal allowance against her income after the separation.

If you have been separated or divorced during the past six years, remember that you can claim that far back if you missed out on this full allowance then.

Additional personal allowance for children

£1150. Anyone with children who is not entitled to the married personal allowance, such as a single parent or a widow, can claim this instead. A 'child' must be either under the age of 16 at the beginning of the tax year or a full-time student.

The category includes legally adopted children and stepchildren. You can also claim for a child who is not your own but who you financially support, provided the child is under 18 at the beginning of the tax year.

You can claim this amount only once, however, regardless of how many children you have.

A divorcée can claim this allowance in the year of divorce if she has custody of the children. The figure of £1150 is the difference between the single and married personal allowances.

Age allowance

£2490 for a single person; **£3955** for a married couple. This is higher than the single and married allowances and is available to everyone, men and women, once they reach the age of 65.

A married man can claim the married age allowance when his wife reaches 65, even if he is younger. You can claim the allowance for the whole of the tax year in which you, or your wife, become 65, even if your birthday is only a few days before the end of the tax year in April.

However, there is a limit to the amount of age allowance you can receive if your earnings exceed a certain figure. In the tax year 1984–85, the point is £8100 whether you are single or married.

Once your total earnings, husband's and wife's together, exceed this figure, the age allowance is reduced by £2 for every £3 of income. So, if you are earning more than £8828 as a single person, or £9300 as a married couple, the allowance drops to the same level as a younger person.

When assessing your income, the taxman will include any building society interest you receive and, moreover, at the grossed-up level and not the amount after tax that the building society actually pays you.

Tax trap

People receiving the age allowance can very easily fall into an iniquitous tax trap. If your earnings are only a few pounds over the £8100 limit, you will be taxed at a very high rate on the money.

For instance, if your income is £8400:

	£	£
Earnings	8100	8400
Age allowance	3955	3755★
	4145	4645
Tax at 30%	£1243.50	£1393.50

★ *The age allowance reduced by £2 for every extra £3 of earnings over £8100; for the extra £300 of earnings you lose £200.*

So, you have paid an extra £150 in tax on just an extra £300 of income. In other words, you are paying tax at 50 per cent on the £300 even though your total income is well within the basic rate tax band.

Widow's bereavement allowance
From the date that a woman becomes widowed, she is entitled, for two years, to an additional allowance worth £1150, to offset against her income. The allowance is available in the year of death and the year following but no unused allowances can be carried over.

If you were widowed in the year before the allowance became payable over two years, you are entitled to claim the £1150 for the second year. So, if your husband died between 6 April 1981 and 5 April 1982, make sure you have received the second year's allowance.

Dependent relative allowance
£100 or **£145**. You can claim this if you are supporting a relative. The allowance is £100 a year if you are a man or married woman; or £145 if you are a single woman.

If you support a relative, then he or she must be infirm or over 65 to claim. However, you can claim for a relative under 65 and healthy if the person is a widow, or divorced or separated, and if she is your mother or mother-in-law.

The dependent relative must have no more income than the state pension and you must contribute at least £75 a year to his or her upkeep, otherwise the allowance is reduced to whatever you pay.

If the relative lives with you, you do not have to provide evidence of handing over £75 a year. If the relative's income is higher than the state pension, the allowance is reduced by £1 for each £1 of income a year more than the pension.

You can claim for each relative you have who qualifies. But if two or more of you support the same relative, the allowance is divided between you. If a man is maintaining his mother-in-law, and his wife is taxed separately, only she can claim the allowance for her mother; each can claim for their own relatives only. However, if they are each supporting a relative, a married woman on separate taxation can claim the £145 single woman's allowance.

Housekeeper

£100. This is for widows and widowers who have to employ someone to look after them. The housekeeper can be a relative but you cannot claim the allowance if she is your daughter who is married to a husband claiming the married man's allowance. Otherwise, it makes no difference to claiming the relief if the housekeeper is a man or a woman.

However, you cannot claim both the housekeeper's and the additional personal allowance for children. Obviously you should claim the additional personal allowance because it is higher.

Son's or daughter's services

£55. If a son or daughter lives with an elderly or infirm parent to look after the mother or father, the parent can claim £55 a year relief if he or she maintains the son or daughter.

However, a married man who is either over 65, or under 65 and infirm, but whose wife is under 65 and healthy, cannot claim this allowance until his wife becomes 65.

Again, you cannot claim this allowance at the same time as the housekeeper allowance and in this case it is better to claim the housekeeper allowance because it is higher.

Blind person's relief

£360. Anyone who is registered as blind can claim this allowance of £360. It is available to anyone who is single or if one partner in a marriage is registered as blind. If a married couple are both blind, they can claim twice the allowance, £720.

To register as blind, you do not have to be completely sightless. If your partial sight prevents you from working, you may be able to register.

As you cannot claim both the blind person's allowance and the son's or daughter's services allowances, you should, of course, claim the higher blind person's allowance.

HOW TO CLAIM TAX ALLOWANCES

If you are not receiving an allowance that you think you are entitled to, write to the tax inspector who looks after your affairs. If you do not know who this is, contact the tax office nearest to your home or place of work (the address is in the telephone directory). The tax office will then send you a form telling you how to claim.

Do not forget that you can claim back relief for up to six years. If you have missed receiving an allowance, you will get a tax rebate plus the interest owed to you at 8 per cent a year.

HOW TO FILL OUT A TAX RETURN

The first rule is: honesty.

If your tax affairs are simple, you will be asked to fill out a tax return, a P1, about every three years. If your finances are more complicated, you may have to do so every year on a form 11P or, if you are self-employed, form 11.

If you have received any additional income one year and the taxman has not sent you a form, you should ask for one. Conversely, if your income goes down, unless covered by a PAYE code, you should complete a new tax return to ensure you are not paying too much tax.

Tax returns, which are sent out during April, ask for information about the money you earned in the year just ended and the allowances you want to claim for the new tax year. The subject headings cover: income, outgoings, and capital gains for the past year and allowances for the coming year.

If you are a married couple the form is sent to the husband to fill in. Married women can ask to be assessed separately (see below). Anyone else who is single, widowed, divorced or separated should complete the 'self' column on the tax return.

If you receive the simple form, a P1, you need only sign the form and give the name and address of your employer. If not, you must write down all the money you have received in the previous tax year.

This includes your salary or wages, overtime, holiday pay, sick pay, bonuses, commission, fees, advances, tips, free gifts, share options, maternity pay, fringe benefits, leaving and compensation payments.

If you are employed and have no other earnings, the figure is the same as the one on form P60, supplied by your employer at the end of the tax year.

Also, your 'income' includes any money from pensions, letting property, untaxed interest, dividends, building society interest, money from settlements, estate, alimony and maintenance payments.

The next section concerns the outgoings on which you are allowed tax relief and include: interest on loans for home improvements and other qualifying loans, such as those used to buy an annuity or a share in a partnership.

Then add on money paid under covenants, maintenance payments and UK rent paid to anyone abroad where you act as a tax collector. The capital gains section must include details of all the gains both husband and wife have made in the year.

What is called your total income equals all your earned income plus investment income minus allowable deductions (charges or outgoings).

When filling in the tax form, you do not need to specify pennies for most entries. You round each sum down to the nearest pound. Only with dividends and tax credits should you be more precise.

You can claim for certain expenses which are incurred as part of your job. These include:

- protective and functional clothes
- tools and musical instruments which you have to provide
- books and stationery if they are essential to your job
- if you work from home, part of the cost of heating, lighting, etc
- interest on loans to buy equipment necessary for your work
- travelling costs but only those incurred in the course of your job and not the cost of getting to work
- sometimes the cost of a spouse accompanying you
- entertaining overseas customers
- hotel and meal expenses incurred while working
- union or professional association fees if a condition of your employment

Once you have filled in a tax return, and sent it back to your tax office, the Inspector of Taxes will give you a code number on a notice of coding. Your employer uses this coding to make the correct deduction from your pay each week or month.

The inspector adds together all your allowances and deducts taxable state benefits such as the state pension. He then crosses off the last figure in the number he is left with, adds a code letter, and this is your tax code for the year.

The code number indicates the allowances you receive; the code letter indicates your tax status, that is whether you are single, married, on emergency tax, etc.

For example:

Married man's age allowance	£3955
Less pension	£2834
Tax code	112V

QUERYING YOUR TAX BILL

If you do not agree with the taxman's assessment, you have 30 days in which to appeal. If, after writing and querying his workings, you still disagree, you can appeal to the general commissioners or the special commissioners. See p. 250 for addresses.

The general commissioners hear local appeals and are not usually tax experts themselves. But special commissioners are tax experts and they hear the more complicated cases.

If you are still unhappy with the findings, you can appeal to the High Court and then to the House of Lords. However, you cannot appeal to the High Court about a PAYE coding.

Although filling out a tax form is a chore, it is a duty and you should do it as quickly as possible. In practice, the taxman will allow you longer than the statutory 30 days to react before sending you a reminder. He may, however, decide to take his own action and put you straight onto emergency tax, which means he will take away all allowances of any kind. This invariably prompts a quick response from the taxpayer.

PAYMENT DATES

Tax is generally due to be paid on 1 January in the year of assessment. This includes investment income not taxed at source, Schedule A and Schedule B tax. Profits from being self-employed are due in two tranches on 1 January and 1 July. Capital gains tax and higher rate tax on investments should be paid by 1 December in the year of assessment.

If you are on PAYE, the tax is taken away from your salary before you receive it.

If you have missed claiming an allowance, you can claim as far back as six years. If, for whatever reason you have not paid tax you owe, the taxman can also claim back tax for up to six years but if he suspects you have deliberately evaded paying, there is effectively no limit to the time over which he can delve back.

On top of this he can fine, or sue, you. In any case, he will charge interest on what you owe (a sum which he decides) at 8 per cent for the period since the tax became due.

ACCOUNTANTS

You may decide that the whole business of filling out a tax return is too tedious and prefer to hand the whole job over to an accountant. You will have to pay for his services, of course, but you hope that an accountant can squeeze a bit more out of the taxman than you could yourself. However, this is not necessarily the case.

When looking for an accountant, one tip is to use a small- or medium-sized firm because large firms of accountants with more expensive overheads and higher-paid staff, will need to charge more to cover their costs.

The cost also depends on whether your affairs are handled by a partner, a senior manager or a junior.

How do you find an accountant if you have never used one before? The best method is word of mouth: ask your friends and colleagues if they can recommend someone. Otherwise, your bank manager or solicitor will be able to put you in touch with someone.

The local district branch of the Institute of Chartered Accountants will give you a list of accountants in your area.

HOW THE INLAND REVENUE TREATS WOMEN

In the eyes of the Inland Revenue, a woman loses all responsibility for her own tax affairs when she marries. In the first year of marriage, the rules do not apply. For that year only, a woman who continues working still gets the single person's allowance.

Her husband will receive the married man's allowance for a full year if they marry before 6 May (one month after the start of the tax year).

After that date, he is docked one-twelfth of the difference between the married man's allowance and the single person's allowance for every month before the marriage. See p. 182.

Once the new tax year starts, the wife is granted the wife's earned income allowance on her husband's tax return. This is the same figure as the single person's allowance but can be used only against earnings and not against investment income.

Her earned income in this case includes the state pension if she has made her own national insurance contributions.

But a wife can ask for her earnings to be taxed separately from her husband's if she wishes – and her husband agrees.

There are two different methods of separate taxation and it is important to understand which is which. One simply means the wife fills out her own tax return; the other way she has her own personal allowances but these are still included on her husband's return. It is possible to have both methods of separate taxation.

The first way will not affect the amount of tax either partner pays and is called separate assessment. The wife receives her own tax return to fill out independently of her husband but, when both forms arrive back with the taxman, he adds them together again to work out the bill.

The second option is called wife's separate election and is worth while only if a husband and wife have sufficiently high income. In this case, the wife is assessed as a completely separate person and the joint tax bill will be lower than it otherwise would. In the tax year 1984–85, a husband and wife's joint income needs to be at least £23,793 to make this worth while. The husband has to agree to the change because his own tax position will be affected.

A wife paying tax under wife's separate election will receive the single person's allowance; her husband will lose the married man's allowance and receive the single person's instead.

Unless the couple ask for separate assessment as well, the tax return will still be sent to the husband.

But note that the wife's investment income will still be treated as her husband's income; even under the wife's separate election.

The time during which you can apply for separate taxation and separate assessment is limited. You must ask for separate taxation no sooner than six months before the tax year starts and no later than 12 months after the end.

If you want to be assessed separately, you must decide no sooner than three months before the tax year starts or later than three months into the tax year. This short-time limit is imposed to allow the tax office time to sort out its paperwork.

Once you have asked for separate taxation or separate assessment (or both), it will continue until you decide to cancel it. You should remember this if your earning position changes.

DIVORCE

If you legally separate or get divorced you will revert to single person status for tax purposes. During the year of separation, the woman can claim a full year's single person's allowance; a man is entitled to the married man's allowance for the whole year plus the wife's earned income allowance against his wife's earnings until the date of separation. See p. 182.

If you separate but do not start divorce proceedings, the taxman will still treat you as a single person.

A divorced husband can claim tax relief on two mortgages as long as the total borrowed does not exceed £30,000. But the two homes must be the one he lives in and the one his ex-wife occupies.

MAINTENANCE PAYMENTS

Alimony or maintenance payments must be made under a court order or a legally binding agreement in order to claim tax relief. You will then receive tax relief at your top rate.

If the payments are made to a wife for the children, they are treated as the wife's income and are taxable as such. If the payments are made directly to the children, then each child in its own right, can claim the single person's tax allowance against the payments.

Small maintenance payments are handed over gross; if the recipient has enough income to pay tax then she will have to pay the tax. The donor gets tax relief either through a PAYE coding or by claiming a rebate.

To qualify as 'small maintenance payments' the limits are £33 a week or £143 a month; if the order was made or altered before August 1982 for a child the limits are £18 and £78.

If the payments are for more than this, the husband will deduct 30 per cent basic rate tax before making the maintenance payments. These payments are counted as an annual charge and can be deducted from total income, when filling out a tax return.

A husband who maintains his ex-family by voluntary payments can continue to claim the married man's allowance (unless they are divorced). But if the payments are enforceable, he is entitled only to the single person's allowance.

FRINGE BENEFITS

You may receive a fringe benefit or perk from your employer which is not part of your monetary salary. In some cases, this will be taxable; in others it will not.

First, there are ruled to be two types of employee: one who earns less than £8500 a year, including the value of the benefits and one earning more than £8500 or a director of a company. The first will be taxed more leniently than the second.

Cars
This benefit is taxable according to a fixed scale if you are a higher earner but tax free for others as long as you do make some business use of it.

Rent-free accommodation
You are taxed on the annual value, unless it is a condition of your job that you live there.

Clothing
The higher paid will be taxed on the full cost of smart clothes but others on the second-hand value only. Working clothes are tax free to both.

Other
Other fringe benefits with varying tax rules include: private health insurance; interest-free loans; share options; luncheon vouchers; subsidised staff canteen; cash vouchers; season ticket and credit cards; assets at employee's disposal.

CAPITAL GAINS TAX (CGT)
Capital gains tax is payable on any gain you make by disposing of an asset but with certain exceptions. You can make gains up to a certain level before tax is due and some items are tax exempt.

If you are a resident of the UK, or normally live here, you will be liable wherever in the world you make the sale. However, you can offset a capital loss against any gains before calculating the tax due.

Tax is due not just from selling an item but 'disposing' of anything. 'Disposing' means giving away, or even accidentally losing. If an item is destroyed by fire, for example, then it is still regarded as a disposal. Also, if you sell the right to an asset, such as by granting a lease, you can be liable to CGT.

Transfers between husband and wife, as long as they are living together at the time, do not count for tax purposes. But they will have to pay tax on any subsequent disposal.

This is how to work out your CGT liability: add up all the chargeable gains less allowable losses during the tax year. The first £5600 is tax free; any excess is taxed at 30 per cent.

In dealing with the losses you can bring forward any earlier losses and use them to offset the gains to the level of £5600, at which point you do not have to pay CGT. You can ignore the gains you make on chattels if you sell them for less than £3000 per item.

For assets you owned before 6 April 1965, you have a choice about which figure to use for assessing the capital gains tax due.

The most usual method is known as 'time apportionment'. Here you take the gross gain between buying and selling the item and assume that the increase arose evenly throughout the period. The gain is apportioned equally over the years both before and after 6 April 1965; the amount falling before that date is not taxable, but the amount falling afterwards is.

Alternatively you can choose to use the market value of the asset at 6 April 1965 instead of time apportionment. To do this you have to make a special election and, once you have done so, you cannot change your mind, even if you end up paying more tax.

Capital gains tax is now indexed for inflation. You calculate the gain by taking the original cost away from the proceeds and you also make an allowance for the effect of inflation on the original cost. The allowance is calculated by taking the percentage increase in the retail prices index from 12 months after the date of acquisition up to the month of disposal and applying this percentage to the original cost.

This is to ensure that the gain on which you are charged is a gain in real terms and not just a rise caused by inflation. You must have owned the item for at least one year to benefit from the index-linked relief.

Because the inflation allowance was introduced only in 1982, any assets that you acquired before April 1981 have their cost indexed from March 1982 only.

ITEMS FREE FROM CAPITAL GAINS TAX
- private motor cars
- gains from gifts to an individual up to £100 in a tax year
- goods sold for less than £3000 each
- your own home (but only one)
- national savings certificates
- gambling winnings
- gilts held for more than one year
- an asset with a limited life (not more than 50 years) such as a boat or a horse
- gifts to the National Trust or otherwise given to the nation
- compensation for damages
- foreign currency for your personal use
- gifts to charities

CAPITAL TRANSFER TAX (CTT)
You pay capital transfer tax (CTT) when you give something away as a gift or it is paid on the value of your estate when you die. CTT has replaced the old estate duty.

Capital transfer tax is payable on gifts you make beyond £64,000 both during your lifetime and when you die. Transfers made after March 1974 are accumulated throughout your lifetime and added to the amount you leave when you die.

There is now a ten-year limitation on accumulations. This means that any transfer you make is added to previous transfers within the last ten years. Transfers are deducted from the accumulation as soon as they reach the tenth anniversary.

The bands of tax are now index-linked and will increase in line with the retail prices index. Different tax rates apply to transfers made during your lifetime and those made on your death: you will pay twice the rate when you die.

When making a transfer, you can choose to pay the tax yourself or leave it to the recipient to pay out of the amount you have given. Either way, it is your responsibility to tell the taxman.

On death, the tax is payable on the net value of your estate, not forgetting the accumulated gifts within the previous ten years. Certain transfers are exempt (some of them similar to those during a lifetime) including donations to charity, the nation and political parties.

Then, to arrive at the net value of your estate, you can deduct funeral expenses, debts owed by you in the UK; and liabilities for income tax and capital gains tax.

There are various ways to reduce the bill.

For example:
- make gifts during your lifetime because the tax rate is far lower
- use the ten-year rule
- give away as much as possible under the tax-free rules
- miss one generation and pass your assets over to your grandchildren to avoid one layer of CTT

The death rates of CTT also apply to gifts made within three years of death.

On the first £21,000 above the £64,000 starting point, you will pay tax at 15 per cent during your lifetime or 30 per cent on death. At the top rate you will pay 30 per cent tax while you are alive, 60 per cent on death, on transfers over £285,000.

ITEMS FREE FROM CAPITAL TRANSFER TAX
- transfers between husband and wife
- total transfers in any one year of £3000, the unused portion of which can be carried forward for one year
- small sums up to £250 in addition to the £3000
- normal expenditure such as regular life insurance premiums
- gifts up to a certain amount on marriage
- gifts to charity
- gifts to the nation
- gifts to political parties

There are special concessions for business property and agricultural land and woodland and for an asset transferred twice in short succession because of death.

HOW TO REDUCE YOUR TAX LIABILITY

- buy your own home: there is tax relief on the mortgage interest repayments and your home is a tax-free investment
- take out a large pension if you are not in an occupational scheme; there is tax relief on pension contributions. See p. 206.
- arrange a deed of covenant: there is tax relief on the payments. See p. 164.
- capital transfer tax: a parent can give £5000 free of CTT when a son or daughter marries
- and each year you can give away £3000 plus £250 in small gifts free of CTT. But do not give away money unless you have sufficient to live on and your spouse will be well provided for
- do not spoil your way of life just to save tax
- remember that the law can (and will) change; do not make inflexible arrangements that mean you might be caught out in future
- tax planning involves spending capital sometimes, as well as saving income.

VAT

The tax you pay on your income is known as 'direct' tax. There is also 'indirect' taxation which is value added tax, commonly called VAT. You have to pay this on nearly everything you buy.

There are some VAT free or zero-rated items such as children's clothes, food, books and gas and electricity. The rate of VAT is 15 per cent and you pay it at the same time as you buy the goods.

Finally

If you are worried about tax problems and cannot afford, or do not want to see, an accountant, you can call into a PAYE enquiry office near your home and ask questions free of charge. The address is in the telephone directory under Inland Revenue.

The Inland Revenue has published a large number of leaflets on all aspects of tax which you can pick up at PAYE offices. Or you can call into a Citizen's Advice Bureau which can give you advice on simple problems.

TAX-SAVING TIPS

For everyone

- make sure you claim all the allowances you are entitled to. Basic rate taxpayers can save £30 in tax on every £100 of allowances they claim. Higher rate taxpayers can save even more.
- make sure you claim all the outgoings and allowance expenses you can.
- if you think you may have previously missed out on some of these allowances, write to the taxman. You can claim back for the last six

years to rectify a mistake. You may even receive interest on the money from the taxman.

- check your PAYE code.
- apply for any new relief immediately. Inform the taxman as soon as your circumstances change so you will receive any rebate as quickly as possible.
- you do not need to include genuine gifts of money in your tax return: the donor is responsible for declaring tax.

Married couples

- a wife can earn an amount equal to the married woman's allowance before she pays tax. If her husband is self-employed, she can earn up to that amount by working for him without paying tax. Or she can earn the same amount from another source.
- if the husband has no income, the wife can claim the married man's allowance.
- similarly if a husband and wife could both command a similar salary by working but one has to stay at home to look after children, it pays for the woman to work. She can offset both the wife's earned income allowance and the married man's allowance against her earnings. But a man cannot claim the wife's allowance.
- a wife earning a reasonable salary should opt for the wife's earnings separate election.
- but consider divorce if the wife has a large element of investment income. Under no circumstances can this be assessed separately from her husband's money.
- divorce is also a way of receiving greater tax relief on mortgage interest payments. Two single people can each claim the £30,000 maximum but a married couple are limited to that sum between them (except in the year of marriage when they can claim relief on payments for one unsold home).
- in the year a woman is divorced she can claim the single person's allowance in full in her own right, regardless of when she and her husband part. The same applies to widows.
- no tax relief is available to anyone making voluntary maintenance payments. You can claim only if the payments are enforceable.
- if you receive any money net of tax but pay little or no tax yourself, claim a rebate from the taxman.
- children are entitled to the full single person's allowance. Save tax by making maintenance payments direct to each child.

Savings

- if you pay tax at a higher rate, look for tax-free savings such as national savings certificates.
- alternatively, go for an investment that gives a capital gain rather than income (you can make £5600 gains a year before tax).

● if you do not pay tax but your interest or dividends are taxed before you receive them, make sure you claim the money due to you. But, remember you cannot reclaim the tax on building society interest or, from April 1985, bank interest.

Gifts
● gifts made to charities are free of capital transfer tax.
● gifts between husband and wife do not usually attract capital gains tax or capital transfer tax.
● tax on capital transfers is far higher when you die than during your lifetime. If you can afford it, reduce your assets at least three years before you die.
● for the elderly, buying an annuity will provide an income and, at the same time, reduce the value of the estate.

At work
● could you become self-employed? If so, you could claim far more expenses and settle your tax bill later.
● pay in lieu of notice, as long as it is not stated in a service agreement, is tax free up to £25,000 and beneficially taxed to £75,000.
● consider taking a fringe benefit as part of a wage rise. Many are tax free, or at least taxed favourably.
● if you travel abroad on business, try to go for at least 30 days in a tax year. In 1984–85, 12·5 per cent of what you earn while overseas could be tax free but from 1985–86 this relief will be withdrawn.
● tell the taxman in the year before you retire that you are about to start drawing your old age pension. This will save paying too much tax and having to reclaim it later.

These reliefs are deducted from your income before assessing the amount of tax you pay 1984–85

	£
Personal allowance: married man	3155
single person	2005
Wife's earnings allowance	2005
Dependent relatives' allowance	100 (or 145)
Housekeeper	100
Additional personal allowance for children	1150
Services of son or daughter	55
Blind person's allowance	360
Widow's bereavement allowance	1150
Age allowance: married man	3955
single person	2490
Age allowance limit	8100

You do not have to pay any tax on the following:
- gambling winnings, such as football pool or racing winnings
- premium bond and lottery prizes
- interest on national savings certificates; SAYE contract bonuses
- wedding or other presents from an employer as long as they are genuine presents and have nothing to do with your work
- retirement or redundancy pay-offs up to £25,000
- scholarships or educational grants
- war widows' pension
- the following social security benefits:
  supplementary benefit
  sickness benefit (not statutory sick pay)
  maternity grant and maternity allowance but not maternity pay
  death grant
  attendance allowance
  child benefit
  family income supplement
  mobility allowance
- housing grants from local authorities
- disability pensions
- allowances paid for extra service in the armed forces
- the first £70 of interest from a national savings ordinary investment account
- allowances paid under a job release scheme
- additional pensions paid to holders of gallantry awards

The old age pension is, however, taxable.

You can claim tax relief on the following:
- loan to buy or improve your home up to £30,000
- loan to buy an annuity if you are over 65 and the loan is secured on your main residence
- money given under covenant (see p. 164)
- maintenance payments under a court order

PAYE CODE LETTERS
L	single person's allowance or wife's earned income allowance
H	married man's allowance
P	single person's age allowance
V	married man's age allowance
T	your employer will not know how much tax allowance you are entitled to
F	taxed at a higher rate
D	higher rate tax
BR	tax collected at basic rate on part-time or casual jobs

LETTER

Q. Please can you tell me what is meant by my 'marginal' rate of tax?

A. *This is the highest rate of tax you pay. The basic rate is 30 per cent, but if you have a larger income and pay, for instance, tax at 45 per cent, then that is your marginal rate. If you are on the borderline between two rates of tax, you are on a tax 'threshold'.*

16/Pensions

Pensions / tax • The state pension • *how the state pension is made up / the basic pension / the earnings-related pension / widows / what it costs you / how to claim / when to retire / retiring early / supplementary benefit / graduated pension* • Private pensions • Company pension schemes • *what it costs you / tax* • How the pension is calculated • *final salary scheme / average earnings scheme / flat-rate scheme / money purchase / death benefits / scheme benefits / inflation-proofing / when you retire / taking cash / widows / extra payments* • When you leave a job • *how you lose by changing jobs / your rights* • Self-employed • *loanbacks* • What you should know about your pension • Glossary of pension terms

Today's pensioners are paid out of today's national insurance contributions. This puts a question mark over how good or bad tomorrow's pensions can afford to be. Private pension schemes, as well as paying today's pensioners, are putting money aside in investments so they know that they should have enough money in the fund to pay everyone.

The Government is in the process of improving the position of the early leaver. They are the people who leave jobs before reaching retirement age. Traditionally, they have had a bad deal on their pension but this has now reached such a large proportion of all workers that the Government has decided that all these frozen pensions will have to be revalued by up to 5 per cent each year.

As pension law now stands, both your basic and earnings-related pensions are price-protected. Every summer, the Social Services Secretary announces the increase to take effect from the following November. The rise will be the rate of increase in the retail prices index for the 12 months up to May.

If you are self-employed and have already made pension arrangements, then whoever set it up for you will understand your situation. If you are self-employed but have not yet organised a pension for yourself, start planning straightaway. You will need the help of a specialist pension adviser, whose name you can find in the *Yellow Pages* under 'life assurance and pension scheme consultants'. Or you can contact insurance companies direct and ask for information.

Pensions

First, there is the state pension which everyone is entitled to receive in some degree or another, if they have worked and paid national insurance contributions.

Second, there are occupational pension schemes which are set up by employers. If you have had a number of different jobs, then you will most probably receive a small pension from several sources when you retire. It is crucial that you remember each of these, particularly if you have moved house, because a previous employer may not be able to find you when the pension becomes due. Your family should remember too, because there is usually some kind of payment if you die before retirement.

Employers often go to a great deal of trouble tracking down potential pensioners who left the company years before. But if the letters come back marked, 'Gone away, address unknown' and the DHSS cannot help trace you, there is little more they can do.

If you have been self-employed, you may have taken out a private pension along the way. New schemes regularly come on to the market which make the choice today quite complicated but you will be able to find a deal that suits your individual circumstances.

Tax

Unkindly, all pensions, including the state pension, are taxable. If you receive no more than the flat-rate pension, you will pay no tax because your income will be no higher than the personal allowance. But you will pay tax on any income you receive above that. The company responsible for paying your occupational pension will have to make sure you pay all your income tax through the code number allocated to you. Since state pensions are payable gross and the DHSS has no way of deducting tax, your occupational pension will appear to bear an extortionate amount of tax because the tax due on your state pension will be taken off your occupational pension. If you have no occupational pension you will deal with the taxman direct.

THE STATE PENSION

Nearly everyone will receive this. If you paid enough contributions while you were working you will receive the full basic state pension. If you have not paid enough, you will get a scaled-down amount.

Women are entitled to receive the state pension when they reach 60 and men at 65. However, you do not have to stop working at these ages and, if you delay drawing your pension, you will receive more when you finally give up work. But you cannot delay past 65 for a woman and 70 for a man.

How the state pension is made up:

The state pension comes in several segments:

1. Flat-rate basic pension
2. Earnings-related pension
3. Supplementary benefits
4. Graduated scheme

The basic pension

This is paid to both the employed and self-employed. The basic pension (November 1984) is £35.80 a week or £1861.60 a year for a single person and £57.30 a week (£2979.60) for a married couple when the wife has no state pension rights of her own. To receive this you must have made sufficient national insurance contributions during your working life.

The minimum calculation is an average of 50 contributions a year between the ages of 16 and retirement. If you missed making contributions because you were ill at some stage, or were unemployed, or (in some circumstances) still in full-time education then you will have received a 'credit'. But if you have been working abroad, or if as a married woman you either did not work or paid the lower rate national insurance contribution, then you will receive nothing in your own right.

The earnings-related pension

The earnings-related scheme which operates today came into being in April 1978. It is known as the 'Castle' scheme after the Rt Hon Barbara Castle who introduced it. On top of the basic pension it allows you to receive an extra pension depending on how much you earned while you were working.

The formula is complicated partly because the scheme will not come into full operation until 1998.

Your extra pension will be 25 per cent of your 'upper tier earnings' if you were under 40 for women, or under 45 for men, in April 1978. This means everything you earn over £34 a week up to £250 a week. These are the lower and upper earnings limits for 1984–85 – the lower figure is always about the same as the basic state pension and the higher figure is always about seven times as much. The figures increase automatically each April.

For example, if you earn £234 a week, your upper tier earnings are £200 a week and your 25 per cent pension will bring you in an extra £50 a week when you reach state pension age. In fact, the DHSS computer will revalue your earnings in line with the way earnings levels generally increase and select the best 20 years of them before calculating your extra pension.

If you were over 40 (or 45) in 1978, your extra pension is scaled down according to the number of years you have left before reaching state pension age.

This part of the state pension does not apply to anyone who is self-employed. If you are, you should make your own arrangements if you want to receive any more than the basic state pension. If you are in a job where your employer runs an occupational pension for you, then he may have chosen to contract out of this part of the state pension. If so, you cannot by law be any worse off as a result.

If you have missed out on some of your contributions, you may be able to catch up later.

Women

Like men, if women are to claim a basic state pension in their own right, they need to have clocked up an average of 50 contributions for each year of their working life, between the ages of 16 and 60 and paid the full national insurance contributions.

It is highly unlikely that the older generation of married women, in particular, will have made so many contributions. It will not be a problem if they are still married and their husbands are five years older than they are, because then the husband would be entitled to draw his pension and the married couple's allowance just as his wife retires at 60. But if the gap is less than five years or he is younger, she will have to wait until he reaches 65 before she gets any money on his pension.

A married woman may have devoted her middle years to staying at home and bringing up a family. If she has a full record over the rest of her working life, she is entitled to spend time at home bringing up a family without losing her pension rights. But she will need to have been paying full national insurance contributions during the outside years. Married women who, in the past, chose to pay reduced rate national insurance contributions will not be earning any pension rights at all on their own behalf. Since 1978 only those who had already opted to pay lower contributions can continue to do so.

Even if she had been working, and paying full contributions she may not have been entitled to join an occupational pension scheme, because it is only recently that employers have been forced to give women doing the same jobs as men equal access to company pension schemes.

But even single women who have worked all their lives will almost certainly be worse off than men at retirement because women's average salaries are lower than men's.

Widows

Widows are entitled to a pension when their husbands die, within certain limitations. If a woman is widowed after she is 50 she will receive the full state widow's pension of £35.80 a week; if she is between 40 and 50 when her husband dies she will get a smaller pension unless she has dependent children in which case she will receive the full pension.

For the first six months after she is widowed she will receive the widow's allowance. This is higher than the state pension which she will receive when the widow's allowance stops after six months. See also p. 160.

If her late husband had not been contracted out of the earnings-related pension, then she will receive a little more. She will probably get further help if her husband belonged to an occupational pension scheme. See p. 209.

Ask your husband now who to get in touch with at his place of work should he die. If your husband dies and you do not know whether he belonged to a pension scheme, contact his employer anyway, to find out if you are entitled to anything. Do this even if your husband has already retired. There may also be some benefits from your husband's previous employers.

What it costs you

A percentage of your pay is deducted automatically by your employer for national insurance contributions. Your employer then chips in with a larger percentage in national insurance contributions on your behalf. The amounts are laid down by the Government.

At present employees pay 9 per cent of their gross income, as long as this is above the lower earnings limit. If you earn less than the lower earnings limit, you pay no national insurance contributions. You pay nothing on earnings over and above the upper earnings limit. Employers contribute 10·45 per cent.

How to claim

Four months before you reach retirement age, the DHSS will contact you with a claim form. If you are nearer to the date of your retirement and you still have not heard from them, get in touch with your local DHSS office quickly. Then you will be sure of receiving your pension as soon as it is due. You should do this even if you intend to carry on working.

When to retire

Men can retire at 65 and women at 60 and claim the state pension from that date. But you do not have to. You have two choices. You can draw the pension at that age and continue to work, or you can delay receiving it until you actually stop work.

You will not make any more national insurance contributions after 65 for men or 60 for women but you will get a larger pension when eventually you do start drawing it.

Once men reach the age of 70, and women 65, then there are no longer any penalties for working and they must take the state pension then or lose the money. There is no longer any advantage in delaying, even if you are still working.

Men between the ages of 65 and 70 and women between 60 and 65 whose earnings are over £70 a week (November 1984) will have their state pension cut back. This is known as the earnings rule and it works in two stages.

Stage 1 Your basic state pension is cut by an amount equal to half of you earnings between £70 and £74 a week.
Stage 2 Your basic state pension is cut £ for £ for earnings over £74 a week.

One further cutback that exists is if the wife is under 60 and earns more than £45, then the married women's addition to the state pension will be reduced. Certain expenses can be deducted from the weekly pay before looking at the £70, £74 and £45 limits.

So, it is worth holding back and waiting for the higher pension later.

Retiring early

Unless you are disabled, you cannot claim the state pension any earlier than 65 for men or 60 for women. And also, if you stop making national insurance contributions, your pension may be considerably smaller when you do come to draw it. It may be worth while continuing to pay the fixed-rate national insurance contribution to make sure you receive the full basic state pension. If you retire close to retirement age, then check with your local DHSS office to see whether you have already paid enough contributions to qualify you for the full rate of basic state pension.

Supplementary benefit

Anyone who has only the basic state pension to live on is entitled to supplementary benefit, even if you have £3000 in savings. In fact, if you are in this position it is worth while bringing your savings down to £3000 so that you can claim supplementary benefit. The DHSS allows you to make certain purchases to reduce your savings as long as they do not raise your standard of living. So, you would be allowed to trade in your old Ford Escort for a fairly new one but you could not replace it with a Rolls Royce.

Graduated Pensions

These were in existence from 1961 to 1975 and when you retire you will be entitled to a pension calculated on any contributions deducted during those years. At the very best, the sums involved are extremely small.

PRIVATE PENSIONS

Since the Castle pension scheme started in 1978, companies which run their own pensions for employees have had the option of 'contracting out' of the earnings-related part of the state pension.

If your scheme is not contracted out, then you will pay towards the earnings-related part and you will receive both elements of the state pension when you retire. You will also pay towards your company pension, unless the company meets the whole cost itself.

If your company has contracted out, you will not receive an earnings-related pension from the state. Instead, your company scheme must give you a pension which is at least as good. If you are contracted out, both you and your employer will pay less in national insurance contributions: the employer pays 4·15 per cent less and you pay 2·1 per cent less on your upper tier earnings. This rebate is adjusted every five years, with the next adjustment due in 1988.

To be contracted out your company scheme must fulfil certain minimum conditions:

- the pension must provide at least 1/80th of an employee's 'final earnings' for each year he is contracted out
- the pension must be at least the same as the state earnings-related pension and the scheme must always guarantee that it has the financial resources to do so
- employees must be able to start claiming the pension at the ages of 65 for men and 60 for women. If they continue working after those ages the pension must be increased by at least 7·5 per cent a year.
- if the employee leaves the job before retiring the part of the preserved pension which is equivalent to the state earnings-related pension must rise in line with the level of earnings generally over the years to retirement. Anyone who is not entitled to a preserved pension will be brought back into the state earnings-related pension
- whether an employee dies in service or after retirement, his widow must receive a pension
- women must have the same right to join a scheme as men if they do the same kind of job. This condition applies to all schemes, not just contracted out ones

When you first started working, you would have been very unusual if you had worried about your pension, or paid much attention to the terms of your employer's pension scheme. However, you should have done. Contrary to popular belief, the single most expensive investment you make in your lifetime is not your home, it is your pension.

The average person probably pays 5 per cent of a gross salary each month into a pension fund. If you started work at the age of 20 in 1950 and stayed on average earnings you will have paid a good £8000 by the time you retire in 1995.

Just what you get for this money depends on various factors. Twin brothers starting from the same point in 1950 can very easily find themselves with greatly different pensions when they retire, depending on what they do during their working lives. If you change jobs twice in your career, you will retire on half the pension of someone who stayed in the same job.

Pensions are a complicated subject to understand in detail but the basic principles are fairly straightforward and a knowledge of these can help you make the right moves, or at least avoid making the wrong ones. If you want to understand your own pension position better, ask for help: your employer or trade union will be able to give you the information.

COMPANY PENSION SCHEMES

Even if your company runs its own pension scheme, this does not automatically mean that you can join it. Many schemes insist that you work for the company for a minimum period (such as six months) before you are allowed to join, or that you are a certain age, say 21 or 25. Sometimes you will have a choice about whether you join at all but most are compulsory.

What it costs you

With some schemes you contribute nothing at all – your employer meets the whole bill. But a scheme where you pay nothing, though it sounds good, is not necessarily the best deal because you might find yourself receiving cut-price benefits.

The more usual system is for the employee to pay 5 per cent of his earnings and the employer to pay whatever balance is needed to fund the scheme, usually between 7 and 12 per cent of earnings.

The most you yourself are allowed to put into a pension scheme is 15 per cent of your gross salary. This limit is a real constraint only if you want to boost your pension by hefty extra voluntary contributions. (See p. 210.)

Tax

One great bonus of pension contributions is that you are allowed tax relief on the money you invest. Your own contributions are deducted by your employer from your gross salary before calculating the tax. And you do not, of course, have to pay tax on your employer's contributions. So, if you put £10 a week into a pension scheme it is really costing you only £7, and even less if you pay tax at a higher than standard rate.

Your employer qualifies for tax relief on his contributions. Moreover the interest which both contributions earn is free of income tax and capital gains tax.

The state pension pays today's pensioners from contributions made by today's workers. This is called an unfunded scheme or a pay-as-you-go scheme. Most private pension schemes work differently and are 'funded', that is, contributions are paid during an employee's working life and, together with the investment returns, are used to pay for the pension at retirement.

HOW THE PENSION IS CALCULATED
Final salary scheme

The amount of pension you will receive under a final salary scheme is based on how much you are earning when you retire, or in the few years just before. Most schemes covering more than 20 employees or so use this formula nowadays. It is sometimes called a 'final pay' scheme.

Make sure you know exactly what the term 'final pay' refers to in your pension scheme: it could be the last year you work before you retire, or it could be the average earnings over the last few years, which will probably be less. You might find that any commission you earn, or bonuses, are excluded when your pension is calculated.

Your pension will be expressed either as a percentage or a fraction of your final salary for each year of service. If it is a percentage, say 1¼ per cent, and you have worked for the company for 30 years before you retire, your pension will be 30 × 1¼ per cent which is 37½ per cent of your final salary. If you are quoted fractions, the fraction will usually be either 1/60th or 1/80th according to the terms of the scheme. Say it is 1/60th, and you worked for the same company for 30 years then you will receive 30/60ths of your final salary, or in other words a half.

Average earnings scheme

This kind of scheme quotes you a percentage or a fraction too, but it averages your earnings as you go along year by year, rather than waiting until the final years. You will be told each year how much you have earned towards your pension and, when you retire, you will receive each year's amount totalled together. Some such schemes copy the state earnings-related pension by revaluing the averages in line with some index, such as earnings or prices. There are very few average earnings schemes.

Flat-rate scheme

Here you will be quoted a flat rate and you simply multiply this number by the number of years you have worked for your firm, or more accurately the number of years which count as pensionable service. Assuming the flat amount is £10 and you have worked there for 30 years, you will receive a pension of £300 a year. Again, there are very few such schemes.

Money purchase

This works differently from the other schemes: instead of deciding how much pension will be paid at the end, a money purchase scheme decides how much the company and, often, how much you, contribute to the scheme (usually a certain percentage of salary) and you have to wait until the time comes to see how much pension this will provide. Money purchase schemes are popular with companies that have small numbers of employees.

Death benefits

Nearly all pension schemes provide death benefits of some kind. The typical scheme pays out a lump sum of two years' salary if you die before retirement age but some pay out the tax-approved maximum of four years' salary. It also pays a pension to your widow (sometimes, but not often, to your widower) of half the pension you would have received if you had lived to retirement on your current salary. Occasionally, there are special additions for dependent children.

The typical scheme also pays out a widow's pension if you die after retirement, usually equal to half the pension you were getting. With money purchase schemes, it is often left to you to decide how much personal pension and how much widow's or widower's pension you want to buy with the contributions invested for you.

Scheme benefits

The precise terms of pension schemes vary quite considerably. This is partly because the schemes are tailored to each company and also because some schemes have larger funds than others.

Whenever you change jobs ask closely about the new pension scheme. It may seem a totally unimportant facet of your salary (particularly when you are young) but really it is not. The money you will be paid when you retire is just as much part of your salary as the money you receive today. It is often difficult to see just how good a pension scheme is without showing the rule book to a pensions expert. Your trade union, if you belong to one, should be able to help.

However, here is a typical private sector scheme against which to measure your own. In this scheme, women are treated the same as men, except that they retire at 60, not 65, and are not covered for widowers' pensions.

- it promises a pension of 1/60th of your final salary for each year you work with the firm. Final salary is defined as the basic salaries of the best three consecutive years in the last ten years before retirement.
- it increases pensions after retirement at a guaranteed rate of 3 per cent. Occasionally, when the firm's profits have been allowed, discretionary supplements have been added.
- it allows you to take part of your pension as a tax-free lump sum.
- for death in service, it pays out a tax-free lump sum to your family of two years' salary plus a widow's pension of half your prospective pension.
- for death after retirement, it pays out a widow's pension of half your actual pension, or what your pension would have been if you had not taken part of it as cash.

Inflation-proofing

If you work in the public sector, the chances are that your pension will be increased each year in line with retail prices. There has been a great deal of debate about this highly valuable feature, largely because it is very rare in the private sector.

Otherwise, you may be lucky enough to be in a scheme which manages to increase your pension each year at, say, two-thirds of the inflation rate without guaranteeing to keep doing so. Or you may be in a scheme which promises you increases, usually at 3 or 5 per cent, which looked pretty sick when inflation was running high. Some schemes which make this pledge, however, try to do even better than they promise. A great many schemes, though, never pay increases at all.

When you retire
The usual retirement age is the same as the state scheme, 65 for men and 60 for women. Some schemes fix it earlier for men and a few at a later age for women. As long as your employer allows it, you can carry on working and if you delay drawing your pension it will be increased when you eventually stop work.

You may have the option of retiring early under your occupational scheme. If you do, the amount of money you receive will be less. The choice depends on what you want to do at the time. You may be able to take less money earlier, in which case you will be paid a smaller pension for longer years, or your pension may be calculated as if you had left the firm, and held until you reach retirement age. If ill health forces you to retire early, you may find your scheme pays you what you would have received by staying on until the normal retirement age.

Taking cash
When you retire you may have the option of taking a cash lump sum and then receiving a lower pension. The maximum lump sum you can take is 1·5 times your final pay. The advantage is that the money is tax free whereas, if you take the money in a pension, it is taxable.

But remember that you may not just be giving up part of your pension. You would also be forfeiting the future increases that might be given, though you would not normally lose any widow's pension.

If you do take cash, you could use the money to buy an annuity to increase your income later on. See p. 48.

Widows
Although women doing similar jobs to men have equal rights to join a pension scheme, the equality often ceases when she dies. If a man dies while still in employment, his widow will nearly always be entitled to a proportion, often a half, of his prospective pension. But if a woman dies, her husband is unlikely to receive any part of hers. Only the most far-sighted schemes pay out to widowers. Much the same happens when a woman pensioner dies before her husband.

The argument used as an excuse for this is that women retire earlier, and on average live longer, so they get more out of the scheme than men anyway.

Extra payments

If you will not have been with a pension scheme long enough to build up a full career's worth of pension rights before you retire, or if your pension scheme pays out low benefits, you may be able to put in extra payments to boost your pension. These are known as Additional Voluntary Contributions (AVCs).

You are not allowed to contribute more than 15 per cent of your gross salary to a pension scheme, and this includes the ordinary scheme contributions you may be making.

AVCs will boost your pension in a tax-efficient way: as with your basic contributions, you get the same tax relief on every pound you put in. Your employer is unlikely to match your additional voluntary contributions. Once you have agreed to make extra payments into your pension scheme you have to continue them for at least a minimum period.

WHEN YOU LEAVE A JOB

Unless you work within the public sector, changing jobs will have a marked effect on the pension rights you have built up in a final salary scheme. It always means that you will be worse off than if you had stayed in the same job until you retired.

As far as pensions are concerned, the whole question of people moving jobs (or early leavers as they are known) has become a subject of wide debate because pension schemes work unfairly against those who change jobs.

This is because the pension that will be kept for you until you reach retirement age is calculated on your salary when you leave. Until now, unless some special protection had been built in, the pension lost part of its value to rising prices.

However, the Government is legislating a new deal for early leavers. It will include abolishing the 26 year age qualification for a preserved pension; revaluing frozen preserved pensions at 5 per cent a year or the rate of inflation if lower (this will benefit only people changing jobs from a future date yet to be announced); giving the right to transfer to another pension scheme.

How you lose by changing jobs

This is how you lose out: if you work for the same employer for 40 years and retire when you are earning £10,000 and you are in a scheme giving 1/60th for each year of service, your pension will be 40/60ths of £10,000 or £6666. But, if you had worked somewhere else for 20 years and left there earning £5000 a year, then spent the next 20 years in a job finally earning £10,000 your pension will be 20/60ths of £5000 (£1666) plus 20/60ths of £10,000 (£3333) giving you £4999 a year pension instead of £6666.

Your rights

You may be entitled to a refund of your contributions when you leave a job. If you have fewer than five years ranking for pension rights, then you have the right to take the money out. This saves you having a number of extremely small pensions coming in when you retire. You can nearly always take out contributions you paid before April 1975.

But you can take out only the money you yourself have put in. You will not receive the contributions made by your employer. If you were contracted out you will have to be bought back into the earnings-related state scheme and part of the cost will be deducted from your refunded money. You will also have to pay tax at the rate of 10 per cent on any money refunded to you.

You may, however, be able to transfer your pension rights to your new employer. It does not necessarily follow that you will receive exactly the same rights from the new employer (they may be better or they may be worse). It depends on how the two companies' actuaries have based their calculations and on differences between the two schemes' benefit features.

Even so, you can transfer a pension only if both pension schemes' trustees agree. There are three ways that it can be transferred. Most probably your old employer will put a 'transfer value' on your pension rights. This is a formula which tells him how much they are worth in his scheme today. He passes on this transfer value to the new employer who in turn interprets it into the new pension scheme where it might buy less pension or more. So, you may have been entitled to a pension of £1000 in your old job. You might get more or less than this in the new one.

Another possibility is that your new employer will translate the transfer value into 'added years'. If you had worked in the old job for 15 years, the new employer may agree to credit you with ten years in his scheme. Remember, though, that these ten years will produce extra pension based on your final salary at retirement. Your new employer is not likely to credit you with more years than you had in the old job.

The last possibility applies only to the public sector. Usually, if you switch from one part of it to another, you receive full rights for the number of years you have worked. This is very expensive for the employer, that is, the taxpayer eventually.

SELF-EMPLOYED

Under the state scheme, the self-employed are entitled to the flat-rate pension only. Their national insurance contributions reflect this: they pay 6·3 per cent of their profits each year. So it is vitally important that the self-employed make their own pension arrangements while they are still working or they could find themselves in a very impecunious position when they do retire.

Like the employed, the self-employed are eligible for tax relief on any pension contributions they make. They can switch up to 17½ per cent of their earnings into a pension, and get full income tax relief on it. Anyone born before 1934 is allowed to pay an even larger percentage.

There are numerous schemes on offer for the self-employed and many insurance companies offer plans with all sort of combinations of benefits. You will need expert advice to choose one. In a self-employed scheme you will be able to invest differing amounts year by year. This allows you to adjust your outgoings according to how much money you make.

The types of benefit will be broadly similar to those from an occupational pension: you can delay the start of your pension and you can take part of the money as a tax-free lump sum if you wish. The big difference is that you choose how you divide your total investment at retirement between the lump sum, personal pension, widow's (or widower's) pension and regular post-retirement increases.

Loanbacks

One added advantage of having a personal pension plan is the opportunity to borrow money. You are not actually borrowing your own money back, though it may feel like it. But, because the insurance company knows you to be a good risk, with security, it may agree to make you a loan out of its vast coffers.

This is a painless way of borrowing money because you do not have to pay it back until the pension falls due. The insurance company normally takes what you owe away from your tax-free cash sum at retirement. Any remaining balance must be paid back separately.

And there you can see the obvious drawback: your pension is going to be very diluted by the time you receive it if you have been borrowing money on it along the way.

WHAT YOU SHOULD KNOW ABOUT YOUR PENSION

The Company Pensions Information Centre recommends the following questions as those which workers should ask about their pension schemes:

- who is eligible to join?
- if there are changes to a scheme, who is affected?
- how is the pension calculated at normal retirement?
- what length of service ranks for pension?
- what contributions, if any, are payable by the members?
- what benefits are payable on death before retirement?
- what benefits are payable on death after retirement?
- what provision is made for early retirement in ill health?
- what provision is made for early retirement not in ill health?
- what provision is made for late retirement?
- what provision is made for 'commuting' some or all of the pension for a cash sum?
- what provision is made to increase pensions in course of payment?

- what benefits are available to anyone leaving service?
- who can provide advice for individuals if it is needed?
- is the scheme contracted out?
- when does the scheme start?
- in the case of a change, when does the change take effect?
- what arrangements are made for collecting contributions from members?
- what tax relief is allowed on contributions?
- what provisions are made for approval by the Inland Revenue and what effect does this have?
- how are the various benefits taxed?
- what is the basis for calculating the employer's payment?
- what options are available to provide benefits for widows and/or dependants?
- what benefit is provided for a member who is disabled?
- what happens if a member is temporarily absent from work?
- what discretion, if any, arises over eligibility, calculation of benefits or the channels through which they are paid?
- are the benefits in any way modified to allow for state benefits?
- what is the position on discontinuance or partial discontinuance of the scheme?
- how is the pension money invested?
- how are the benefits paid for?
- how does one join?

GLOSSARY OF PENSION TERMS

Accrued pension   the amount you are entitled to when you retire for the years worked so far

Actuarial report   shows the financial state of your pension fund at a given date. It also recommends to the employer what contribution he should make. It is expensive to produce so is done every few years only

Actuary   the person who works out how much has to be paid in to meet the cost of the pensions that will eventually be paid out

Added years   when you move jobs, you sometimes gain additional benefits in the new scheme in terms of more years in exchange for transferring the value of your old pension scheme rights

Additional voluntary contributions (**AVCs**)   you may have an option to buy extra benefits by paying in more money as AVCs

Annuity   in this context, it means the same as your pension

Approved scheme   to qualify for tax relief, your scheme must be approved by the Inland Revenue

Average salary scheme   There are not many of these around. They assess your eventual pension on the average salary you have earned over the whole of the time you have been part of that particular scheme

Castle plan   The state earnings-related pension now in operation which was introduced by the Rt Hon Barbara Castle

Commutation or cash option. Your option to take a tax-free cash lump sum when you retire and a lower pension

Contracting out An employer who provides a pension at least as good as the state earnings-related pension can contract his pension scheme members out of that part of the state scheme if he chooses

Deferred pension The pension from a job you have left which will be paid to you at some date in the future; or the pension you will receive later because you have delayed retirement beyond the normal date.

Early retirement If you stop working before the normal retirement date you may be able to draw an occupational pension, but it will probably be less than you would receive by waiting

Final salary scheme the most common form of pension which bases the amount you receive on your salary in the last year, or few years, that you worked

Frozen pension the amount held for you, when you retire, from a job you have left some time before

Graduated pension this is what you receive from a scheme run by the state between 1961 and 1975. It is added to the rest of your state pension

Guaranteed minimum pension (GMP) if your employer is contracted out of the state scheme, he is required to provide at least a minimum amount of pension which is roughly the same as the earnings-related state pension

Insured scheme any scheme that has an insurance company looking after it and gives guarantees on investment

Late retirement if you retire after the normal age, your pension will build up and when you draw it you will receive a bigger pension than you would otherwise have done. Or you can take your pension and carry on working

Lower earnings limit Only people earning less than this figure do not have to pay national insurance contributions

Managed fund A fund managed by any outside institutions such as a bank or insurance company. This money is pooled with money from other pension funds and invested as the organiser decides, often in consultation with the pension scheme trustees

Money purchase This scheme dictates how much money is paid in rather than how much is paid out. You will not know how much pension you are going to receive until you retire

Occupational Pensions Board Supervises contracted out schemes

Paid-up pension A pension which is totally paid for in advance but will not be paid out until a future date

Pay as you go This is how the state pension works. Today's pensioners are paid out of the money today's contributors make

Pensionable earnings or pensionable salary The amount of your earnings used to calculate your pension; it may be different from your total earnings. For example, your bonuses, commission and overtime may be excluded

Pensionable service   You may not be eligible to join the company pension scheme until you have worked for the company for a number of years. Those early years may not then count towards your pension

Portable pension   One that you take with you whenever your change jobs and is not tied into an employer's scheme

Preservation   When you leave a job, if you have worked there for five years, any pension you have earned will be 'preserved' until you retire

Self administered scheme   A scheme which the employer runs himself without outside help

Superannuation   Pension

Transfer value   When you move jobs, if your new employer agrees to accept the pension rights you have built up already into his scheme, the amount handed over is called a transfer value

Trustees   Those responsible for looking after the pension fund

Upper earnings limit   You pay no further national insurance contributions on any earnings above this figure

Widow's pension   This is paid to the widow of a member. It is less common to have a widower's pension

17/A Car

Buying new • Buying second hand • Selling privately • How to pay
• *cash / hire purchase / bank loan* • Insurance • *minimum cover / third
party / third party, fire and theft / comprehensive / cost / no-claims
discount / cutting the cost* • Hiring a car • Pooling lifts • If you have
an accident • Costs of running a car • Letters

A new car loses 20 to 30 per cent of its value in the first year; by the end
of year three its value will have halved; to keep a 1500cc car on the road
costs 30p a mile. But despite the expense more people are buying cars
every year.

Your first decision is whether to buy a new or a second-hand car, and
the deciding factor will be how much you can afford. For the same
amount of money you can choose a smaller, brand new car or a larger,
faster, second-hand one.

BUYING NEW

It is easy to compare prices of new cars: the car you are buying should be
in immaculate order, though it may not be in practice. But, if it is not,
then you are covered by the manufacturer's guarantee.

Certain extras like a radio, or carpet, may be included in the basic
price or they may cost extra; if a garage is running a special promotion,
it might pay a year's road fund licence for you, or fill up the car with
petrol. These are incidental perks which are simply meant to catch your
attention.

You will probably have to pay extra for seat belts, which are
compulsory, a delivery charge and number plates.

The disadvantage of buying new cars is that they drop so much in
value in the first year. And if there are any inherent faults in the car, you
will have the hassle of getting them put right as well as being without the
car while the garage works on it.

BUYING SECOND HAND

This is an extremely tricky exercise. If you do not know much about cars yourself, make sure you have the advice of a friend who does.

Better still, if you are a member of the AA or RAC, you can ask them to check over a second-hand car for you. A vehicle inspection for ordinary family cars costs £32 and for this they give your car a two-hour inspection including road test.

If the inspector finds any faults, the seller is under no obligation to put them right but you are in a stronger bargaining position to ask. However, if you go ahead and buy the car knowing that there are faults, you have no case for complaining later.

The test will be carried out at a garage or, if it is a private deal, at the owner's house. The tests are recommended even if the car is less than a year old so that you can pick up any likely faults before the manufacturer's warranty runs out.

Again, if the car has been involved in an accident, it is worth while having a test carried out in the hope of showing up problems which otherwise might not become apparent for some time.

But be careful if you are buying privately. There will be very little you can do if anything goes wrong with the deal, whereas if you buy from a garage or dealer you are covered by a range of consumer protection laws. See p. 236.

SELLING PRIVATELY

You will almost certainly be able to obtain a higher price if you sell your old car privately rather than trading it in at the garage. The drawback is the time and expense of advertising, seeing prospective buyers, and receiving the money safely.

Make sure you have the cash before handing over your car or, if payment is by cheque, make sure the cheque is cleared.

Then, if you cannot manage without a car for a day or two, there is the problem of co-ordinating the selling and buying dates.

HOW TO PAY

You have several choices when it comes to finding the money for a car, some more advantageous than others.

Cash

If you offer a garage cash, you will very likely be able to negotiate a discount. This will depend on how well car sales are going at the time and how anxious the garage is to shift its stock.

You may have an old car to sell, in which case you can either negotiate a part exchange or sell privately. The part-exchange deal you agree will depend on how keenly you fight for what you consider to be the car's value and how anxious the garage is to sell.

Prices offered by the trade for second-hand cars are based on *Glass's*

Guide which lists all cars in all stages of decrepitude. You will be lucky if you can look at a copy yourself because garages obviously do not want to show their hand in negotiations.

But you can get an idea of current second-hand car prices by looking at car magazines.

Hire purchase

If you do not have enough cash to buy a car, or simply do not want to pay in cash, the garage will be more than happy to arrange hire purchase for you.

It works out as an expensive way of borrowing money but the only thing you have to do towards arranging it is to sign your name. The garage will have an arrangement with a particular HP company and will do all the paperwork for you.

Garages are not just providing an efficient service; they receive commission from the HP company for every contract they sign up. When the garage is quoting the rate of interest, make sure you know what the Annual Percentage Rate (APR) is, see p. 52.

There is now no legal requirement to put down a deposit but, in practice, garages will ask for one, just to make sure you are serious about going ahead.

You can repay the loan over any agreed period but the usual time is two or three years. To be covered by consumer credit law, the amount of credit must be no more than £7500 and rising to £15,000 in May 1985.

You do not have to agree to use the HP company suggested by the garage. Telephone several to see if anyone else is offering a better deal and make sure you know how much is being charged for arranging the loan. Also, ask how much it will cost if you repay the loan earlier than stated in the agreement: it can become surprisingly expensive.

But always work out the figures for yourself. Do not take anyone's word that he is giving you a bargain, either by offering more for the trade-in of your old car, charging you less for a new one, or providing you with 'free' credit.

The important sum is the total cost to you of buying that car, allowing for all the incidentals.

Bank loan

A cheaper way to borrow to buy a car can be to ask your bank for a loan. The principle for evaluating the cost is just the same as with HP: ask what is the APR. This figure will be lower than the HP company charges.

It is worth putting a little spade work in before you see the bank manager, deciding exactly what you want, and how you are going to repay it.

As with HP you will repay the loan in equal monthly instalments.

INSURANCE

A minimum amount of cover is required by law but you can opt for some additional cover which is more costly.

So, is it worth paying out for extra insurance cover over and above the minimum you need? In practice very few people opt for the minimum cover and, if they do, it is probably because their driving record is so bad that they cannot obtain any more.

There are four types of motor insurance to choose from:

- the minimum legal cover
- third party
- third party, fire and theft
- comprehensive

The insurance company is the 'first party', you are the 'second party' and 'third party' means anyone else. If you have an accident, and injure someone, he or she is the 'third party'.

Minimum cover

This does not include the cost of damage to your car if you have an accident. Neither will it pay the cost of repairing another car which you may hit, nor the replacement value of your car if it is stolen.

The cover is limited to accidents which happen on the public roads – not even those in your own driveway. All it does is to insure for the liability of the driver in case they injure or kill someone.

The amount of this liability is unlimited. However, these policies are very rarely issued.

Third party

If you have an accident, a third-party policy covers you for injury to others, including passengers, and damage to other cars or property.

Additionally, there is an indemnity to passengers in your car. So if they cause an accident, perhaps by opening the door carelessly, your policy will pay out to the injured person and for any damage.

Third party, fire and theft

This type of policy goes further and covers loss or damage to the car by fire, explosion, theft or attempted theft. The policy will also cover the theft of accessories fitted to the car.

Comprehensive

Comprehensive policies cover everything mentioned so far plus accidental damage to the car whoever is to blame, although they will not cover you for breakdown. There is limited cover for personal accident benefit.

With all these policies, legal defence costs are included.

Cost

How much you will have to pay in insurance premiums depends on a mix of factors:

- the type of car
- where you live
- your driving experience
- what you use the car for
- any accidents or claims you may previously have had

The money the insurance company collects in premiums is pooled to pay out when drivers make a claim. Very simply, the actuary gauges how much he will need by equating the number of accidents against the cost of repairs.

If you use your car in the course of work, the rating is higher. And if you want to use your car for motor rallies or competitions, you will have to pay an even larger premium.

No-claims discount

Insurance companies reduce their premiums to more experienced, safer drivers by allowing a no-claims discount, the amount of which depends on your number of claim-free years. In practice, very few drivers, except the young and totally inexperienced, or extremely bad drivers, have no discount at all.

The usual penalty for making a claim is to go back two steps on the discount scale. You then move back up the scale one step at a time each year when you renew your policy.

When you reach the top rung, usually a 60 per cent discount, for a small additional premium you can obtain a protected no-claims bonus which will allow you, for example, two claims every five years without the penalty of losing some of your discount.

Your comprehensive policy should allow you to claim whenever you break a windscreen without affecting your no-claims discount. Some companies allow you only one free windscreen claim a year.

Cutting the cost

To cut the cost of motor insurance you can limit the scope of the policy. Restricting driving to yourself is the first step, and here it is female drivers who earn the greatest discount. If you have just one driver and a spouse named on the policy, this will save about 10 per cent over a policy which allows anyone to drive the car.

But think carefully before asking for these discounts. Circumstances may arise when you need someone else to drive your car.

Then, if you agree to a voluntary excess, that is paying the first agreed amount of any claim yourself, you can reduce the premium by up to 25 per cent.

Some insurance companies give a special discount to the over 50s or the over 60s.

A standard private motor insurance policy might cost something like this a year:

Driver: aged 35 years; comprehensive cover; nil accident damage excess; driving a new Ford Escort 1300L (Group 3); with full no-claims discount; any driver

living in Cornwall	£104
living in Nottingham	£114
living in Watford	£137
living in Central London	£154

Driver: aged 55 years, comprehensive cover; with a £35 accidental damage excess; driving a new Ford Escort 1300L (Group 3); with full no-claims bonus;
His wife also drives the car; is aged 55; and has had a full licence for more than three years

	with no-claims discount protection	without no-claims discount protection
living in Cornwall	£70	£63
living in Nottingham	£76	£70
living in Watford	£92	£84
living in Central London	£103	£94

HIRING A CAR

Even if you own a car, you may need to hire one on occasions: you may need a larger car than you own, or yours may be in for repair.

If you do not use a car very often, it may be cheaper to hire one when you need one rather than buying a car which sits in the street or in the garage rusting away for most of the year.

Shop around to compare rates. Obviously you will pay more for larger and newer cars and you will pay twice as much if you hire one at an airport.

Rental companies will ask you to pay a deposit before you take the car away, unless you pay by credit card or charge card.

Outside Central London you will pay around £17 a day to hire a car, with unlimited mileage. You should add on insurance and VAT to this and you will have to pay about £35 in advance. The weekly rate will be about 20 per cent cheaper.

POOLING LIFTS

It used to be against the conditions of motor insurance policies to accept money for giving people lifts. This is no longer the case, as long as you do not make a profit out of it and the lift is for a social purpose.

So, if several of you want to share a car to get to work, you can each use your car in rotation and save money.

But you must take no more money than necessary to cover the price of petrol and the other costs of motoring, otherwise you will still invalidate your insurance policy.

IF YOU HAVE AN ACCIDENT

First, talk to any witnesses who may have seen the accident. Before they disappear, write down their names and addresses so they can back up your story later. If anyone has been injured you must exchange insurance details.

Then, take the name and address and car registration number of any other drivers involved in the accident. They are legally required to give you this information but, in case they give false names and addresses, make sure you have the licence number.

If the other car does not stop, try to take down his licence number and report him to the police immediately.

Next, make notes describing the scene of the accident, including the position of all other vehicles and the road conditions at the time, the weather, and the speed at which you were travelling.

Lastly, admit to nothing. It is difficult not to keep saying 'sorry, sorry' just after an accident but you really should not. In fact, your insurance contract forbids you to accept liability.

Call the police if anyone has been injured and, if necessary, an ambulance. If someone else was to blame for the accident, he will either have to pay out of his own pocket or through his insurance policy.

If you have to pay, you may find it less expensive to pay for the repairs yourself rather than claiming on your insurance policy and losing part, or all, of your no-claims discount. If you decide to claim, or even if you think you may, telephone or write to the insurance company and they will send you claim forms to complete. In any case you should inform them that you have had an accident, even if you do not claim.

Most insurance companies have knock-for-knock agreements to reduce the administration costs of dealing with motor claims. Under these agreements each insurance company pays for the damage to the car it insures without apportioning blame. This saves the time otherwise spent in establishing blame and it costs the insurance company less money. Therefore do not expect an insurance company to pursue a claim on your behalf very aggressively.

If you have an accident, the insurer may ask you to take the car to one of its approved garages to have it repaired, or they may ask you to supply them with two quotations before sanctioning payment.

If the repair work is going to be more expensive than replacing the car, then it will be written-off and you will receive what the insurance company decides was the value of your car at the time. If you had a new carpet or very low mileage, make sure you tell the insurer because your car will be worth more than the standard second-hand value.

COSTS OF RUNNING A CAR

The AA produces figures showing how the total running costs add up:

	Engine Capacity (cc)				
	Up to 1000	1001 to 1500	1501 to 2000	2001 to 3000	3001 to 4500
Standing Charges per annum (£)					
Car Licence	90.00	90.00	90.00	90.00	90.00
Insurance (i)	241.40	255.70	317.80	419.80	606.20
Depreciation	510.42	697.56	895.85	1575.00	2157.04
Interest on Capital (ii)	255.21	348.78	447.93	787.50	1078.52
Garage/Parking (iii)	156.00	156.00	156.00	156.00	156.00
Subscription to AA	35.00	35.00	35.00	35.00	35.00
	1288.03	1583.04	1942.58	3063.30	4122.76
Cost a mile (in pence)					
10,000	12.880	15.830	19.426	30.633	41.228
5000	25.760	31.660	38.852	61.266	82.456
15,000	8.587	10.553	12.951	20.422	27.485
20,000	6.440	7.915	9.713	15.316	20.614
Running Cost a mile (in pence)					
Petrol*	4.425	4.929	5.618	8.196	9.279
Oil	0.330	0.327	0.347	0.383	0.626
Tyres (iv)	0.458	0.573	0.705	1.295	1.692
Servicing	0.666	0.656	0.592	0.834	1.243
Repairs and Replacements	3.828	4.053	4.737	7.167	8.907
Total (pence)	9.707	10.538	11.999	17.875	21.747

*At £1.84 a gallon (40.5p a litre). For every penny more or less add or subtract

	0.024	0.027	0.031	0.045	0.050

Total cost a mile – based on 10,000 miles

Standing charges	12.880	15.830	19.426	30.633	41.228
Running costs	9.707	10.538	11.999	17.875	21.747
Total (pence)	22.587	26.368	31.425	48.508	62.975

(i) Insurance: average rates for Class 1 policies. No allowance is made for no-claims discount

(ii) Interest on capital: new car value if invested at 6·25 per cent a year; second-hand cars will be less

(iii) Garage/parking: at £3 a week

(iv) Tyres: estimated tyre life of 30,000 miles

LETTERS

Q. I am confused by petrol prices being quoted in litres instead of gallons. It looks far more expensive. How do the figures convert?

A. *One gallon is equal to 4·5 litres; one litre is equal to 1·76 pints (8 pints to the gallon). The prices compare like this:*

price a gallon	price a litre
175p	38.5p
180p	39.6p
190p	41.8p
200p	44.0p

Q. Can a garage sell a second-hand car in any old condition?

A. *If the garage belongs to a trade association, it must comply with a Code of Practice which says the car must be checked and a copy of the checklist given to the customer.*

Q. I cannot afford to be without my car for a single day. Does my insurance include the cost of hiring a car if mine is stolen or if I have an accident?

A. *Only if you are insured with General Accident. Otherwise it is unlikely that you will even be given the option. If you have an accident and the other person is held to blame, you can claim the cost of hiring a car against his third-party insurance.*

18/**Holidays**

Foreign money ● *cash / travellers cheques / Postcheques / eurocheques / credit cards / charge cards / how should you take your spending money on a foreign holiday?* ● Insurance ● Timeshare ● Duty-free allowances ● Letters

Brighton or Barbados; Blackpool or Biarritz. Once you have decided where, you will start wondering how? After agreeing where to go and how to book it, there are two more important issues to decide: do I need insurance and, what do I do about foreign money?

FOREIGN MONEY

You can take this in the form of cash, travellers cheques, Postcheques, eurocheques, credit cards. Each has its own advantages and disadvantages.

Cash

This is the most versatile and cheapest method but it is also the riskiest. You can take sterling abroad with you (you will need some change when you come home anyway); you can buy the foreign currency before you go; or you can pick it up while you are travelling, at the airport or on the boat although watch the rates here. Remember too that you will need some cash as soon as you set foot on foreign soil.

But whether to buy the bulk of it before you leave or when you arrive is debatable. For the amount of money you will be taking on holiday, really you may as well buy wherever is most convenient for you because any potential gain will be too small to worry about.

Similarly, there is no point in buying your currency six months before you go away in the hope of beating the foreign exchange rates and making a killing. You just might. But, unless you put the money in a foreign currency deposit account, you will probably lose more by forfeiting the interest you could otherwise have earned.

Maybe you prefer to wait until you arrive to buy your holiday money. When deciding, remember you might get a marginally better rate if you buy 'hard' currencies before you go and 'soft' ones when you arrive. 'Hard' currencies are those that are doing better than sterling, so once you are abroad, sterling will be less welcome and the rate not so good. 'Soft' currencies are weaker than the pound, so sterling, as a stronger currency, will be wanted abroad.

Carrying large sums of cash around is extremely risky. But if you take out holiday insurance, you can claim on the policy if your cash is lost or stolen. However, do check the small print before you sign, to make sure you are covered and to see what the limitations are: you may have to pay the first £5 or £10 of the loss and you may not be able to claim more than £200. In any case, you will have to wait until you arrive home to claim for the money. You will also need proof that you really did lose the money; a statement from the local police is best.

Travellers cheques
You can buy travellers cheques from banks, some building societies, the post office and large travel agents. They come in various demoninations, currencies and names. Each bank has its own; other well-known names are Thomas Cook, American Express, and Diners Club.

If you order travellers cheques in the currency of the country you are visiting, you may not have to pay anything to cash them but each bank in each country has its own scale of commission charges. Sterling travellers cheques will cost about 1 per cent to exchange but conversely you will suffer if you have any unused foreign currency travellers cheques to bring back. You can buy travellers cheques over the counter at bank branches with large foreign exchange departments. But usually you have to order them in advance, say ten days or two weeks. When you collect them you will be asked to sign each cheque in one corner before leaving the premises. Once this is done, the money is guaranteed and will be refunded if you lose the travellers cheques.

To cash travellers cheques, you date them, insert the name of the payee and countersign them in the presence of a cashier who checks your two signatures tally before handing over the money.

Sometimes you will be able to use travellers cheques to pay for goods in shops, as well as withdrawing cash from the bank. In the United States, you can receive change in dollars.

You can cash travellers cheques in various places: at banks, of course, where you will probably get the best rate; in large hotels where the exchange rate is not as good; and in some shops.

Postcheques
This is a facility offered by Giro systems throughout Europe. The main

advantage is the enormous number of outlets where you can cash Postcheques – including small post offices in out-of-the-way villages.

You need to have an account with Girobank first because it is essential to have a cheque guarantee card. Then, at least ten days before you are due to leave, ask Girobank to send a book of Postcheques printed with your name and account number. There are five Postcheques to each book and you can ask for as many books as you think you will need (and your account will stand).

Postcheques are accepted in 28 countries throughout Europe and the Mediterranean area. In the United States you can cash them at 200 public offices of Western Union. Each cheque has a maximum limit in the local currency of approximately £50 and you can cash up to two cheques a day. You pay no charge at the time but 50p will be debited from your Girobank account for each cheque cashed and the foreign currency is converted at the rate of exchange ruling roughly halfway between the time you write out the cheque and the day it is debited to your account.

Eurocheques

You can withdraw cash from your own bank account nearly anywhere in Europe. You now need a special eurocheque encashment card to do so and, if you bank with Midland Bank, Allied Irish Banks, Bank of Ireland, Clydesdale Bank or Northern Bank, you will also have to buy special eurocheques.

Under the straightforward system at National Westminster, Lloyds and Barclays, the banks will give you a free plastic card, similar to the familiar cheque guarantee card. This enables you to write out cheques in sterling with your usual cheque book. But this method can be used only to withdraw cash from a bank and the fee is around 0·5 per cent of the value with a minimum of 75p payable when you write out the cheque.

The system which Midland and some other banks have joined means that, with the special eurocheques you can pay for goods in stores as well as drawing cash, in the same way as you would with an American Express or Diners Club cheque.

The uniform eurocheque encashment card from Midland Bank costs £3.50 a year and the special eurocheques are 28p each plus 1¼ per cent of the amount you write out. You can use these cards in some cash machines on the continent.

Credit cards

You can use Access, Barclaycard, Trustcard or any other credit card to pay for goods abroad and to obtain cash. Just look for the familiar Mastercard and Visa logos displayed in shop and bank windows. If you buy goods, you will pay for them when you receive the monthly bill at home and at the exchange rate ruling when the bill is presented.

You can use Access and Barclaycard to withdraw up to £100 worth of foreign currency a day at banks showing the Mastercard or Visa signs. With Access you pay the usual interest rate starting immediately you take the money; with Visa you pay a straight 1·5 per cent handling charge and then interest is due as usual when the bill arrives at home a few weeks later.

Access and Barclaycard are accepted in most countries, but if you intend visiting an out-of-the-way spot, make enquiries before you leave.

Charge cards

You can use American Express or Diners Club charge cards almost anywhere in the world. These cards do not allow you credit; you have to pay the full bill when it arrives back home, probably six weeks after you have had the goods. The cards can be used to pay for goods and to get cash at their companies' offices.

If you lose your card, or it is stolen, you should report it as soon as you can to the company through the local office.

How should you take your spending money on a foreign holiday?

This table shows the relative advantages and disadvantages of the various options. The best method scores 1 down to the worst at 7.

	cost	convenience for cash and goods	security	outlets
cash	1	1	7	1
travellers cheques	4	4	1	5
Postcheques	3	6	2	2
eurocheques: *Midland*	6	3	3	3
other banks	2	7	4	7
credit cards	5	5	5	6
charge cards	7	2	6	4

INSURANCE

Should you take out insurance before going abroad on holiday? Yes, probably you should. The highest risk you will run is having to pay for medical treatment abroad and this can quickly grow to staggering amounts.

For example, if you need an X-ray and stitches in a deep cut by an American doctor, this alone could cost you £40 to £60.

The most useful advice, before taking out holiday insurance is to read the small print. **Make sure that you are covered for all the eventualities you want and that there are no exclusion clauses cutting out anything you might need or any activity you might take part in.**

If you are buying a package holiday, the brochure will almost certainly include an insurance application on the back page. It could be that the insurance is reasonably priced and comprehensive, but do not assume that it is. You should shop around.

If you have an all risks policy for your house contents, you may find that this covers your possessions while you are on holiday abroad and you may not need any extra insurance. It will be worth while putting a little effort into finding insurance that meets your needs for the least cost.

Particularly if you have been ill or consulted a doctor recently, you might find that the insurance company says this invalidates a claim. They call it an 'existing' condition and may not pay out if you were already ill before you went on holiday, even if you are claiming for a quite different problem.

It is a question of what the insurance companies call 'material' facts. The onus is on you to declare all information about yourself and your state of health that might affect the company's decision to insure you. Even if there is no specific question on the application form, it is your responsibility to tell them. This is unsatisfactory, but it is the way the companies are allowed to operate.

To find out more about holiday insurance, call into an insurance broker and ask for several quotations. Or contact an insurance company direct. The Association of British Travel Agents (ABTA) recommends its own comprehensive insurance policy following complaints a few years ago about the inadequate policies available.

You should expect to pay about £27 for two weeks' cover world-wide under a policy giving £100,000 worth of medical expenses, cancellation compensation, delay, lost baggage, money, personal liability, and personal accident. Two weeks' holiday insurance in Europe will cost about £12. You will have to pay at least twice as much if you are going on a high-risk holiday such as skiing, so be sure you have the appropriate cover. Some holiday insurance policies include a get-you-home air ambulance service. The insurance company arranges a tie up with an air ambulance organisation which provides emergency repatriation.

If your plans do not fit in with a 'package' insurance, ask for 'selective' travel insurance which allows you to insure for exactly what you want.

Before you leave, make sure you know how to claim, should you need to. If you are unlucky enough to have an accident, while you are lying unconscious is not the time to start wondering where the insurance policy is and how you set about making a claim.

Make sure, before you go on holiday to an EEC country, that you know what to do if you fall ill. Some EEC countries have reciprocal arrangements under which UK residents can receive free, or reduced cost, medical treatment. Pick up a leaflet SA30 from your local social security office. This is called: 'Medical costs abroad: what you need to know'.

Four weeks before you are going to an EEC country, complete a form E111 which comes complete with an explanatory leaflet. This will entitle you to medical treatment in EEC countries. You apply for form E111 by completing a form included in leaflet SA30. When E111 arrives, you will also receive SA36, telling you how to get medical treatment on holiday abroad.

Another useful leaflet is SA35 'Protect your health abroad'.

But even in EEC countries, private insurance cover is still recommended. You may be able to recoup only part of the cost of treatment. And worse, if you had an accident, there would be no time to look around for another doctor if the one treating you does not take part in the reciprocal arrangements.

Then, think of the extra hotel accommodation and travel expenses you might have to meet.

When motoring abroad, whichever country you visit will have its own insurance regulations and these will almost certainly demand a certain minimum level. All UK motor policies have some provision for the minimum requirements of EEC countries. But it is worth while taking out insurance beyond this minimum requirement, which you can do by extending your UK motor insurance policy. Only for driving in remote places will this not be possible.

When you ask for your UK insurance to be extended you will be issued with a Green Card. This is an internationally-recognised document indicating that you have the same level of cover abroad as you do in the UK. Without a green card you are covered only for the minimum insurance in the EEC.

In Spain the police can detain a driver and his car after an accident unless a deposit is paid. For an additional premium, you can take out a Bail Bond, which acts as surety if this happens to you.

If your car is stolen abroad, or damaged beyond repair, you may have to pay import duty in that country. This is because the duty is payable on any car that is not taken back out of the country within a certain period of time.

If you have a caravan, your existing policy may include travelling with it abroad. If not, get the policy extended and note the caravan separately on the green card. In the UK, caravan insurance can either be taken out as a separate policy or as an extension to a package household policy.

Similarly, a household policy can be extended to cover horse riding. But more usually this insurance is taken out separately. The premiums will differ depending on the type of riding – the more hazardous, the more expensive.

Most of the large insurance companies will underwrite insurance for pleasure boats. Small craft under 16 feet, including speedboats and racing dinghies, can either be included in a household policy or treated separately.

Boats over 16 feet, including yachts and motor boats, have a more complicated rating basis and need a separate quotation.

TIMESHARE

An increasingly popular form of holiday is timeshare. You buy the right to stay one or more weeks of the year in a property for the next 50 to 80 years, depending on the agreement. Overseas or in Scotland you buy in perpetuity.

So, instead of booking into a hotel, or renting a holiday home, you buy your accommodation for a few weeks every year for the next so many years.

The timeshare companies make expansive claims for the advantages but you should remember that this is a comparatively new idea in this country. The only overseer is the British Property Timeshare Association; address on p. 248.

The usual selling points given include:
- you are buying a good investment
- you are buying holidays for the next 80 years at today's prices
- you can swap your weeks with other timeshare holidays in other parts of the world
- you can rent out any unused weeks
- you can sell your timeshare weeks at any time you want
- you can live in more luxurious accommodation than you could afford at home
- you are inflation proofing your holidays

What the salesmen will not emphasise is:
- you are buying 'weeks'; you are not buying a property
- service charges will increase each year; and once the developer has sold all the weeks, this will be his only source of income
- you may not be able to swap with what you ideally want

- there is no guarantee that you can sell later on – you will have to find a buyer first and no one knows how much in demand timeshare weeks will be in a few years' time
- so there can be no guarantee that you will get any money back, let alone a higher price
- remember to add VAT to any prices you are quoted
- you still have to pay the fares to the holiday home
- you have to rely on the developer to maintain the standard of the property and once all the weeks have been sold he may not be so interested in the property
- other timesharers may not share your standards of cleanliness
- there is no control over timeshare developers
- the property should be completely closed for at least two weeks each year for maintenance and repair; make sure it is
- there will be legal fees to pay when you buy
- the developer might sell out after all the weeks have been sold
- timesharing may suit you and your family now, but will it when your children have left home?

DUTY-FREE ALLOWANCES

	goods bought in ordinary shops in EEC countries	goods bought outside the EEC, or in a duty-free shop in the EEC
TOBACCO		
cigarettes	300	200
cigarillos	150	100
cigars	75	50
tobacco	400g	250g
ALCOHOL		
over 22 per cent	1½ litres	1 litre
or fortified	3	2
or sparkling wine		
plus		
still table wine	4 litres	2 litres
PERFUME	75g	50g
TOILET WATER	375cc	250cc
OTHER GOODS	£163	£28

LETTERS

Q.   I seem to have an awful lot of insurance one way or another. I am not bothered about obtaining a few pounds' compensation if the plane is delayed, so is there really any need for me to take out holiday insurance?

A.   *The biggest cost you might face is medical expenses. But if you already have private medical insurance, you might find that your policy will cover you for the hospital's and doctor's bills while you are abroad. And if you have an all risks household policy, your possessions will be covered while you are on holiday.*

Q.   How can I be sure I am getting the best rate when I buy my holiday money?

A.   *Go to a bank. No one undercuts the banks' rates though some operations charge considerably more. Shop around to see exactly what rates the different banks are quoting if you wish, but steer well clear of the 24-hour* Bureau de Change *where you will most probably get a bad deal. And try to avoid changing money or travellers cheques in a hotel. You will almost certainly be given a worse rate than at a bank.*

19/The Law

Buying goods ● *sale goods* / *changing your mind* / *buying privately* / *buying at auction* / *buying second hand* / *disclaimers* / *pay a deposit* / *guarantees* / *doorstep salesmen* / *mail order* ● Buying services ● *estimates* / *quotations* / *disputing the bill* / *completing the work* / *descriptions* ● Buying food ● *food labelling* ● Buying on credit ● *door-to-door salesmen* / *faulty goods* / *paying off early* / *guaranteeing a loan for someone else* / *licences* / *credit cards* / *unsolicited goods* / *credit card responsibility* ● How to complain ● *small claims* / *where to go for legal advice* / *how to find a solicitor* / *law centres* ● Legal aid ● *legal advice and assistance or green form scheme* / *civil legal aid* / *criminal legal aid* / *£5 for half-an-hour scheme* ● Bankruptcy ● *discharge* ● Letters

If you buy a Japanese radio in a sale, can you take it back if it is faulty? Can you return an armchair if you find the colour does not match your curtains? If a pair of shoes falls apart, should you complain to the manufacturer or the retailer?

Your rights as a consumer are laid down by law but the interpretation of the law is sometimes unclear. The broad guidelines are designed to protect the consumer. However they are effective only if you use them.

BUYING GOODS

Every time you buy something, whether you pay by cash or by credit, whether it is something as small as a packet of sweets or as large as a car or a house, your rights are protected. The consumer is able to buy goods knowing that, if they are in any way faulty, or if you have been deceived about the quality, you can complain with the full back-up of the law.

Different laws cover different situations, but the whole basis of buying is that you make a contract with the shopkeeper. He displays goods for sale; you offer to buy them; you agree the price; you hand over the money; he hands over the goods. In the eyes of the law, both of you have made a contract and if either of you breaks the contract, the other has redress.

If you find that the pair of shoes you just bought fell apart the first time you wore them, go back to the shop. And if your cheque bounces, the shopkeeper will come back to you.

You both have to agree the terms of the deal before a contract is struck. So, if the shopkeeper displays a video recorder in his window with a £244 price tag, that does not automatically give you the right to buy at that price. When you go inside the shop, the shopkeeper may say that the price ticket is wrong and the real price is £422. You then have to decide whether or not you will buy at £422.

But if the trader had no intention of selling at the lower price and was deliberately trying to mislead you to tempt you into the shop, then he is breaching the Trade Descriptions Act which is a criminal offence.

Sale goods

You have exactly the same rights if you buy goods in a sale as you do at any other time. Unless the items are specifically labelled 'damaged', the retailer cannot refuse to give you your money back simply because you bought them at a reduced price.

Even if he displays a sign saying: 'sale goods cannot be exchanged' or 'no refund on sale goods', if you were allowed to believe that they were 100 per cent sound, you can take them back if they turn out to be faulty. But you cannot expect exactly the same quality of goods as if you had bought them at the full price.

Changing your mind

You cannot ask for your money back simply because you have changed your mind about an item. Some retailers will allow you to do this for the sake of goodwill, but you do not have any statutory rights. Only if you change your mind before you hand over the money does the shopkeeper have to accept your decision. Similarly, the shopkeeper cannot withdraw the goods once he has accepted your offer to buy.

If you are buying on credit or mail order, the timing is a little different (see below).

Buying privately

Here you do not have quite the same rights: the only responsibility of the seller is that the goods are 'as described' and correspond with any sample given. Beyond that the onus is on you to ask the questions which will establish the condition of the article.

Buying at auction

Here it really is up to you to make up your mind about the condition of what you are buying. You will have the opportunity to examine the items before the bidding starts and the catalogue will give some indication of condition. The initials A.F. mean 'as found' and are a warning that the goods are likely to be in a poor condition.

The contract on this occasion is made as the auctioneer's gavel hits the table and whoever has made the last bid (which will be the highest) has to buy.

Buying second hand

Unless you are buying privately, you are fully protected by the consumer laws. But they do take account of the fact that second-hand goods are not expected to have the same quality or length of life as new ones, and the older they are, the poorer in quality they will be.

There are a number of overlapping laws that protect the consumer. They cover the quality, condition and safety of the goods. If you buy on credit, you are further covered by the Consumer Credit Act, 1974.

The shopkeeper's side of the contract demands that he:
- sells goods that are suited to their normal purpose, even if you have bought them in a sale or second hand.
- sells goods that are capable of doing what he says they will.
- sells goods that conform to his description of them.

In the first place, if you are not satisfied with any items you have bought, you should take them back to the shop where you bought them. You should not at this stage send them to the manufacturer because your contract was with the retailer.

If the object is too heavy to carry, tell the shopkeeper and ask him to come and collect it. If you are right and the item is seriously faulty, the retailer's only obligation is to give you your money back. If the goods are slightly faulty or damaged you may be able to negotiate a partial repayment and keep the goods.

The trader can offer to repair the item, or to replace it. But if he offers you a credit note in exchange for faulty goods, do not accept it. You are entitled to the cash and you may not see anything in his shop that you wish to buy with a credit note.

There are some instances when you cannot claim your money back for faulty goods:
- if you knew the fault was there when you bought the item.
- if the salesman told you about the fault before you bought the goods.
- if you bought an item in the hope that it would suit your purpose even though the salesman had told you he did not know if it would or not.

If you are given a present that turns out to be faulty, then the person who bought the item for you must take it back to the shop. Even if this is embarrassing, you do not have the right to return it yourself as you are not the person who has a contract with the retailer.

Disclaimers

If a tradesman displays a notice in his shop saying 'no money refunded', you can ignore it. In fact this notice is illegal and you can report the shop to the Trading Standards Officer. A shopkeeper cannot escape his legal responsibilities this way and, despite any notices, you still have your usual consumer rights. For example, if the notice reads 'items left at owner's risk' in a dry cleaners, the trader can enforce it only if it is reasonable for him to do so.

Pay a deposit
There is no necessity to pay one, but it is a sign of your good intention to buy. You should expect to pay a deposit if you want to reserve a dress until you can afford it on payday, or if the shop is out of stock and ordering one in your size specially for you. If you pay a deposit, the trader is obliged to reserve the dress for you until the balance is paid.

If you change your mind later about buying, the trader could keep your deposit because you have already made a contract. He could even sue you for the balance of the purchase price.

A builder adding an extension to your house may ask for a deposit, or money in advance, to buy the materials he needs. You will have to make up your own mind about paying it.

Guarantees
Some manufacturers give a guarantee with the goods they sell. This cannot in any way take away your statutory rights, but it may increase them. A television manufacturer might guarantee all parts for five years. But if you need to claim, read the terms of the guarantee closely. You may be better off returning the television to the shop (which you should do in the first place anyway) rather than paying postage or labour charges to the manufacturer.

Doorstep salesmen
Always be extremely wary of anyone knocking at your door trying to sell. He will be hoping to catch you off your guard and talk you into buying something you otherwise would not.

If you are tempted, make a note of the price he is charging and his name and address, then ask him to come back later. That will give you time to check his price against those of other retailers. If you do buy, you cannot change your mind afterwards, unless you bought on credit.

Mail order
To be safe, buy from well-known names only, or at least make sure you keep a copy of the original advertisement promising the quality of the goods. The descriptions must conform to the same standards demanded of retailers.

BUYING SERVICES
When you are paying for services rather than buying goods, you are protected by different laws. These say that the trader must do the work properly, as you have agreed. In most cases it is obvious whether you are buying services or goods:

- you are buying a pound of potatoes; or you are paying a gardener to dig them up.
- you are buying a pair of shoes; or paying to have them mended.
- you are buying a new coat; or having it dry cleaned.

But there are some instances where it is not so clear cut, or that involve buying both services and materials, for example if you are having your car repaired.

If you walk into an art gallery and buy an oil painting, are you paying for services (the artist's talent) or for goods (the paint and canvas)? The answer is that you are buying goods, unless you have commissioned the painting, in which case you are paying for the artist's skill.

The difference is important because, if it comes to a dispute, you are covered by different laws. Services cover such things as: dry cleaning; shoe repairs; hairdressing; travel agents; repairs; car servicing; taxis; hotels; solicitors; accountants; estate agents; builders; banking; and insurance.

When you pay someone to carry out a service for you, his responsibility is:
- to work to a reasonable or laid-down professional standard.
- to use good quality materials which are suitable for the job.
- to look after your property while it is in his care.
- to carry out the work as agreed.
- to charge a reasonable price (unless a price has been agreed).

If he fails in any of these areas, you have cause for complaint, although the terms are extremely vague. The 'reasonable standard' you would expect from a gardener trained by the Royal Horticultural Society would be different from the one you could fairly expect from an odd-jobman who will turn his hand to anything. And of course, you will pay appropriately.

What happens if your watch is stolen while it is at the jewellers for repair? If the jeweller can prove that he took all reasonable measures to secure his premises, he owes you nothing. Unless you can claim on an all risks insurance policy, you have lost your watch. But if the jeweller cannot show that he has taken proper care and so, in a way, contributed to the theft, then you can sue him for compensation.

Printed on the receipt you are given when you first leave the goods for repair, you may see words to the effect of: 'goods left at owner's risk'. This inclusion clause is an attempt by traders to avoid their responsibility. But, if you were not made aware of the clause at the time of the transaction, or if the court decides the wording is unreasonable, then it has no effect.

Estimates
Very often when you take in goods for repair, the shopkeeper will not be

able to tell you exactly how much the job is going to cost. If you ask, he will give you an estimate before he starts work.

The difficulty is knowing how precise this figure is going to be. The trader can charge you more, or less, when the work is finished and you have no firm basis for disputing the cost. If in doubt, always ask for a written estimate as this prevents the trader telling a different story later.

Quotations
These can be regarded as firmer indications of the eventual cost. And if the quotation is stated to be a fixed price quotation, then that is the figure, and the only figure, you will have to pay. The exception would be if you subsequently asked for more work to be done.

Disputing the bill
If you feel that the trader is charging too much, and you did not agree this price beforehand, then, to prove your point you should ask for quotations for the same job from other traders. But you must expect to pay a 'reasonable' amount, even if you are not satisfied with the job at the end. You must at least pay for the work that has been done.

For instance, should a builder walk off the site leaving your extension only half built, you do not have to pay the full agreed price for the job, because he has broken the contract. But you do have to pay him for the amount he has done (if he has the nerve to come and ask you) less an appropriate sum to compensate you for his breach of contract.

Completing the work
You should agree the time in which you expect the job to be finished so that, if it is unreasonably late, you can claim recompense. If you have not mentioned timing, you cannot complain as long as the time taken is 'reasonable'.

Descriptions
The Trade Descriptions Act rules also apply to services. The trader is liable if he knowingly or recklessly makes a false statement. Thus, '24-hour dry cleaning', 'same day service', 'repairs while you wait', and 'sea view' must mean exactly that.

BUYING FOOD
Very strict regulations cover the sale of food: it must be fit to eat; correctly labelled; and manufactured and stored in hygienic conditions. You cannot sell short-weight items.

Food labelling
Food labelling laws set out very strictly just what must be included on the label: all the ingredients for pre-packed foods must be shown in order of quantity and this includes water. If one ingredient is singled

out for special mention: 'cake made with butter', then the amount of butter used must be shown: 'contains 10 per cent butter'.

Labels on all food that is advertised especially for slimmers must explain which ingredients are beneficial and also give the number of calories. Branded foods must say what the packets contain beyond a brand name.

The name and address of the manufacturer or distributor must be clearly shown and also the date by which the food is best eaten. It is illegal to fail to display a price on foods and no foods past their 'sell by' date should be on offer unless they are sold at a reduced price and clearly labelled as having passed the 'sell by' date.

BUYING ON CREDIT

Here again strict rules have been laid down to protect the customer. Anyone selling goods on credit must display certain information very clearly:

- the rate of interest according to the APR
- the basic price without the interest
- the total cost including interest
- what the repayments are and how frequently they must be paid
- the length of the loan
- the deposit
- if you have to put down any security.

For details of the various methods of buying on credit see pp. 53 to 58.

When you sign a credit agreement, you are signing a legally binding contract so be very sure you understand what you are doing. The agreement must show the relevant information as above and, if it does not, then the trader cannot enforce the contract.

You become absolutely bound to maintain the agreement once whoever is granting you credit approves your application. This will take several days while he checks out your references, so during this time you can, if you wish, change your mind and pull out.

If you sign the contract in your own home, or at least not on the shopkeeper's premises, and the trader has discussed the transaction with you beforehand, you have extra time to think about it. This cooling-off period is designed to protect people against unscrupulous door-to-door salesmen who often have a very smooth line in sales talk.

With any agreement signed in your home, you have a five-day cooling-off period during which you are quite free to back out even if you have signed a contract. Moreover, the five days start from the time you receive a copy of the agreement in the post from the salesman, which will be a few days after you have signed the contract.

He must leave a copy of the agreement with you at the time he makes the sale and then post another one later on. If you decide you want to back out, you should send a letter in writing to the company and, ideally, send it by registered post so there can be no argument about whether it arrived.

If you cancel an agreement, any money you have paid over must be refunded although under certain circumstances the trader is allowed to keep a £1 administration fee.

The consumers' watchdog is the Office of Fair Trading, or OFT. The OFT looks after the interests of both consumers and businessmen, and protects them against unfair practices.

The Director General of Fair Trading keeps in contact with trade organisations, encouraging them to maintain Codes of Practice; he monitors traders who consistently offend; he issues licences to credit traders; he watches estate agents; and he looks out for unfair practices.

The OFT cannot take up individual complaints but this can be done through the Citizens Advice Bureau or a Trading Standards Department.

The Trading Standards Officers are also known as consumer protection officers; they are employed by the local council to enforce the Trade Descriptions Acts and consumer legislation.

Door-to-door salesmen
No one is allowed to knock on your door, or stop you in the street, and offer you credit. But what they can do is to knock on your door and offer to sell you goods which, surprise, surprise, you can buy on credit.

Faulty goods
You are protected against substandard goods when you buy on credit in the same way as you are with cash transactions. Moreover, whoever has provided you with the credit is, in some circumstances, liable equally with the shopkeeper for goods which cost between £100 and £10,000 including VAT. The upper limit rises to £30,000 in May 1985.

But this applies only where you have borrowed the money to buy specific goods. An overdraft from the bank does not involve the bank in liability for the goods because the money has not been lent for any one item. But if a personal loan is tied in with the purchase of a particular item, then the bank is responsible with the supplier.

Paying off early
If you wish, you are fully entitled to pay off the whole amount for the goods at any time. And you should not pay interest beyond then.

Guaranteeing a loan for someone else
If a friend asks you to sign a guarantee enabling him to take out a loan or buy on credit, be very, very, cautious before agreeing. Remember that, if he does not pay up, then you will have to pay – and moreover for goods which you have never received.

Unless you are happy to pay off someone else's debts, the best advice is DON'T SIGN.

Licences

Everyone who offers credit in whatever form must be licensed by the Office of Fair Trading. Before giving them your business you should check that the company is indeed licensed and, if you find someone operating without a licence, then you should report them.

If you have already signed an agreement with someone who is unlicensed, stop paying immediately but hold on to the goods. The agreement is not enforceable without a validation order from the OFT and it serves them right for acting illegally.

But this applies only if the credit is below £5000 (rising to £15,000 in May 1985). A licence is not necessary if the trader only ever provides credit above this amount. And it is the amount of credit that matters, not the cost of the item, and house purchase is excluded.

Credit cards

When you buy goods using a bank credit card, such as Access or Barclaycard, the credit card company is liable too if the goods are faulty or if the service fails and the credit is between £100 and £10,000 rising to £30,000 in May 1985.

Credit card responsibility

Until you receive the card and sign it, you have no responsibility whatsoever for the card. If it is stolen and misused, that is not your worry. But once you have signed the card, you are theoretically liable for the first £30 if anyone uses your card without your permission. However, in practice, the banks do not charge you this £30 if your card is stolen and misused. But, if you have lent the card to a friend, then you are totally responsible for whatever is spent.

Once you have notified the credit card company of the loss of the card, they take total responsibility for the debts run up. Obviously, it is crucial to notify them immediately you realise you have lost a card, and to make a note of exactly when you contact them.

Unsolicited goods

If goods are sent to you which you have not ordered, do nothing. You should not use the goods but put them to one side where they will not be damaged. You can, if you wish, write to the sender, saying that these goods were unsolicited, and ask him to take them back.

If you ask and he does not come to collect them within 30 days, the goods are yours. If you do absolutely nothing, the goods become your property after six months.

HOW TO COMPLAIN

The attitude you adopt when you first complain can make an enormous difference to the eventual outcome. If you are calm and reasonable when you talk to the people involved, you are far more likely to reach an amicable conclusion than if you rant and rave and force them into a defensive corner.

But you should never fail to complain when you have just cause. If you don't, you are making it easier for the slack standards to continue and so others will suffer.

First of all, take the item back to the shop where you bought it. If it is too large, telephone and ask them to come and collect it. Take the receipt or some other proof of purchase with you, if you have it, but the shopkeeper cannot wriggle out of his responsibility simply because you do not have one.

You can, if you prefer, write a letter. Address it to the senior person or position at the company and make sure you keep copies of all correspondence. Or you can telephone, in which case note down the name of the person you spoke to and what was said.

If you have a complaint about the quality of food, contact your local Environmental Health Officer immediately. The address is in the telephone directory under the name of your local authority.

Should you get no satisfaction at this stage, you can ask for further help from your local Trading Standards Officer, Citizens Advice Bureau or consumer advice centre. You might find that a letter from one of these bodies will persuade the shopkeeper to reach a settlement.

If you still cannot reach agreement, you should contact the trade association which monitors the business you are in dispute with. Many of them have a Code of Practice which the shopkeeper may be breaking. In any case, the trade association's staff will be anxious that you should be satisfied with the services of their members and will try to sort out the problem. They may have an arbitration scheme which will pronounce a binding decision.

The final resort is to go to court, though you cannot do this if you have already accepted binding arbitration. Going to the law can be expensive and time consuming so make sure this is what you want to do before starting. You may be able to apply for Legal Aid to help meet the costs, or for small amounts use the small claims procedure in the County Court.

Small claims

You may think it is not worth suing for a small amount of money because of the costs involved. But, if the value of the disputed item is £500 or less, then it is classified as a 'small value' claim and will not be as expensive as a full-scale claim.

The case will not be treated as a full trial: there is no judge or open court, simply an arbitrator. No legal costs are allowed and the only cost to pay is the court fees which are 10p in the £ up to a claim of £300; £35 between £300 and £500.

Where to go for legal advice

As well as using a solicitor (see below, for advice on how to choose one) you can go to a local law centre, Citizens Advice Bureau, or Advice Centre for help. Look in the local telephone directory for the address.

How to find a solicitor

You will probably feel quite bewildered wondering how to find a solicitor for the first time. You will want someone you find sympathetic; someone who has specialist knowledge of your problem; and someone who will not charge too much.

The best starting point is to ask friends, neighbours, and colleagues if they have used a solicitor and what they thought about him or her.

Your bank manager may be able to suggest someone he knows locally or you can write to the Law Society which will send you a list of solicitors in your area, although it cannot, of course, give you a recommendation.

Before finally deciding, ask for an estimate of the fees and also ask if the solicitor regularly handles your sort of case. If you are fighting a divorce case, it is less use going to a solicitor working in a district of happily married people who deals only in commercial matters or with conveyancing and wills.

Citizens Advice Bureaux and local libraries keep a list of solicitors who operate legal aid schemes. The CAB will be able to give you the names of solicitors in the area that their clients have used satisfactorily in the past.

Law centres

These are voluntarily staffed by lawyers to help people in dire need and with little money. The service is free if they agree to handle your case.

LEGAL AID

There are four different schemes broadly known as legal aid and you need to ask for the one most appropriate to your circumstances.

Legal advice and assistance or green form scheme

This is for those with simple legal problems who have very little money. See p. 159 for divorce cases. If you qualify, you will receive free legal advice. You should look for a solicitor who displays the legal aid logo. You will be able to find a list of solicitors who do legal aid work in your local public library.

Anyone on supplementary benefit or family income supplement is automatically entitled to free legal aid, unless you have more than £730 of possessions, excluding your house, furniture and clothes and minus an allowance for dependants.

If your weekly disposable income is below £49 you will also receive totally free advice. If it is between £49 and £103 you will have to contribute a certain amount on a sliding scale.

Civil legal aid

This is a common form of legal aid. Anyone who is involved in a civil case, whether they are suing or being sued, can apply. Whether or not you will be granted legal aid depends on your income.

Very broadly, you may be entitled to legal aid if your disposable income, that is your income after all your regular, essential outgoings, is less than £4925 a year and your disposable capital is below £4500. You certainly will if the figures are £2050 and £3000. But you will also need to satisfy the solicitor that the merits of your case warrant legal aid. Generally you must show that you are justified in bringing, or defending, the case and that you stand a reasonable chance of winning.

You may be entitled to receive all your legal costs free or just a proportion of them, depending on how much money you have.

Criminal legal aid

You can ask for this aid if you are defending a criminal case but not if you are bringing one. Again, there is a means test to decide if you qualify.

Account will be taken of the seriousness of the offence with which you are charged and the likelihood of you losing your liberty. A rich man charged with murder may well be granted legal aid whereas he would not if charged with a trivial offence, say, giving short weight in his sweetshop.

£5 for half-an-hour scheme

As long as the solicitor agrees, anyone, regardless of means, can ask for an interview under the scheme. The first half hour will cost £5 including VAT, but after that, normal rates apply.

BANKRUPTCY

You can be declared bankrupt if a court makes an adjudication order against you. But, before that can happen, you will already have passed through a long process of creditors trying to reclaim their money.

Before anyone can start bankruptcy proceedings against you, you must have committed one of the following acts:
● you have already been ordered by a court to pay a debt of £200 or more and failed to comply.
● you have disposed of property in order to avoid paying your creditors.

● you have fled the country to avoid paying your debts.
● you yourself asked to be made bankrupt.

If you start bankruptcy proceedings against anyone, you will have to pay court fees of £12 for the notice, £25 for the petition and 50p search fee, plus a deposit of £90.

If you are declared bankrupt, a trustee will sell off everything you own and distribute it to your creditors. All you can keep is your bedding and clothing for yourself and your family.

First, the legal fees are met; then secured creditors are paid (this will be a mortgage and any money you have borrowed against security); next come 'preferential' creditors which means paying tax to the Inland Revenue, rates to the local authority; and finally the ordinary creditors who may receive only so many pence in the pound rather than the full amount.

Discharge

Once you have been discharged, which means that all your debts have been paid off, you can start again with a clean sheet. The disadvantages of being an undischarged bankrupt are:

● if you earn any money you must hand it over to the trustee; you keep only a small amount for yourself.
● you cannot become a Member of Parliament.
● you cannot obtain credit for over £50 without disclosing the fact.
● you must tell the trustee if you want to open a bank account.
● you cannot manage a company or become a company director.

LETTERS

Q. My next-door-neighbour has invited me to a party where she will be selling underwear. If I buy anything from her will I still have the usual consumer protection?

A. *Yes. You are covered by the Sale of Goods Act 1979. Moreover, there is a Code of Practice which anyone selling goods at parties in private homes must adhere to. Even so, make sure you know the name and address of the firm selling the goods and the agents who will be at the party.*

And do not feel embarrassed if you do not want to buy anything. There is no reason why you should spend money if there is nothing you want.

Q. I thought the practice of 'recommended' retail prices had been banned but I still see it around. Are these people acting illegally?

A. *On certain items retailers are no longer allowed to show a 'recommended' retail price and these are: beds, carpets, furniture, electrical appliances and electronic items. It is still permitted on other goods.*

The whole consumer legislation is taking a very long time to come completely into force. It started way back with the Consumer Credit Act 1974 and finally comes on to the Statute books in May 1985.

Q. We used to have a furniture store down the road which was open on Sundays but it had to close down. But there is one near my sister which still opens all day Sundays. Has there been a change in the law?

A. *Not yet, although it is possible. If a retailer takes his day of rest on a Saturday, then he is allowed to open on Sundays. Otherwise he is acting illegally though a local authority will usually wait until someone complains before taking any action and some authorities are more lenient than others.*

The Sunday trading laws are totally illogical: you can buy gin but not babies' milk; pornographic magazines but not a bible; a Chinese takeaway but not fish and chips.

USEFUL ADDRESSES

Age Concern, Bernard Sunley House, 60 Pitcairn Road, Mitcham, Surrey CR4 3LL (01-640 5431)

Air Transport Users' Committee, 129 Kingsway, London WC2B 6NN (01-242 3882)

Associated Scottish Life Offices, 23 St Andrew's Square, Edinburgh EH2 1AQ (031-556 7171)

Association of British Credit Unions, PO Box 135, Credit Union Centre, High Street, Skelmersdale, Lancs, WN8 8AP (0695 31444)

Association of British Travel Agents, 55–57 Newman Street, London W1P 4AH (01-637 2444)

Association of Investment Trust Companies, Park House, 16 Finsbury Circus, London EC2M 7JJ (01-588 5347)

Association of Manufacturers of Domestic Electrical Appliances, AMDEA House, 593 Hitchen Road, Luton, Beds LU2 7UN (0582 412444)

Automobile Association, Fanum House, Basingstoke, Hants RG21 2EA (0256 20123)

Banking Information Service, 10 Lombard Street, London EC3V 9AP (01-626 8486)

British Association of Removers, 277 Gray's Inn Road, London WC1X 8SY (01-837 3088)

British Insurance Association, Aldermary House, 10–12 Queen Street, London EC4P 4JD (01-248 4477)

British Insurance Brokers' Association, BIBA House, 14 Bevis Marks, London EC3A 7NT (01-623 9043)

British Property Timeshare Association, 4–5 Shilling Street, Lavenham, Suffolk CO10 9RH (0787 247930)

Building Centre, 26 Store Street, London WC1E 7BT (01-637 1022)

The Building Societies Association, 3 Savile Row, London W1X 1AF (01-437 0655)

Child Poverty Action Group, 1 Macklin Street, London WC2B 5NH (01-242 3225)

Citizens Advice Bureau, National Association, Myddleton House, 115–123 Pentonville Road, London N1 9LZ (01-833 2181)

Company Pensions Information Centre, 7 Old Park Lane, London W1Y 3LJ (01-493 4757)

Consumers' Association, 14 Buckingham Street, London WC2N 6DS (01-839 1222)

Cruse National Widows' Association, 126 Sheen Road, Richmond, Surrey TW9 1UR (01-940 4818)

Domestic Coal Consumers' Council, Gavrelle House, 2 Bunhill Row, London EC1Y 8LL (01-638 8929)

Electrical Association for Women, 25 Fouberts Place, London W1V 2AL (01-437 5212)

Equal Opportunities Commission, Overseas House, Quay Street, Manchester M3 3HN (061-833 9244)

Families Need Fathers, 37 Carden Street, London SE15 (01-639 5362)

Federation of Private Residents' Associations, 11 Dartmouth Street, London SW1H 9BL (01-222 0037)

Finance Houses Association, 18 Upper Grosvenor Street, London W1X 9PB (01-491 2783)

Gas Consumers Council, National Estate House, 130 Jermyn Street, London SW1Y 4UJ (01-930 7431) (see local telephone directory for regional councils)

Gingerbread, 35 Wellington Street, London WC2E 7BN (01-240 0953)

Housing Corporation, 149 Tottenham Court Road, London W1P 0BN (01-387 9466) and 24 Cathedral Road, Cardiff CF1 9LJ (0222 384611)

Incorporated Society of Valuers and Auctioneers, 3 Cadogan Gate, London SW1X 0AS (01-235 2282)

Industrial Life Offices Association, Aldermary House, Queen Street, London EC4N 1TL (01-248 4477)

Industrial Tribunals, Central Office, 93 Ebury Bridge Road, London SW1 (01-730 9161)

Institute of Chartered Accountants in England and Wales, Chartered Accountants Hall, Moorgate Place, London EC2P 2BJ (01-628 7060)

Insurance Brokers Registration Council, 15 St Helen's Place, London EC3 6DS (01-588 4387)

Insurance Ombudsman Bureau, 31 Southampton Row, London WC1B 5HJ (01-242 8613)

Land Registry Headquarters, Her Majesty's, 32 Lincoln's Inn Fields, London WC2A 3PH (01-405 3488)

Law Society, 113 Chancery Lane, London WC2A 1PL (01-242 1222)

Law Society of Scotland, PO Box 75, 26 Drumsheugh Gardens, Edinburgh EH3 7YR (031-226 7411)

Life Offices Association, Aldermary House, Queen Street, London EC4N 1TN (01-236 1101)

Lloyds Advisory Division, London House, 6 London Street, London EC3 7HA (01-623 7100)

Local Authority Loans Bureau, 65 London Wall, London EC2 (01-920 0501)

Motor Agents' Association, 201 Great Portland Street, London W1N 6AB (01-580 9122)

National Association of Conveyancers, 2 Chichester Rents, Chancery Lane, London WC2A 1EG (01-405 8582)

National Association of Estate Agents, 21 Jury Street, Warwick CV34 4EH (0926 496800)

National Association of Funeral Directors, 57 Doughty Street, London WC1N 2NE (01-242 9388)

National Consumer Council, 18 Queen Anne's Gate, London SW1H 9AA (01-222 9501)

National Council for One Parent Families, 255 Kentish Town Road, London NW5 (01-267 1361)

National Federation of Credit Unions, The Cottage, 18 The Downs, London SW20 8HR (no telephone)

National Federation of Housing Associations, 175 Grays Inn Road, London WC1X 8UP (01-278 6571)

National Home Improvement Council, 26 Store Street, London WC1E 7BT (01-636 2562)

National House Builders Federation, 82 New Cavendish Street, London W1 (01-580 5588)

National House Building Council, Chiltern Avenue, Amersham, Bucks HP6 5AP (02403 4477)

Office of Fair Trading, Field House, Breams Buildings, London EC4A 1PR (01-242 2858)

Personal Insurance Arbitration Service, Chartered Institute of Arbitrators, 75 Cannon Street, London EC4N 5BH (01-236 8761)

Post Office Users' National Council, Waterloo Bridge House, Waterloo Road, London SE1 8UA (01-928 9458)

Rating and Valuers Association, 115 Ebury Street, London SW1 9QT (01-730 7258)

Royal Automobile Club, 49 Pall Mall, London SW1Y 5JG (01-839 7050)

Royal Institution of British Architects, 66 Portland Place, London W1N 4AD (01-580 5533)

Royal Institution of Chartered Surveyors, 12 Great George Street, Parliament Square, London SW1P 3AD (01-222 7000)

Royal National Institute for the Blind, 224 Great Portland Street, London W1N 6AA (01-388 1266)

Scottish Child Poverty Action Group, 50 Kerrycroy Avenue, Glasgow GL2 0BH (no telephone)

Shelter Housing Aid Centre (SHAC), 189a Old Brompton Road, London SW5 0AR (01-373 7841)

Society of Motor Manufacturers and Traders, Forbes House, Halkin Street, London SW1X 7DS (01-235 7000)

Society of Pension Consultants, Ludgate House, Ludgate Circus, London EC4A 2AB (01-353 1688)

Solid Fuel Advisory Service, Hobart House, Grosvenor Place, London SW1X 7AE (01-235 2020)

Special Commissioners of Income Tax, Turnstile House, 94 High Holborn, London WC1 (01-438 6622)

Stock Exchange, London EC2N 1HP (01-588 2355)

Unit Trust Association, Park House, 16 Finsbury Circus, London EC2M 7JP (01-628 0871)

Credit reference agencies:
United Association for the Protection of Trade, Zodiac House, 163 London Road, Croydon CR9 2RP (01-680 7400)

CCN Systems, Lincoln Chambers, Lincoln Street, Nottingham NG1 3DJ (telephone number is ex-directory)

Self-employed advice:
Co-operative Union, Holyoake House, Hanover Street, Manchester M60 0AS (061-832 4300)

Council for Small Industries in Rural Areas (CoSIRA), 141 Castle Street, Salisbury, Wilts SP1 3TP (0722 336255)

Crafts Council, 8 Waterloo Place, London SW1 (01-930 4811)

London Enterprise Agency, 69 Cannon Street, London EC4N 5AB (01-236 2676)

National Federation of Self-Employed, 32 St Annes Road West, Lytham St Annes, Lancs FY8 1NY (0253 720911)

Small Firms Centres, Freefone 2444 and ask for your regional centre.

Index